T0288001

STORIES THROUGH THEORIES | THEORIES THROUGH STORIES

North American Indian

Writing, Storytelling,

and Critique

EDITED BY

GORDON D. HENRY JR.,

NIEVES PASCUAL SOLER, AND

SILVIA MARTÍNEZ-FALQUINA

Michigan State University Press • *East Lansing*

⊗ The paper used in this publication meets the minimum requirements
of ANSI/NISO Z39.48-1992 (R 1997) (Permanence of Paper).

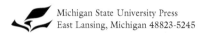 Michigan State University Press
East Lansing, Michigan 48823-5245

Printed and bound in the United States of America.

15   14   13   12   11   10   09   1   2   3   4   5   6   7   8   9   10

LIBRARY OF CONGRESS CATALOGING-IN-PUBLICATION DATA
Stories through theories/theories through stories : North American
Indian writing, storytelling, and critique / edited by Gordon D. Henry
Jr., Nieves Pascual Soler, and Silvia Martínez-Falquina.
p. cm. — (American Indian studies series)
Includes bibliographical references.
ISBN 978-0-87013-841-6 (pbk. : alk. paper) 1. American literature—
Indian authors—History and criticism—Theory, etc. I. Henry, Gordon.
II. Pascual Soler, Nieves. III. Martínez-Falquina, Silvia.
PS153.I52S76 2009
810.9'897—dc22
2009014698

Cover design by Erin Kirk New
Book design by Charlie Sharp, Sharp Des!gns, Lansing, Michigan

g green press INITIATIVE Michigan State University Press is a member of the Green
Press Initiative and is committed to developing and
encouraging ecologically responsible publishing practices. For more
information about the Green Press Initiative and the use of recycled paper
in book publishing, please visit *www.greenpressinitiative.org*.

Visit Michigan State University Press on the World Wide Web at
www.msupress.msu.edu

STORY: historical relation or anecdote, historical writing XIII; recital of events XIV; narrative designed for entertainment, tale XIV; account XVII. Aphetic—AN. estorie (OF. estoire, mod. histoire)—L. historia HISTORY

—*The Concise Oxford Dictionary of English Etymology*

I posit a what and a way. The what of narrative I call "story"; the way I call its "discourse."

—Seymour Chatman, in *Story and Discourse*

Contents

■ Critical Traces

■ Of Good Listeners

Allegories of Engagement: Stories/Theories —A Few Remarks

GORDON D. HENRY JR.

I was pulled in three directions. My readings in Native literature opened a world of language and self-representation that helped me see some of the ways Native writers had found to represent their realities in writing. My ongoing interest in and love of theory reminded me of how far I and other Native scholars needed to go in confronting the intellectual challenges the Native world was facing. My increasing awareness of the complexities and varieties of Native communities was a constant reminder that a real world was at stake in the process.

—Robert Warrior, "Native Critics in the World"

In any spectatorial situation, a subject is distributed within a larger circuit of engagement determined through technological systems of communication, storage, sorting, and retrieval, contoured under the social and institutional construction of knowledge. A viewing subject is linked or inserted into larger networks of seeing and linguistic meaning.

—Jordan Crandall, "Precision+Guided+Seeing"

THEORY: mental conception, scheme of thought. XVI.—late L. theōria—Gr. theōríā contemplation, speculation, sight. f. theōrós spectator, f. thea- base of theâsthai look upon, contemplate.

—*The Concise Oxford Dictionary of English Etymology*

My coeditors and colleagues, Nieves Pascual Soler and Silvia Martínez-Falquina, and I began this collection with the hope of furthering conversation on the seemingly contentious relationships surrounding the study of American Indian literature in view of contemporary critical theory. On one hand contemporary American Indian writers, literary critics, and scholars have expressed various degrees of "resistance" to Western discourse and theory. Yet, in different strains of discourse and narrative, American Indian scholars, critics, and writers have embraced, acknowledged, or tended to methodologies and terminologies of theory to advance certain intellectual interests and cultural perspectives in their writing. Thus, the energy and idea for this collection grew out of a sense, perhaps too speculative, that American Indian literature and the study of such often stands in a contentious yet complicit relationship with "Western Eurocentric literary theory." Initially, this general sense/speculation was informed, in part, by specific trace references to theory in works by highly successful, widely read American Indian writers, Leslie Silko and Sherman Alexie. In those works from the 1990s both writers refer directly to terms or important figures in "Western theory." In *Indian Killer* Alexie titles one of his chapters "Deconstruction,"[1] and in *Almanac of the Dead,* Silko makes multiple references, by name and in critique, to both Sigmund Freud and Karl Marx. While both authors turn the terms and ideas of theory to their own narrative ends, perhaps to dismiss theory, or to critically adapt theories to Native knowledge systems and concerns, these trace references raised questions for us about the incidence of theory in Native literary texts and in readings of American Indian literature.

Our interest in relationships between theory and American Indian critical work was further fueled by the words and work of Gerald Vizenor. Over the years Vizenor's creative use of theory and his intellectual presence have recast academic discourse on American Indian literature at almost every turn. In some respects, even resistance to theory might be attributable to the ways Vizenor's stories and theoretical perspectives have shadowed serious academic work on American Indian culture and literature for the last twenty-five years. To that point Penelope Myrtle Kelsey writes:

> As a graduate student, with the exception of Gerald Vizenor's continental-inspired trickster theory, I often found that this historical materialism was simply the best approach available for practicing a criticism that was responsible to tribal peoples in its potential to approximate an indigenous perspective. Vizenor's introduction of key concepts such as "survivance," "postindian," and "tribal striptease" represents a critical first step in the evolution of indigenous literary frameworks, however one that is notably dated by its reliance on postmodern and poststructuralist theory. (Kelsey 2008, 3)

It is notable that even while Kelsey acknowledges Vizenor's groundbreaking theoretical work, she goes on to cite the tension in categorizing Vizenor's ideas. While she claims the "continental" inspires the "trickster," it seems the trickster did not, or could not, inspire or transform or even reveal the "continental" under her readings of Vizenor. In an oblique, rather strange turn, this privileges the influence of western theory over the power of the trickster. Further, even as Kelsey goes on to cite Vizenor's "success in writing in the oral tradition"[2] and his "greatest critical success in developing ideas of 'Native Transmotion,'" she still tempers his influence by associating him with "dated" theories, as if the importance or relevance of developing indigenous critical frameworks for critique runs parallel to some historical belief about theoretical relevance in time (Kelsey 2008, 3). In short, she may be seeing passé theories in Vizenor's work even as she and other native critics often look to the past to create a more contemporary critical perspective. Again, in some sense, this sets western theory as some kind of standard not only of how we apply critique, but also of when we deploy theory: that is, theory in movement and trend may transform and determine the relevance of critique, according to some ingrained idea of historical sequence.

In any case, the range and array of Vizenor's critical, literary, production illustrates not just a strong engagement with theory, but also a willingness to contest the theoretical assumptions of particular deliveries of western theory and the unimaginative presumptions of readers and critics who would frame tribal stories within the enclosures (material or otherwise) and limits of texts, ideologies, and reductive representational depictions of Native people and their stories. From his early essays on Jacque Derrida to his later work in *Narrative Chance*, from *Manifest Manners* to *Fugitive Poses*, Vizenor has informed and transformed the culture of reading and critiquing Native texts and the cultural work of "westerners" who have relied on Native subjects for their material productions.

■ Ethnographing Theory: The Allegory of the Deconstructive Trickster

Another view of trickster engaged theory lies almost dormant in the spring 1979 issue of *Boundary 2*, which predates Owens, Vizenor, and Youngblood Henderson's trickster discourse. Therein Karl Kroeber pairs "trickster-transformer" with deconstruction.[3] On the first page of the article Kroeber relates his critical intent.

> Trickster-Transformer occurs in many of the world's literatures and my-
> thologies. He does, though, present special difficulties for conventional
> literary criticism, and my purpose here is to outline a range of procedures
> which might make aesthetic analysis of such material possible. Since
> my aim is to distinguish parameters of method, I shall not undertake
> exhaustive exegesis of any one story. I shall try, instead, to suggest how
> any Trickster-Transformer tale might be criticized usefully—that is, in
> a way helpful both to developing improved techniques of criticism and
> to enriching appreciation of the literary accomplishments of American
> Indians. (Kroeber 1979, 73)

Though Kroeber mentions the difficulties of using "conventional" criti-cal techniques to liberate trickster from a world of confused readers, he sets out to provide the tools to read trickster material as trickster material has never been read before—as "possible" to read and interpret. Yet, to do so Kroeber circles back, in his outline of purpose, to the language of procedure, aesthetics, analysis, and method, to spin and turn trickster-transformer to material, critical means for what he claims in the end will lead to an enriched appreciation of American Indian literature. Initially, under Kroeber's gaze, such appreciation can only be realized in conjunction with an understanding of terms of interpretation that are associated with Eurocentric literary critique. Trickster-transformer and the stories about trickster and American Indian literature can only be appreciated in the view of existing literary formulations of western discourse. The critical understanding and aesthetic enrichment Kroeber sets out remains contingent on comparisons to literary works in the western canon and to critical methods he draws from deconstruction. At this juncture, there are no surprises. Native Literature and Native story are formed and evaluated under the comparative, critical eye of a non-Native scholar.

But, to be fair, the story turns, and by the end of his essay Kroeber privileges the sophistication of Native stories over the modern stories he compares them to, just as his final turn to deconstruction tells another tale. In the end, Native story and tribal systems of transmission remain preferable to European critical theory. In Kroeber's view we find an argument for taking on theory with the tools, sensibilities, and performative power of Native storytellers. Under Kroeber's gaze, Tribal stories and story contexts are morally and culturally more effective than deconstruction, and tribal stories suggest ways deconstruction might go beyond meaningless activity of critique which often ends in an abyss of nothingness. So, an attempt to relate "tricktster-transformer," with critical theory, led Kroeber from a limited sense of the importance of deconstruction as outlined in the following passage.

Miller's version of Derrida's position presupposes the "interminable activity" of text-deconstruction as pointless, purposeless, intrinsically unmeaningful.[4] And even the most metaphysically naive and ethnologically ignorant can at once perceive this view to be alien to any of the Indians among whom Coyote/coyote tales were (or, indeed, are) popular. One fashion of learning how and why a critical method apparently so useful for the analysis of Trickster-Transformer stories can be so incommensurate with the social realities out of which the tales emerge is to examine the nature of Indians' literary criticism. A brief task. The Indians had no literary critics.

From there Kroeber suggests the following possibilities for deconstruction, based on its ways of bringing readers through the filmy bounds of the opaque (to see the light) and based on its propensity for attacking concepts he associates with western doctrine.

> One virtue of deconstructionism is that it brings us to what Blake called "the limit of Opakeness," beyond which there has to be light. Thus "teaching" in the West has often been thought of as conveying a doctrinal message; in attacking the concepts of univocity and fixed, rational meaning the deconstructionists shatter this narrow idea of education and, inadvertently, allow us to reconsider the efficacies of performance. It is literary performance that ensures a heterogeneity of meaning educationally effective, rather than the mere rendering of mise en abyme.

Rather than continuously gazing at its object in an infinite regression then, deconstruction can go beyond meaningless activity and fulfill a culturally relevant educational purpose, if it can effectively perform, either symbolically or literally—we imagine—as a kind of literature. The inspiration for Kroeber's revelation on another, better path for deconstruction developed from certain readings of tribal stories. Whether one agrees with Kroeber or not, his interpretations of the efficacy of tribal stories and their moral, cultural, and participatory ways of conveying "heterogeneity" of meaning stands stories up tall, perhaps taller than literary critical traditions of the west. For Kroeber, stories are better teachers than theories and stories can teach theory how to work beyond pointless critique.

Whether, Kroeber's critical process ever leads to his promise of an "enriched" appreciation of American Indian literature remains muted, since at this end of this allegory, tribal stories, in all their transformative energy and cultural potency, suggest additional possibilities for understanding and expanding deconstructive readings. Whatever deconstruction seems to lack in meaningless readings toward an abysmal end, trickster stories might be able to reinvigorate with some expanded (performative?) purpose. According to this allegory, engaging Native story/subjects with theory may lead to privileging of Native story/subjects, though transformation of views of theory, though the use of Native story in this manner may not constitute resistance, in the minds of some critics.

In *Theory Matters*, Vincent B. Leitch explores the ground of struggle over theory with fine, insightful personal, historical, and methodological overviews of the development of theory in cultural and literary studies. Therein he writes,

> Let me clarify what I mean by "theory." In its contemporary context "theory" refers to a body of texts, ancient and modern, concerned with poetics, interpretation, rhetoric, textual commentary, and models of culture. More recently we have added to this list semiotics; media and discourse; race, class, and gender codes; and visual and popular culture. Yet "theory" also designates a mode of logical, skeptical, and judgmental inquiry. In recent times, theory, influenced by psychoanalysis, poststructuralism, and cultural studies, has added other dimensions, especially a "hermeneutics of suspicion," characterized by interest in ineradicable distortions and contradictions; distrust in common sense, social institutions, and hidden agendas; and preoccupation with linking up local phenomena to globalizing forces. (Leitch 2003, 30)

Leitch's extended, array of definitions (in characteristics, functions and dimensions) of theory, insightful and expansive as it is, also points to one of the major drawbacks in writing or talking about theory. Theory suggests many different things to many different people. Some scholar/critics may hold an expanded view of theory, as in Leitch's example, and some scholars may perceive theory in much more limited ways (as associated with only deconstruction, for example). Further still, it seems possible that views of theory can grow more expansive or more reductive—perhaps by chance—for any individual or any community in the space of a conversation, or even in limited readings or writings on a passage of text. For example, in *Tribal Theory in Native American Literature,* Penelope Myrtle Kelsey writes:

> If we take theory to mean a lifeway or way of considering one's world, suddenly the field for studying Native American Literature possesses a wide range of theoretical strategies. How many Indigenous scholars have at their fingertips a body of knowledge about the specific tribal tradition that they might now employ legitimately as a theoretical framework for considering a given text? (Kelsey 2008, 10–11)

In this transformative passage "tribal tradition" may become theory to legitimize tribal traditions as foundational knowledge for reading texts. In some respects legitimization has been turned around, then. Kelsey's momentary formulation of the possibility for legitimizing tribal knowledge, by seeing tribal knowledge as theory, by considering one as the other, makes the legitimization of tribal knowledge seem dependent on a particular view of theory that at once expands theory and contracts tribal knowledge to frameworks of legitimization.

From strategy to strategy, text to text, story to critique, word to word, theory seems strangely protean, capable of lodging and dismantling thousands of shapes, applications and formal dispersions. We may be drawing on theory in what we believe to be our arguments against it; we may be dragged through it by law, process, or system on our way to collective freedom, sovereignty, and empowerment. Even as we write or read theory or speak of theory, it draws us forward, pushes against us, turns our consciousness, tropes us, turns us away, angers us, signs us, frustrates us, or seems compatible to us, among so many other possibilities. But if we accept Leitch's broad depiction of theory—even when culturally or theoretically we can't or shouldn't—then we may also understand the wide range of reactions to theory in American Indian literary studies; the ideas and terms, in part or on the whole, Leitch has outlined above remain relevant to how people have written and still write about American Indian literature and cultural production—if we accept his definition.

■ Thinking against Theory: The Allegory of the Anti-Trickster

Interestingly, James (Sákéj) Youngblood Henderson relates another view of trickster, a tribal storied being, and theoretical discourse. In a telling critique of Eurocentrism and colonization, Youngblood Henderson positions trickster against an insidious other, in the guise of a European force, called "anti-trickster."

> Among some Indigenous peoples, Eurocentrism is known as the twin of the trickster, or imitator, or the "anti-trickster." Similar to the trickster who emphasizes Aboriginal thought and dramatizes human behaviour in a world or flux, the "anti-trickster" appears in many guises and is the essence of paradoxical transformation. The "anti-trickster" represents a cognitive force of artificial European thought, a differentiated consciousness, ever changing in its creativity to justify the opposition and domination of contemporary indigenous people and their spiritual guardians. (Youngblood Henderson 2000, 58)

In this assessment of Aboriginal and European thought, Henderson offers representations, in an abstract summary of a contest, as a sort of storied relationship where contrary sensibilities and forces are allegorically named to reveal the contextual ground and cognitive alliances of "twin" thought-characters. Trickster corresponds to Aboriginal thought, anti-trickster to Eurocentric thought; anti-trickster to artificial thought, trickster to the un-named (natural thought) opposite of artificial thought.[5] Aboriginal trickster thought is also associated with "behaviour in a world of flux." More than that, the play of opposing forces, the motive in this contest stems from the Eurocentric desire to dominate, in this example "contemporary Indigenous people" and "their spiritual guardians." Behind the allegorical anti-trickster lies theoretical, abstract, Eurocentric thought, as though in a metonymical mask for a totalizing context of a dominating "artificial" paradigm. In that respect, Henderson's remarks on the play of trickster and anti-trickster points to at least one obvious factor driving Native resistance to critical theory. Theory represents discourse, interpretations, worldviews, systems, and models that are implicated in Eurocentric attempts to dominate Native people. By this allegory, theory must be resisted. It represents domination of Indigenous people and their relations to spirit(s).

In *The Columbia Guide to American Indian Literatures of the United States since 1945,* Eric Cheyfitz proposes resistance to critical theory in the field of American Indian literature, as follows:

> The resistance to theory comes from two fronts. With the notable exception of Krupat, some of the first wave of Euro-American scholar/ critics of Native American Literatures, like Charles Larson, Kenneth Lincoln, Elaine Jahner, and Andrew Wiget, have from the 1970's onward grounded their criticism in a combination of ethnographic and formalist methods, which for what may be fundamental philosophical differences have not opened themselves to critical theory. At the same time, the group of nationalist Native critics, associated with the notion of "intellectual sovereignty," have been suspicious of a body of theory that is grounded in Western philosophy and has with few exceptions overlooked Native American literatures in its formulations. (Cheyfitz 2006, 5)

On the one hand, "the ethnographic-formal," as Cheyfitz names it, "places a strong emphasis on the formal or aesthetic properties of native texts in limited cultural contexts, while deemphasizing or ignoring the social, political and historical contexts in which U.S. American Indian literatures take shape" (5). Cheyfitz goes on to define the features of this particular theory-resistant strain of reading, in the following way:

> I term this work "ethnographic-formal," because it derives its agenda from two sources: Boasian anthropology's focus on ethnographic details of specific cultures, independent of the colonial histories of these cultures; and academic literary study's focus during the same period (roughly 1920–1960) on literary work, with poetry as the paradigm of literature, as a self contained artifact independent of its social and political context—work typified by a movement known as New Criticism. (71)

For Cheyfitz to position New Critical readings and ethnography, associated with social science theories of anthropology, against theory, as if they don't involve strategies, worldviews, or ways of reading, seems contrary to Vincent Leitch's aforementioned remarks on theory. Once again this may inflect a disconnection between what one critic considers theory and theoretical and what another critic considers, shall we say, just closer (to a cultural) reading. Such a disconnect may also point to the ways some critics associate critical readings of texts with historical periods that have been marked by particular schools of criticism that don't seem to apply theory per se, but still involve beliefs, methodologies, and critical philosophies that in the broadest terms are theoretical.

Ironically, Cheyfitz's first theory resistor-type, "ethnographic-formalism," with its cadre of non-Native interpretive critics, may have set the ground for debates over postcolonial readings and the so-called nationalist critiques, to follow. In *Anti-Indianism*, Elizabeth Cook-Lynn contends:

> The examination of Indian/white relations in America by academics in the disciplines has always been a contentious matter but for a few brief decades, from 1960 to 1990, when there seemed to be an empathetic and mutually supporting relationship between publishers and scholars and Indians who had begun to provoke reassessments in the emerging postcolonial debates. (Cook-Lynn 2001, 196)

In the same text Cook-Lynn goes on to detail how academics have systematically silenced or taken authority over authenticity of native literary works. She claims white post colonial scholars have silenced or subsumed native voices in the process of interpreting or imposing certain methodological and theoretical frames around Native texts. In one passage which unfolds a bit more on Cook-Lynn's position on the rise of postcolonial theory, Jody Bird offers the following.

> The nascent connections between Native American literary studies and postcolonial theory that Cook-Lynn gestures toward demands that scholars consider how British and then deep settler colonialism inform

discussions of citizenship, diaspora, and authority in the U.S. Yet, on the other side of the terrain, those involved remain guarded, tenuous and occasionally resistant, which may account to some degree for Cook-Lynn's own ambivalence about the theory. (Bird 2006, 85)

Theory, in this case with a postcolonial perspective, bears a trace or whiff of considerations which are connected to the interests of Native writers and critics. Moreover, those connected considerations express the "demand" to read Native texts in certain ways—under this example, in light of language, organizations and systems of colonization and its residual effects. But to engage with theory, to gesture with postcolonial tools, for example, "those involved" as Native critics and readers remain resistant, hesitant, as if viewing the theory from another place, from another side of the "terrain" of text and critique. This view from the other side reflects an ambivalence about what one sees in theory. Whether in gestures of acknowledgement or denial, engagement with theory, with the view from another terrain winds theory with ambivalence.

Still, to differentiate, Cheyfitz's second resistor-type, the "nationalist critic" is associated with advocating "intellectual sovereignty," also expressed in the work of Cook-Lynn, who wonders whether "native literary traditions and contemporary works will have much relevance" in the canon, given their

own unique set of aims—the interest in establishing the myths and metaphors of sovereign nationalism: the places, the mythological beings, the genre structures and plots of the oral traditions; the wars and war leaders, the treaties and accords with other nations as the so-called gold standard against which everything can be judged. These are the elements of nationalism which have always fueled the literary canon of tribal peoples and their literary lives. . . . Reference to a body of nationalistic myths, legends, metaphors, symbols, historical persons and events, writers and their writings must form the basis of the critical discourse that functions in the name of the people; the presence of the Indian nation as cultural force, a matter of principle. (Cook-Lynn 1996, 84–85)

Under such views American Indian literary critique should develop from inside our unique tribal, community, and family experiences and from our relationships with specific "national" cultures, stories, and songs, from particular memory, life, storied relations, inside and with structures, activities, and methodologies of transmitting knowledge within and through Indigenous cultures in time and space. While we may have questions about the appropriateness of the use of terms such as *nation* and *nationalism*,[6] some elements of the nationalism Cook-Lynn outlines for us seem to resonate through the work of many American Indian writers and artists.[7]

In, *Red on Red,* nationalist designate Craig Womack goes deeper into the heart of what Cheyfitz refers to as "intellectual sovereignty."

> Native literature, and Native literary criticism, written by Native authors, is a part of sovereignty: Indian people exercising the right to present images of themselves and to discuss those images. Tribes recognizing their own extant literatures, writing new ones, and asserting the right to explicate them constitute a move toward nationhood. (Womack 1999, 14)

Just as the term *sovereign* rose up to buttress nationalism in Cook-Lynn's reflections on American Indian critical discourse, *sovereignty* informs Womack's assertions of the rights of Native people to produce, discuss, and explain "themselves." In this passage, sovereignty entails struggles over images and demands self-determination over image production and critical discourse about those images. Further, Womack suggests Natives writing with sovereignty will push sovereign-seeking tribes a bit further down a path toward nationhood. Nationhood inheres in sovereignty, and the current expressions of sovereignty, not yet realized nationhood, will eventually lead to nationhood. Yes, Womack tempers that perspective, by writing, "While this literary aspect of sovereignty is not the same thing as the political status of Native nations, the two are, nonetheless, interdependent (14)." But Womack leaves little doubt: he binds writing with sovereignty, as he intertwines writing with political status.

Womack also circles back to the passage (cited above) by Elizabeth

Cook-Lynn, prefacing his quote of Cook-Lynn in this way: "The point that Cook-Lynn makes so well is that there already exists a Native Literary school" (14). In this light, the sovereign critical ground for discourse on American Indian literature and culture already exists in extant oral and written cultural expressions and experiences of tribal people as passed down through generations. At the same time, cultural, artistic, and written expression "contributes to keeping sovereignty alive in citizens of a nation" (14). It follows, then, that this "gives sovereignty a meaning that is defined within the tribe rather than by external sources" (14). Other implications are clear here. Given the existence of a Native literary school and sovereignty defined from within, there is no compelling reason for external readings of Native texts through Euro-American theory—whether through formalist interpretations or otherwise. Moreover since people inside sovereign tribes should provide the interpretative, expressive force for critical literary readings, sovereign readings seem to exclude nontribal outsiders and outsiders from other tribes. An outside reading in theory, or in fact, under the wrong eyes, with the wrong interpretation, could inhibit tribal sovereignty.

But the limits of reading Womack this way are tempered by earlier remarks in his introduction to *Red on Red*. The inner tribal theory he advocates also acknowledges at least a trace presence of theory in Native critical circles.

> I hope this study provides a positive example of why looking toward primary Native cultures, authors and histories can enrich Native literature. If we Native critics share the fault of being "theoryless," my contention would be that this comes from not looking *enough* at our home cultures, not from looking *too much* at them. Naturally, this process does not call for abandoning literary theory, and if one examines the work of most Native critics, one will find few of us have anyway. (13)

Ironically, or perhaps naturally, Womack sets out with a parcel of the same intent as Karl Kroeber does. Both intend to "enrich" readings of American Indian literature. Significantly, both attempts to enrich the literature and readings of Native literature return to involving theory. Womack makes a point of directing part of that enrichment (under the acknowledged impoverished lack of theory) back to closer readings, energized by a Native critic's return to a tribal/cultural home to find theory, even though he doesn't see an enriched primary Native reading of texts in the absence of theory. Ultimately, reading and critiquing Native texts should be an assertion of sovereignty, or an act of resistance for Native writers and critics; yet somehow, someway, readings by Native critics should not abandon theory, even if tribal story or performance becomes the privileged mode or method for undermining, or recasting theoretical perspectives and methods.

Womack's and Cook-Lynn's concern over primary readings and sovereign interpretations of tribal literatures may engender the politics of discourse, by advocating tribal/community-centered influences for writing and interpretation while forging just arguments about issues of discourse and justice in writings by and about American Indians. No doubt culturally rooted American Indian ways of knowing and of receiving and transmitting knowledge should inform interpretative discourse on American Indian literature and culture. And certain lasting views about the efficacy of words and about the importance of applying Aboriginal experience, thought, and cultural tools to critical work should rise to the surface in much of the critical discourse produced by Native scholars. But such acknowledgments rarely engender empirical experiences and critical processes, which, for some undisclosed reasons—perhaps fear of essentialist, or irrationalist, or mystical labels, or perhaps taboo against revealing ancient tribal secrets—should not or cannot be offered as the primary tools for critical interpretation. Thus, the deeper understandings we receive through cultural knowledge are almost never directly referred to in our writings as Natives. Perhaps giving primacy to such tools and cultural knowledge would, among other dangerous possibilities, reconfigure certain power dynamics in the academy and critical studies, as Craig Womack suggests in "Theorizing American Indian Experience."[8]

Still, to be sure, Womack's acknowledgment of the use of "theory" by Native scholars may not reflect surrender to theory, or to theorists who would delegitimize and constrain Native perspectives with theoretical constructs. For Womack and many other Native critics theory and terms associated with theory (such as *hybridity*) have often been used to discount the experiences of Native scholars, writers, and people. It's just that the use of theory may sometimes help advance the argument and cause of resistance. This seems to be the case for a number of "nationalist" readers and indigenous scholars. Perhaps Devon Mihesuah makes it clearest: "While utilizing non-Indigenous ideologies is not problematic in itself, it does become an issue when they are used exclusively" (Mihesuah 2004, 40).

From another perspective, Native critics' ambivalent relationship to theory may be empowering resistance-discourse on some undisclosed, perhaps discreet or subterfugal, levels. In *Post-colonial Transformation* Bill Ashcroft claims:

> If resistance is *never* a simple and transparent polarity, if textual resistance is necessarily a mediated act, then our notion of what resistance actually means, what it entails, what kind of act it implicates, must undergo a radical readjustment. . . . If resistance is sometimes ambivalently situated, it is also open to a wide horizon of possible forms, forms which often look very different from resistance. (Ashcroft 2001, 32)

On some ground, in some context, perhaps inside the academy more than anywhere else, Native critics' use of, engagement with, and overturning of theory may signify the most efficient, resistant, or effective use of the methodological tools, or formal applications at the site of intellectual struggle and political discourse. For more, much more on resistance, theory, and Native nationalist critique, readers might turn to *American Indian Literary Nationalism*, by Jace Weaver, Craig Womack, and Robert Allen Warrior (2006). More recently, the collective volume *Reasoning Together* (Acoose et al. 2008) circles around and treats questions raised here as well. Further, one of the best critical texts on Native literature to come out for a long time, Michael Wilson's excellent book *Writing Home* (2008), also ties resistance to theory in a wealth of perceptive readings of a broad range of Native literature.

In the end, all this push and pull against, then with, then against, then with theory, suggests too briefly, of course, that while Cheyfitz may be right in pointing to resistance to theory in nationalist Native critical writing, resistance in such writing often directly acknowledges—for better or worse, to dismiss or employ—a relationship with theory, with Western literature or with theories about what Native theories and literatures should or do entail. So the larger shadows, the same old questions and issues, still seem to loom out there: for example, what aspects of reading and interpretation are not informed in some way by Western models, particularly in the field of literary and cultural studies? How do Indigenous, Aboriginal, Native, First Nations, tribal, American Indian, Mixed- blood, Full Blood, No blood, believed-to-have-blood, imagines-blood writers/scholars/critics/teachers/ culture workers escape the "prison house," (Jameson 1972) of Western discourse, methodology, and thought—since reading and writing may, arguably, be some creative "anti-trickster," some sign, some meme or some function of all that? And what is not tied to theory when it relates to interpreting cultural production, from where most of these interpretive issues of contention arise—such as in the academy? Further, how have more recent critical calls for Indigenous or nationalist readings of American Indian literature sublimated or subsumed the terms, methods, tactics, strategies, and technics of theory, or so-called Western depth models?[9] Further still, why have the most vehement tracts against theory not carried over as vehemently to dismissal and resistance to applications and cultural technics in other areas of cultural production in which Natives engage the West—as in references to "Western law" as foundational to discussion of American Indian literature, for example,[10] or as in daily engagements with cognitive forces and functions associated with instruments and technics of old and new media, including visual and performing arts? At the most basic levels we ask, can we avoid theory altogether? Is it possible, in the work we do? And if we must engage theory, on some ground, as most Native writers and scholars have, including those calling for decolonization and return to Native worldviews and nationalist roots, what methodologies of reading, what strategies and tactics of resistance have worked most consistently for tribal communities, or for the "lesser blessed" and the less interested in critical reading? Even the hybrid terms of *survivance*[11] and, more recently, *communitism*,[12] resistant and culturally driven as they may be, implicate an engagement with theoretical predecessions. Finally where would cultural and literary studies' decolonization and Native critique be without engagement with Foucault, Derrida, Fanon, Said, or feminist studies, ethnography, queer theory, theories of the body, chaos theory, the participation mystique, or more simply the reading-extraction-interpretive techniques of New Criticism, formalism and reader response, for example?

As for stories, of course, there are theories about stories: and there are questions about the features, the elements, and the function of stories: such questions and theories involve discussion of where stories come from, what they entail, what makes for a good story, how culture inheres in stories. All such surmise may lead to further questions about the nature of stories, the efficacy of stories, the truth of stories, the power of stories, and so on and so forth. American Indian literature tells us a bit in this regard. Native literature is replete with discourse on the nature and power of stories. Nearly every narrative text by Native writers and nearly every Native storytelling community comments on stories, either directly or indirectly, in formal structures or internal narrative passages, on what a story is or what stories are. Need we remind ourselves of the passages on stories in Leslie Marmon Silko's *Ceremony*? As Betonie refers to stories in calendars, among the varied collection of articles one finds in a room, for example. As old Ku'oosh remands us to the deep cultural implications of telling, of the inherent relationships between words and world. Must we recount or quote the passage from Louise Erdrich's *Tracks* to remind ourselves of how Nanapush claims to have kept Lulu alive, by talking, by recounting, by storytelling? Do we have to open *Dead Voices* to the pages where animal narrators smell as well as tell stories, to be reminded of the sophisticated perceptions Native writers offer in their narrative attempts to tell what we might know if we could further develop our own sensory and intellectual means and qualities of perception?

Yet stories often resist cultural isolation and fixed fields of context. Stories seem to transcend jurisdictions of nation, culture, time and text, irrespective of whether they are spoken, written, heard, smelled, filmed or performed. The "transposability of the story is the strongest reason for arguing that narratives are indeed structures independent of any medium" (Chatman 1978, 20). Stories are intertextual, transcendent, evocative, and arguably efficacious. We could never write enough to say what stories are, how they function, or what methodologies might be best for considering them as primary critical tools, in a sort of meta-storied critical process. In fact stories may lead to, may have already led us to, theories and then back again to stories.

Further, both theory and story imply acts of perception; whereas in theory perception may seem to rely on perception of an object—only in this manner can the perceiving subject arrogate for himself the impartiality of science, or the perceived impartiality of a methodology—in story perception moves to and from, through and with natural, spiritual, animal, plant, mineral, human individuals and communities, transmitters and receptors, naturally, supernaturally, and artificially communicated, among all we know to say, or sense, move, or write, paint, or sing, or dance. It's a great wonder, then, that in some circles theory is codified as truth and assigned a high rank, while fiction and storytelling is associated with lying and fabrications. As it is, current literary critique seems to operate as a kind of negation of primacy of story, and stories seem to operate as a negation of abstract theory, each of the two seeming to exclude the other, negating the other, but inevitably each pushes the other forward, since deep down, what is negated, or denied constantly, threatens to eventually free itself from the restrictions of negation. Moreover both theories and stories establish affiliations, break barriers of media and discourse and live inside us, sometimes insidiously, sometimes transparently, as bodies without organs, as bodies within bodies, to travel beyond limits of texts, or their own perceived filiations or affiliated origins.

So the narrative traces inherent in many theoretical accounts of literature may just indicate the impossible nevers of negation, of never whole, or never true, as if never could be absolute. Perhaps stories authenticate theory in traces of narrative, as well; just as abstract discourse fails, or falls into gaps, with an undisclosed purpose. Or perhaps theory authenticates experience, as a kind of abstract meta-speak, where all the fissures and faults of attempts to explicate eventually fall back in some critical moment to some pause of narrative, to some imagined encounter, to tell more about theory than theory could ever disclose. Theory like story may bring us closer to the impossibilities of reconciling our still extant needs, desires (even undisclosed pressures?) to legitimize our theories through our experiences and vice versa. Even as we seem to be writing about, with, for, or against theory, we cite or narrate our affiliations, and our cultural experiences, as though we now know well enough, now, how to subsume one in the other, or both in neither, to keep writing our way in this strange complex of discourse we have entered into in this engagement with cultures our own and otherwise. At the same time, it may be good, or relevant, to think of the struggles over this complex ground of American Indian literature and critical studies as an indication of the vitality of Native writing and culture and as a sign of the vast cultural and intellectual resources Native scholars and communities have had and continue to have available to them in their work. Yes, individually we seem to have no final, complete, absolute answers. But we have a wealth of personal, communal, and cultural resources and imaginative work behind us, before us, and ahead of us that may open the world and beyond to more thoughtful, beautifully cast, imaginative readings, and perhaps, there in the reading, in the interpretation, we will go on to forge political sovereignty, or at least the imagined sovereignty of more interesting ways of telling what we know and who we are, in our own terms and language.

We followed our initial speculations, then, with a call for essays on Native literary texts that acknowledge or refer directly to theory, initially, to explore the ways American Indian literature treats theory in the imaginary spaces of fiction, poetry, and drama. But after some discussion we decided to turn to broader interests and concerns. We thought we should also include work that considered cultural works, such as stories, songs, oral and written, of so-called traditional and contemporaneous invention, as capable of offering interpretive critique of culture and cultural production. Finally, we thought we might suggest possibilities for understanding critical theories as holding traces of stories, in discourse gaps and breaks, in aporia, in cathartic fissures, in brief surrender to narrative and sublime image, in discourse and exchange between people, in propagation of empathy and affiliation and as vehicles for turning consciousness back to those moments that remind us we are human, whether in folly, in love, or in fear, in desire, or lament, in suffering, or in all those turnings back to trying to tell who we are and what we believe. After we put out a call for papers some years ago, we received a number of essays, some of which dealt directly with the critical issues we outlined in our call, many of which did not, though all addressed, more generally, key terms of our call, in the relations between theory and story.

At some unnameable idealistic moment, though, our work on this book endeavored to resist the either/or forces of essentialist, or theoretical, categorization in favor of a both-and/or-neither approach, creating engagements between storytelling and critique in view of American Indian texts. Stories of theories, theories of stories, stories as theories, and theories as stories are presented in multiple formats, from a variety of perspectives through many different strategies of discourse. The textual relationships between negation and affirmation, absence and presence; the ways in which theory includes vestiges of stories to support assumptions of critical theory and the way stories presuppose theory; the uses of story as critique; the juxtaposition of story elements from different sources; and the relationship between writer, text, reader, and critic are here open to discussion by a group of storytellers and scholars from diverse academic and national backgrounds. These writers/critics/teachers/scholars come from diverse cultural backgrounds and critical perspectives, as well. Thus, *Stories through Theories / Theories through Stories* includes essays by Native and non-Native scholars and writers from the U.S., Canada, and Europe, from citizens of the sovereign nations of White Earth, Cheyenne River, and Spain, among others. Though we may not always agree with the critical positions or ideas advanced by the scholars whose work appears here, we did not ask them to change their essays or ideas based on any national or tribal perspectives or ideologies we may hold about the way and how of their written work. We thank them for their work, and we thank them for their readings.

Megwetch.

NOTES

1. See Sherman Alexie, *Indian Killer*, Part 2, "Hunting Weather," Chapter 17, "Deconstruction" (Boston, MA: Grand Central Publishing, 1998), 245–248.

2. A reference, of course, to the title of Kimberly Blaeser's critical work on Vizenor.

3. There is room for some wonder here.

4. This follows Kroeber's summary and critique of J. Hillis Miller's essay "Stevens' Rock and Criticism as Cure," *Georgia Review* 30 (Spring 1976). According to Kroeber, Miller came to some tough conclusions about deconstruction.

5. In his third note for the essay, Youngblood Henderson writes, "Aboriginal traditions

are taught through a paradoxical force in nature known as 'Trickster'" (2000, 73 n. 3). Youngblood Henderson also delves much deeper into the *artificial* and the *natural*. This is very interesting indeed, as Youngblood Henderson draws on the theories of Brazilian legal philosopher, Roberto Mangbeira Unger to forge resistance to Eurocentric ideologies.

6. We realize Cook-Lynn has tempered the theoretical outside with the use of "myth, metaphor and sovereign" in her reflections on nationalism, but this is language calling for additional readings. For example, resistance to the term *nationalism* may revolve around concerns about the historical associations with the words *nationalism* and *nationalist*. For some readers those terms may bring to mind, in thought and ideology, in some parts of the world, ways in which nationalism bears traces (at some ends of theories) of colonial resistance, postcolonial theory, legal and political theory, and (at other ends) oppressive nationalist states.

7. Of late and of the most influence, Weaver, Womack, and Warrior (2006) have articulated "nationalist" views as well, though in different ways and in more complexity than we will attempt to relate here.

8. For example, Womack rightfully confronts arguments against theories and theorists that deny or question the "validity of any 'pure' Native experience," which emphasize outside influences on Native experiences, as a means of discounting their validity (2008, 383).

9. See Jameson 1991. There Jameson outlines prominent ideologies and theories of Western thought as "Western depth models."

10. Eric Cheyfitz (2006) claims American Indian literature must be read in relation to federal Indian law; this will eventually require "political" readings of Native literature.

11. For more on *survivance* see the Oxford English Dictionary, which dates a form of the word back to 1623. Survivance is also used in reference and relation to French nationalist politics in Quebec and the emigration of French Canadians to New England from 1850 to 1930. See also Derrida 2002, wherein Derrida mentions survivance in reference to the French communist party in the 1930s.

12. See Jace Weaver's essay in *American Indian Literary Nationalism,* as he writes "from the 'community' and 'activism' signifying a proactive commitment to Native community" (2006, 15).

WORKS CITED

Acoose, Janice, et al. 2008. *Reasoning Together: The Native Critics Collective*. Edited by Craig S. Womack, Daniel Heath Justice, and Christopher B. Teuton. Norman: University of Oklahoma Press.

Ashcroft, Bill. 2001. *Post-colonial Transformation*. New York: Routledge.

Bird, Jody. 2006. "(Post)Colonial Plainsongs: Toward Native Literary Worldings." In *Unlearning the Language of Conquest: Scholars Expose Anti-Indianism in America*, edited by Wahinkpe Topa (Four Arrows) aka Don Trent Jacobs. Austin: University of Texas Press.

Chatman, Seymour. 1978. *Story and Discourse: Narrative Structure in Fiction and Film*. Ithaca, N.Y.: Cornell University Press.

Cheyfitz, Eric. 2006. *The Columbia Guide to American Indian Literatures of the United States since 1945*. New York: Columbia University Press.

Cook-Lynn, Elizabeth. 1996. *Why I Can't Read Wallace Stegner and Other Essays: A Tribal Voice*. Madison: University of Wisconsin Press.

———. 2001. *Anti-Indianism in Modern America: A Voice from Tatekeya's Earth*. Urbana: University of Illinois Press.

Derrida, Jacques. 2002. *Negotiations: Interventions and Interviews, 1971–2001*. Edited and translated by Elizabeth Rottenberg. Stanford, Calif.: Stanford University Press.

Jameson, Fredric. 1972. *The Prison-House of Language: A Critical Account of Structuralism and Russian Formalism*. Princeton, N.J., Princeton University Press.

———. 1991. *Postmodernism, or, The Cultural Logic of Late Capitalism*. Durham, N.C.: Duke University Press.

Kelsey, Penelope Myrtle. 2008. *Tribal Theory in Native American Literature: Dakota and Haudenosaunee Writing and Indigenous Worldviews*. Lincoln: University of Nebraska Press.

Kroeber, Karl. 1979. "Deconstructionist Criticism and American Indian Literature." *Boundary 2* 7.3: 73–90.

Leitch, Vincent B. 2003. *Theory Matters*. New York: Routledge.

Mihesuah, Devon Abbott. 2004. "Academic Gatekeepers." In *Indigenizing the Academy: Transforming Scholarship and Empowering Communities*, edited by Devon Abbott Mihesuah and Angela Cavender Wilson, 31–47. Lincoln: University of Nebraska Press.

Miller, J. Hillis. 1976. "Stevens' Rock and Criticism as Cure (Part I)," *Georgia Review* 30.1: 5–31.

Owens, Louis. 1992. *Other Destinies: Understanding the American Indian Novel.* Norman: University of Oklahoma Press.

Said, Edward. 2002. "On Lost Causes." In *Reflections on Exile and Other Essays.* Cambridge: Harvard University Press.

Vizenor, Gerald, ed. 1989. *Narrative Chance: Postmodern Discourse on Native American Indian Literatures.* Albuquerque: University of New Mexico Press.

Warrior, Robert. 2006. "Native Critics in the World: Edward Said and Nationalism." In *American Indian Literary Nationalism,* by Jace Weaver, Craig S. Womack, and Robert Warrior, 179–223. Albuquerque: University of New Mexico Press.

Weaver, Jace. 2006. "Splitting the Earth: First Utterances and Pluralist Separatism." In *American Indian Literary Nationalism,* by Jace Weaver, Craig S. Womack, and Robert Warrior, 1–89. Albuquerque: University of New Mexico Press.

Weaver, Jace, Craig S. Womack, and Robert Warrior. 2006. *American Indian Literary Nationalism.* Albuquerque: University of New Mexico Press.

Wilson, Michael D. 2008. *Writing Home: Indigenous Narratives of Resistance.* East Lansing: Michigan State University Press.

Womack, Craig S. 1999. *Red on Red: Native American Literary Separatism.* Minneapolis: University of Minnesota Press.

———. 2008. "Theorizing Native American Experience." In *Reasoning Together: The Native Critics Collective,* by Janice Acoose et al., edited by Craig S. Womack, Daniel Heath Justice, and Christopher B. Teuton, 353–410. Norman: University of Oklahoma Press.

Youngblood Henderson, James (Sákéj). 2000. "Post Colonial Ghost Dancing: Diagnosing European Colonialism." In *Reclaiming Indigenous Voice and Vision,* edited by Marie Battiste, 57–76. Vancouver: University of British Columbia Press.

Living to Tell

Living to Tell Stories

P. JANE HAFEN

A t the 2003 Lannan Institute at the Newberry Library, Michael Tsosie (Mohave) averred that even using the term "decolonization" acknowledges the success of the conquerors when, in fact, indigenous peoples have survived and resisted systematic and institutionalized colonization. Tsosie's point is well-taken. Many aspects of indigenous life have persisted independent of the colonizing forces that have assailed our cultures and our lives. However, the mere fact that we are having this discussion in written English acknowledges the influences of the colonizers. Rather than submitting or hybridizing, native peoples have, in the phrase of Joy Harjo (Muscogee) and Gloria Bird (Spokane), *Reinvent[ed] the Enemy's Language* to reassert tribal sovereignties. Initially native resistance to colonization was on the expediential levels of mere physical survival. After verging on the edge of extinction, American Indian tribes have revealed their stamina and resistance, particularly in a flourishing production of scholarship and literature.

Asserting tribally centered literature and scholarship presents a number of challenges. Most institutions of higher learning require that critical discourse be conducted according to the prevailing theories with the assumption that such theories are universal. Too often, students are not exposed to native critics and believe application of mainstream criticism is appropriate to indigenous literatures. Such critical approaches constitute literary colonialism. In this essay I will demonstrate some of the complexities of centering critical approaches within tribal apparatus with several concrete examples.

White Earth Chippewa writer Gordon Henry Jr. begins his autobiographical essay in *Here First* with a section titled: "The First Door: I not as I" (146). Beginning with "postmodern or modern; sign or signifier," he then continues with a two page list of things he is not. Only then is he free to address the subsequent doors with an affirmative autobiographical "I am." Henry's pattern seems to be the case where many indigenous scholars spend as much time defining and explaining what they are not and what does not work in the literature as they do asserting indigenousness. This definition against oppression and colonization has long been the hallmark of Native American resistance literature and is a reality of our lives as American Indian peoples.

From the outset, I want to be perfectly clear that I am not being essentialist; I am not saying that only American Indian peoples should study American Indian literatures. I am asserting that academic training analogous to any other field is necessary, perhaps even more so, because the ethical stakes are higher when dealing with indigenous peoples, with ideas about us, and with the five hundred year history of colonialism. The matters of the academy involve how Indian peoples are written about, represented in literature, in institutions, in organizations, and in critical approaches.

Can anyone write about Indians fictively and critically? Of course, but doing it well requires particular insight. American popular imagination has been so infused with romantic images, noble images, savage images, that even some Native peoples play into those expectations. Spokane/Coeur d'Alene writer Sherman Alexie has said: "I believe that non-Natives can write anything they want about Native Americans, but they are writing a colonial literature that merely confirms existing ideas" (ix). Simon Ortiz, Acoma Pueblo, writes of conference venues where Indians sit in the back of the room and listen to what scholars have to say about them and their people. He fictionalizes an anthropology conference where a white archaeologist is trying to raise money for "site" "recovery"; where a white linguist is funded by state and federal agencies to "preserve" Indian languages. The Lakota linguist is left with not enough time to speak on the program. The narrator describes himself as a "show and tell" Indian (133–135). Too often, our participation is "show" but not tell.

Quite frequently I am invited to participate in various presentations, committees, and even anthologies. Often those in charge wish a "native point of view" represented. Much has been written about the service burden of minorities and women in the academy. These women and minorities can find themselves overextended with inadequate time to devote to scholarship and securing tenure. That part of the story is well-known (see Fogg 2003, A14). What is lesser known are the challenges those positions represent. Sometimes they involve Indians 101—a basic introduction to fundamental concepts regarding American Indians, their diversity and complex histories and literatures. Sometimes we are invited because our appearance seems politically correct, but our words are not regarded seriously, nor is our field. We may be invited and then disinvited. Or if we feel a particular venue is not appropriate and we decline, then we are also judged as being uncooperative.

For two years I chaired a Native American Literature Symposium sponsored by the American Literature Association. When I and other organizers suggested our interests were not best served by blending with other minority literatures, when we suggested holding the symposium at a tribally owned venue would serve Indian scholars and students and help educate non-Indian scholars and students, the American Literature Association dissociated from us. The story is a bit more complicated, but when we refused to be colonized by the agenda of the sponsoring association, we were dumped. Fortunately, there was sufficient critical mass and the Symposium has thrived and expanded at its subsequent locations: Mystic Lake, Minnesota, the home of the Shakopee Mdewakonton Sioux, and the Soaring Eagle Hotel and Seventh Generation Center of the Saginaw Chippewa. This is an act of decolonization by refusing to submit to the institutional desires of the ALA and by establishing our own voices and our own conference.

Having the Symposium in a tribally owned venue not only introduces some scholars to the realities of contemporary Indians but also is a commitment to community. Choctaw Devon Mihesuah observes, "[responsibility to the community is] the most serious problem in Native studies today. It also is an ethical and moral issue that is sidestepped by many scholars who focus their careers on studying indigenous peoples. Scholars absolutely do have a responsibility to the people they study." Our resources as a conference about Native peoples go to Native peoples, and in turn the Mdewakonton Sioux and the Saginaw Chippewa have supported us financially and culturally.

In the field of American Indian Studies the issues are complex, perhaps more so than other literary fields. Matters of colonization, language, history and culture cast their shadow on literary questions. Unfortunately, there are generally three types of scholars of American Indian Literatures. There are dilettantes or tourists[1] who may have encountered a literary work in one course in American Indian history or literature, who publish an article or present a conference paper without ever fully understanding the diversity of tribal cultures or contexts. Then there are those who re-colonize the literature through theoretical applications that may work in the intellectual abstract, but have little to do with the tribal contexts that produce the literature. Some of these scholars, and I am not exaggerating, spend their whole careers studying Indians and Indian Literatures without ever meeting an American Indian or understanding the depths of the field, without any contributions to Indian communities. Too frequently these applications contain serious errors and ignore current criticisms by American Indian scholars. They are published and perpetuated by like-minded scholars. These scholars are poachers. Finally, there are those scholars who carefully lay foundations of understanding through deliberate scholarship and through an awareness of the political implications of their work; they are our allies.

Rather than asserting what does not work for native peoples, what we are not, I will follow what Gordon Henry establishes by discussing affirmatively what we are. I will demonstrate a tribal approach with two Diné (Navajo) poets, Laura Tohe and Esther Belin. My methodology of establishing tribal contexts can be used with any tribe and is based largely on what Choctaw writer LeAnne Howe calls tribalography in her essay, "The Story of America." Howe writes:

Native stories, no matter what form they take (novel, poem, drama, memoir, film, history), seem to pull all the elements together of the storyteller's tribe, meaning the people, the land and multiple characters and all their manifestations and revelations, and connect these in past, present, and future milieus. (42)

In the classroom I use a group project to incorporate this methodology.[2] Each class member is assigned to a group. The group presents information that includes the following components: an origin myth, the traditional tribal name, a summary of tribal culture, a description of the tribe's geographical location, significant tribal historical events, current tribal status, and a recent critical article. The results of the group assignment are presented orally to the class. The group decides on the method of presentation, which can include panel discussions, game show formats, cooking demonstrations, and attempts at material culture exhibits. Part of each student's evaluation is based upon how well the group coordinates its information. Additionally, each individual member of the group prepares a seven- to nine-page essay that correlates the information from individual research and/or addresses critical issues of the work selected. Students use MLA style and documentation and include a bibliography of all resources for the essay and the presentation.

By working in a group, students are challenged to reassess their natural individualistic tendencies. While they cannot enter into or completely under-stand the full impact of tribal communities, they may begin to acknowledge group dynamics. Because information in particular categories will overlap, the students also will begin to see the holistic intricacies of tribal cultures.

From this project, students should learn that several origin stories may exist for the tribe. These traditional stories shape tribal world view and are alluded to in various Native texts. The apparent "discrepancies" and mul-tiple versions of stories the students will uncover in this part of the exercise bear witness to the fact not only is there diversity among the more than five hundred Indian nations in this country, but also among the various bands of peoples as well. Likewise, identifying the traditional tribal name will allow students to encounter the significance and power of naming among bands.

The summary of tribal culture is a large category that may encompass many aspects including social structure, gender divisions and constructions, material cultures, foods, dwellings, and arts. Often students discover that in some secondary literatures the historical emphasis in discussing cultures focuses on primarily male behaviors or employs racist or prejudicial language. This discovery provides a good opportunity to discuss the role of historical or anthropological texts in creating and perpetuating negative stereotypes of Indian peoples.

Students can learn about land issues and tribal distinctions through descriptions of geographic locations. Discussion of land is frequently connected with specific tribal historical events. A historical review helps students connect past to current and future events. Likewise, students profit from research on the tribe's current status by recognizing that American Indians are part of contemporary living cultures, not historical relics. Creative students sometimes contact various tribes directly for current and more detailed information. Assessment of a critical article may supplement or contradict the information already gathered by the group. By the time the students complete both the oral presentation and the accompanying essay they should be able to place the literature in a decolonized context.

The Navajo Nation has the largest land holdings of any tribe in the United States. In population the total numbers from the 2000 census are second only to Cherokees. However, those who claim Navajo and other races comprise less than ten percent of the total population of 298,197. Those who claim Cherokee and other races make up more that fifty-eight percent of the total Cherokee population of more than 700,000. The number of Cherokees might explain the preponderance of writers from John Rollin Ridge to Thomas King, Diane Glancy, Marilou Awiakta and Betty Louise Bell, just to name a few. What seems less clear is, if those Navajos are everywhere as they seem to be, apart from Luci Tapahonso and Rex Jim few Navajo writers are known. There are others, actually too many to list here, but they seem not to have yet entered the canon of teaching texts or critical study.

Non-Navajo authors have canonized the most familiar Navajo characters. Tony Hillerman's Jim Chee and Joe Leaphorn are probably most familiar to the reading public, despite criticisms and protests. Sherman Alexie, one of Hillerman's sharpest critics, observes that these kinds of characters are "popular because they're well written and exciting, but equally important, because they do not challenge any mainstream notions about Navajo Indians in particular or Native Americans in general" (xiii). N. Scott Momaday (Kiowa) and Leslie Marmon Silko (Laguna) have each created memorable Navajo characters. Momaday's Ben Benally narrates one section and offers the source for the title of *House Made of Dawn*. Silko's Betonie offers Tayo a sense of healing in *Ceremony* and in the widely anthologized short story from *Storyteller*, "Lullaby," Ayah instills fear in the men in the bar. Additionally in *Storyteller*, Silko establishes that the Navajos interact with their tribal neighbors, particularly the Laguna. After all, those Navajos show up regularly for feast day and they are kidnapped by the Laguna women. Still, as memorable and important as these characters may be, they are limited.

For the Navajo Nation, the following basic information is pertinent, but a scarce representation of a complex culture. Navajos call themselves Diné, meaning "the people." They are matrilineal and have distinct clan definitions. The linguistic foundation of their language, culture and relationships is *bikeh hozho* which signifies balance and beauty (see Witherspoon 1977). At Diné College, history begins with the Navajo creation story. Material culture indicates adaptation through rug and blanket weaving, sandpainting, silversmithing and sheepherding. Major historical events include the Long Walk of 1864, livestock reduction of the 1930s and 40s, the World War II Codetalkers, the consequences of uranium mining and mineral development. The official reservation is 25,000 square miles, but the land they consider sacred is within a matrix of four mountains. Two of the best sources about Navajos are *Language and Art in the Navajo Universe* by Gary Witherspoon and *Diné: A History of the Navajos* by Peter Iverson and Monty Roessel (Navajo).

Laura Tohe was born of the Sleepy Rock People for the Bitterwater clan (Native American Authors, Internet Public Library Project). Her book of poetry, *No Parole Today*, earned Tohe the Wordcraft Circle Writer of the Year in 1999. Additionally, she edited *Sister Nations*, with Heid Erdrich (Ojibwe), a collection of Native women's writing. Her most recent publication *Tseyi/ Deep in the Rock: Reflections on Canyon De Chelly* (2005) is a poetry collection accompanied by photographs by Stephen Strom and evinces the inextricable connection between place and identity. Tohe is author of the seminal essay, "There is No Word for Feminism in My Language" where she defines and explicates gender from a tribal perspective. In a different essay, "A Contextual Statement Surrounding Three Poems of Prejudice," she introduces herself:

I want to make it clear that this narrative is written from the perspective of a Diné woman. . . . I am not speaking for the Hopi, Chippewa or Pawnee, urban Indians or terminated Indians. They have their unique experience to tell, although we share similar experiences with U. S. colonialism and capitalism. (246)

Tohe definitively places herself within Diné traditions, as does her writing. The majority of poems in *No Parole Today* reflect Tohe's boarding school experiences. Others center on contemporary events. I chose the following poem because, to me, it captures the sense of a reservation border town as well as anything I have read.

AT MEXICAN SPRINGS

Up here I can see the
    glimmering lights of Gallup calling the
                Reservation
    like a whore standing under a light post
    the way they do in Juarez
          in Gallup
    when our sons are born they say
    "she gave birth to a wino"
    Gallup steals our children
    returns them empty and crumbled

But here the hills are quietly breathing
    the earth is a warm glowing blanket
    holding me in her arms
        It is here among the sunset in
                    every plant
                    every rock
                    every shadow
                    every movement
                    every thing

> I relive visions of ancient stories
>> First Woman and First Man
>> their children stretched across
>> these eternal sandstones
>> a deep breath
>> she brings me sustenance
>> life
> and I will live to tell my children these things. (47)

Mexican Springs is a small community on the Navajo reservation about twenty-two miles north of Gallup. As the Navajos have transitioned from an economy of complete subsistence to mixed mercantile and subsistence, they have been obliged to trade with towns such as Gallup. Tohe describes the circumstances:

> Border towns, such as Gallup, located near Indian reservations often are the most intolerant of Indian people, as is Gordon, Nebraska; Farmington, New Mexico; and Flagstaff, Arizona, to name a few. In these towns, Indian people experience the most blatant forms of racial intolerance. . . . the kinds of indignity [Diné] received in a town they have helped to support economically for decades: being waited on last or ignored by clerks, paying higher than average interest rates on vehicles and other major purchases, exploitation of Indian people's lack of understanding of business dealings, . . . and so on. (253)

Gallup is well known for selling alcohol that cannot be bought on the reservation, for acquiring "authentic" Indian goods at low prices and marketing them to the world. Billboards on I-40 proclaim the town's affiliation with Navajos and Indian Country, but belie the hostility of the town.

Tohe's counterbalance to Gallup is in the Diné place and traditions. The second stanza reveals the living earth and the sacred nature of place. The comprehensive wholeness of the phrases repeating the word "every" emphasize the unity and balance that comes from *bikeh hozho*. The comforting blanket could be an allusion to Navajo material culture.

The third stanza references a Diné creation story. The "eternal sand-stones" show the ontological nature of place and identity. By connecting, as LeAnne Howe stated, past, present and future, the speaker is free or decolo-nized. She then can declare survival for the future generations. That future is situated in land, Diné Bikéyah, traditions, story and resistance.

Esther Belin resists in a different way. She describes herself as an "U.R.I. (Urban-raised Indian)" (74). She was born in Gallup at the Indian hospital (64). She is of the Zia Clan and for the Bitterwater clan (72). Raised in Los Angeles and educated at UC Berkeley and IAIA, Institute of American Indian Arts, she nevertheless returns "home" to the Navajo reservation. In 1999, her first book, *From the Belly of My Beauty*, won the American Book Award from the Before Columbus Foundation.

Belin's cycle of poems centered around the character of Ruby is most compelling. Ruby's experiences are placed in urban settings and combat the stereotypes and misunderstandings familiar to urban Indians. Ruby is sexual, plays softball, attends art galleries, stands in line at the welfare office, con-fronts ignorance. In "Ruby and Child" her memory takes her back to Navajo images of frybread, weaving and the popularity of the Blackfeet Black Lodge Singers (45). Belin addresses blood quantum and tribal identity in "Ruby in Me #1": "¼ Navajo / ¼ Navajo / ¼ Navajo / ¼ Navajo . . . enrolled = proof / 50 / 80 / 100 if you can stand / it." Ruby is not autobiographical, though, and Belin says:

> Ruby was inspired from the women I've met and especially by dad's younger sister. Ruby is like your older sisters. She can say things I would never want to say. She is "in your face" ("Ruby's Answer"), not like me. I see Ruby as that voice of the people, a mirror for women of both positive and negative. (Jacobs 2000, 9)

Additionally, Dean Rader observes the angry tone and urban imagery are much like Sherman Alexie's writings (17). In "Ruby's Answer," Ruby has a non-reservation experience common to many urban Indians.

> Sunny day, Southern California restaurant, February 11, 1990. While eat-ing lunch, Ruby is confronted by a blonde woman with frosted hair and

gold wire-rimmed Ray-bans. The woman claims sisterhood with Ruby saying, "I know exactly how you feel because I'm part Indian myself." This is Ruby's response:

If you're Indian
I'm a WASP
White Indians aren't Indians, blondie
You mixed and assimilated and trashed and denied your Indian
blood
You want to claim and regain your Indian identity
maybe in another life
Why all of a sudden do you want to be Indian?
Why do you want to be considered a minority?
An insignificant inferior piece of red trash?
Why do you want to go from historically supreme to historically
oppressed?
Why do you want to be a statistic and census number and a
dropout and a drunk and a savage and a squaw or a princess and a
car and a mascot and completely exploited until you no longer want
to be Indian?
Are you on crack or did you just get a vision from your great—great-great-
Cherokee grandma?
Blondie, this isn't the Girl Scouts
This is religious freedom and unrecognition and Big Mountain and
releasing brother Leonard Peltier
Indians don't "come out" like gay people
They are wiped out by the people that gave you most of your
blood!

Ruby didn't mind getting kicked out of the restaurant because she got a free lunch. (42)

On the surface Ruby may appear to be a generic Indian. In the context of the other Ruby poems, and her other writings, she is clearly Navajo. Not having specific Navajo cultural markers does not diminish either Ruby's or Belin's Navajo identity, but demonstrates that indigenous peoples often must confront a general ignorance that is a branch of specific tribal ignorance. With vivid imagery and tight language Belin shows that what Ruby experiences in this poem is common to many urban Indians. Her response reveals a prejudice that parallels the racism of Gallup with denial, ignorance and good intentions.

The two poems by these Navajo authors are but a brief comparison. Many other touchpoints can be established in both poetry collections. Both resist colonization through their writing, their subject matter and their use of Diné language. Clearly, each poet defines herself as Navajo/Diné, but their voices and positions are varied as the landscape. As Dean Rader observes in his comparison between Belin and Tapahonso:

> I would like to suggest, however, that [their] experiences can be quite different from each other and that the tribal reality of the Diné extends beyond the world of the four sacred peaks and into the frenetic urban scene of the city, despite those who would like to keep it isolated in Arizona and New Mexico. (Rader 2000, 26)

With more than two-thirds of Native peoples living off-reservation, residency is hardly a litmus test for tribal authenticity. Nevertheless, the variety of Indian experiences within tribes and among tribes, on and off-reservations, with primarily Native speakers and English speakers, demonstrates that there is no singular Native American or American Indian. As Belin observes: "That I am one voice for Native people. Indian people have such different cultures, and I am Navajo, but I do not represent my whole tribe. Still, what I write is valid and legitimate as history" (Jacobs 2000, 10).

The stories in indigenous literatures are in academic writing as well. As Indian scholars we are constantly aware of our responsibilities. We are aware that studying Native peoples in the academy goes beyond intellectual enterprise. We are aware that what we write and what we present will shape how others perceive Indian peoples. Too much of our energy is spent explaining what we are not. Like Gordon Henry, we are not postmodern or modern, we are not post-colonial. We are not trapped between two worlds. As twenty-first-century indigenous peoples, we are survivors. We are survivors of disease, of violence, of colonization, of boarding schools, of personal racism and of institutional racism.

A number of contemporary critics have laid foundations for ethical criticisms of American Indian literatures. Osage scholar Robert Allen Warrior sets out ideas of tribal and intellectual sovereignties. Choctaw writer LeAnne Howe offers tribalography as a methodology, that is, giving due to tribal cultures and histories. Muscogee writer Craig Womack also argues for a tribally based criticism outside the colonizing mainstream of traditional literary methodologies. Lakota historian Craig Howe models reconsiderations of historiographies. Kahnawake Mohawk Taiaiake Alfred (Gerald R. Alfred) and Mojave Michael Tsosie are young scholars who are arguing for indigenousness, resisting colonialism and starting with an assertion of tribal identity and culture.

We owe and give honor to those who have laid foundations in American Indian Studies, those who have worked hard to establish a place for American Indian Studies with strength and resistance, like Bea Medicine (Lakota), Vine Deloria Jr. (Dakota), and Elizabeth Cook-Lynn (Crow Creek Dakota). We look forward to the day when we can move beyond a reactionary mode, beyond colonial assumptions of Indian identity and romanticized images. We seek out literary criticism that does not perpetuate modes of colonialism with misunderstanding and appropriation. We look to writers who tell our stories of shared experience and tribal distinctions. As the words of Ojibwe writer Louise Erdrich explain from "Jacklight":

> It is their turn now,
> their turn to follow us. Listen,
> they put down their equipment.
> It is useless in the tall brush.
> And now they take the first steps, not knowing
> how deep the woods are and lightless.
> How deep the woods are. (Erdrich 1984, 4)

NOTES

1. I owe the terms "tourist," "poacher," and "ally" to James H. Cox and Daniel Justice, Cherokee.

2. This pedagogical method is discussed more fully in Griffin and Hafen 2004.

WORKS CITED

Alexie, Sherman (Spokane/Coeur d'Alene). 2003. "Introduction." *Watershed,* by Percival Everett. 1996; Boston: Beacon Press.

Belin, Esther G. (Navajo). 1999. *From the Belly of My Beauty.* Sun Tracks, vol. 38. Tucson: University of Arizona Press.

Erdrich, Louise (Ojibwe). 1984. "Jacklight." In *Jacklight,* 3–4. New York: Henry Holt.

Fogg, Piper. 2003. "So Many Committees, So Little Time." *Chronicle of Higher Education* 50.17 (December 19): A14.

Griffin, Gwen W., and P. Jane Hafen. 2004. "An Indigenous Approach to Teaching the Works of Louise Erdrich." In *Modern Language Association Approaches to Teaching Louise Erdrich,* edited by Greg Sarris and Connie Jacobs, 95–101. New York: Modern Language Association.

Harjo, Joy (Muscogee) and Gloria Bird (Spokane). 1998. *Reinventing the Enemy's Language: Contemporary Native Women's Writings of North America.* New York: Norton.

Henry, Gordon, Jr. (White Earth Chippewa). 2000. "Entries into the Autobiographical I." In *Here First: Autobiographical Essays by Native American Writers,* edited by Arnold Krupat and Brian Swann, 164–81. New York: Modern Library.

Howe, LeAnne (Choctaw). 2002. "The Story of America: A Tribalography." In *Clearing a Path: Theorizing the Past in Native American Studies,* edited by Nancy Shoemaker, 29–50. New York: Routledge.

Iverson, Peter. 2002. *Diné: A History of the Navajos.* Photographs by Monty Roessel (Navajo). Albuquerque: University of New Mexico Press.

Jacobs, Connie. 2000. "From California to the Four Corners: An Urban Navajo Returns Home: An Interview with Esther G. Belin." *Studies in American Indian Literatures* 12.3 (Fall): 1–13.

Metz, Andrew. 2003. "Identity Crisis: Survival of Tribes at Stake as Strict Rules Weed Out

Members." Newsday.com. Http://www.newsday.com/news/nationworld/nation/ nyusindi213593131dec21,0,5585606.story?coll=ny-nationalnews-print. December 22.

Mihesuah, Devon (Choctaw). 2003. H-AmIndian Discussion Series-Discussion #1: Scholarly responsibilities to Indigenous Communities. April 16.

Ortiz, Simon J. (Acoma Pueblo). 1999. "What Indians Do." In *Men on the Moon: Collected Short Stories,* 129–140. Tucson: University of Arizona Press.

Rader, Dean. 2000. "'I Don't Speak Navajo': Esther C. Belin's *In the Belly of My Beauty.*" *Studies in American Indian Literatures* 12.3 (Fall): 14–34.

Tohe, Laura (Navajo). 1998. "A Contextual Statement Surrounding Three Poems of Prejudice." In *Communicating Prejudice,* edited by Michael L. Hecht, 246–56. Thousand Oaks, Calif.: Sage Press.

———. 1999. *No Parole Today.* Albuquerque: West End Press.

"Tohe, Laura." 2003. Native American Authors, Internet Public Library Project. http:// www.ipl.org/div/natam/bin/browse.pl/A190. December 22.

Witherspoon, Gary. 1977. *Language and Art in the Navajo Universe.* Ann Arbor: University of Michigan Press.

Taking Turns Breaking Me into Pieces: The Reading of Immiscible Others in Ray A. Young Bear's *Black Eagle Child: The Facepaint Narratives*

ROB APPLEFORD

Autobiography is the subject of personal logistics of knowable selves. How does one put I where one is or was? One needs a center, around which to build. The center is rarely an I.

—Gordon Henry Jr., writing as Bombarto Rose

Young Bear's universe of poetic authority, instead of converting others' labor to his own poetic capital, seeks a place in a communal arena where there is room for his imagination and room for others. Not that anything others might do is okay.

—Robert Dale Parker, "To Be There, No Authority to Anything: Ontological Desire and Cultural and Poetic Authority in the Poetry of Ray A. Young Bear"

Ray A. Young Bear's literary labor rests on a paradox. He sees himself as an inheritor of the traditionalist project of his ancestors, who sought to preserve Mesquakie cultural knowledge from outside encroachment and forced assimilation, and who understood, in Young Bear's words, "what to keep, what to keep away" in the project of cultural survival (2002a). Yet, despite this conservative inheritance, Young Bear's writing experiments with artistic forms, breaches distinctions of genre and identity in its articulation of experience, and thereby interrogates and expands the boundaries of expression that Native writing is commonly understood to encompass. How is it possible to be at once a cultural conservationist and an artistic experimenter? This paradox might be tinctured somewhat if one were to read his work as a syncretic fusion, a keeping and keeping away that mixes sacred and profane according to context and circumstance. But the traditional Mesquakie knowledge and experience "for keeping" that Young Bear either elides or re-presents without explanation for a non-Mesquakie reader will often refuse to be diluted; it is what Young Bear, borrowing a term from classical chemistry, calls "immiscible" (2002b), meaning "of a liquid incapable of forming a true solution *with* or *in* another liquid" (OED). This immiscible tradition both invites and resists the literary tools we might think to apply to it to make its interpretative ambiguity potable. When Young Bear's text resists us and refuses our tools, it is tempting to throw up hands and claim that the text is not for us (*with* us or *in* us), that it frustrates any "Outside World" reader's attempts to theorize the author's commingling of knowable and unknowable. The result of this is foreclosure and silence.

For example, in his discussion of Young Bear's work, Neil Schmitz asks, "How will secular Anglo-American readers engage the Mesquakie supernaturalism (UFO sightings, witchcraft, alien abductions, and meteorological anomalies) that Young Bear constantly sets forth in his text?" He answers with a disclaimer: "This feature of Young Bear's fiction, its signs and wonders, does not address an Anglo-American public . . . . It is straightforward Mesquakie reportage for a Mesquakie literature that exists inside American literature" (2001, 156). Schmitz's evocation of Homi Bhabha's description of the Bible as a book of "signs taken for wonders" (Bhabha 1985, 144) for the nineteenth-century Indian subcontinent suggests that similar dislocation and distortion awaits "Anglo-American" readers, that "the dazzling light" of Young Bear' work "sheds only areas of darkness" (Bhabha 1985, 147). I would ask whether this conclusion is in fact useful or necessary when considering how others might read Young Bear's immiscible "fiction."

In light of this question, I will consider the chapter entitled "The Supernatural Strobe Light" in his experimental autobiography *Black Eagle Child: The Facepaint Narratives*. I will argue that Young Bear's story in this chapter attempts to build a notion of the self around what are a series of unexpected and revelatory "centers" (as Henry's Bomarto Rose epigraph to this essay suggests), including an uncanny encounter with extraterrestrial visitors. "The Supernatural Strobe Light" employs the rhetorical devices of the typical humanist poetics of autobiography, and these devices invite a particular theoretical apparatus. But Young Bear's use of these devices in the story problematizes the reading practice this poetics requires for itself to function, and thus makes occluded relationships visible within this poetics. In "The Supernatural Strobe Light," the relationship between readers and the protagonist Edgar Bearchild is recast, not as a fictive mutual constitution of selves, humanist readers, and humanist writer, but rather as a problematic collision of Others. The Other in the text is defined by its ability to read itself as well as other Others. Given this connection between Otherness and reading, the "ultimate" Other in the text is ambiguously rendered through the narrative devices Young Bear uses; the protagonist Edgar Bearchild, the readers, and the extraterrestrials all help to destabilize the definition of the humanist self and the narrative it tells to know itself. The Mesquakie author both elicits and ultimately thwarts the readers' desire for a self that can be apprehended as a knowable speaking subject, and this desire is refracted through the prism of the popular cultural narrative of extraterrestrial contact. Ultimately, what Young Bear's story accomplishes is to tantalize the "Anglo-American" (in my case, "Anglo-Canadian") reader with potential points of traction that would allow the reader to move in and out of the Other's space in the story with impunity. The story told does not withhold its Mesquakie "secrets," but rather, calls into question the mastery that any syncretic keeping or keeping away would take for granted. Without a confident theory (Mesquakie or otherwise) of interpretation in place to guide us, narrator, reader, and alien are revealed to have immiscible relationships to each Other.

Contemporary Native autobiographers face a number of challenges, not the least of which involves the kind of self they wish to present to readers. Theorists of autobiography have variously understood the self in the autobiographical text as being unified and individual, as split, as textually produced, and as impossible. The notion of the self as a unique and self-evident entity has been severely attacked by poststructuralists, historicists, and psychoanalytic theorists, among others. Yet there is the attendant risk that a self without such inherent cohesion serves to reaffirm, as Biddy Martin warns, "institutional privileges enjoyed by those who can afford to disavow 'identity' and its 'limits' over against those for whom such disavowals reproduce their invisibility" (1988, 78). And since historically, as Arnold Krupat reminds us, "Indian autobiography is a contradiction in terms" (1985, 30), both the narration and the demarcation of the "I that speaks" (Smith 1988, 100) in contemporary Native autobiography are necessarily inventive.

Our selves are returned to us, constantly. This pat observation takes on the force of an operational imperative in the writing and reading of autobiographical texts. In most autobiographies, selves are written to be returned as a kind of gift to the author by the readers. But this is never a simple return; autobiography is constructed using narrative devices to facilitate a particular (preferred) version of the self to be read and returned as a gift.[1] These devices, borrowed from literary and social scientific discourses,[2] signal the readers how to read the self in the autobiography, and signal the success of the return for the readers. Humanist autobiography is a story articulating "coherence, progress, and rationality"—as Janice Carlisle and Daniel R. Schwarz define "humanistic narrative" (1994, 4), and the self becomes a standing figure of the narrative as defined by humanist discourse, what Sidonie Smith calls "the autonomous or metaphysical self as the agent of its own achievement" (1987, 39). If read as a species of dramatic performance, the autobiographical text may employ literary devices to complicate or defer the *anagnorisis* of its protagonist, but this complication or deferral is meant to heighten the dramatic effect of the self-recognition that ultimately must occur. As Shirley Neuman explains, in humanist autobiography, "The autobiographer is seen as discovering meaningful pattern[s] in the flux of past experience in order to arrive at an understanding of himself [*sic*] as unique and unified" (1992, 214). While this (re)discovery of self is necessary to the project of humanist autobiography, this discovery must also be deferred by the autobiographer so that readers can participate in the assembling of details that constitute self-discovery. This humanist model of autobiography invites readers to assemble "the flux of past experience" through close reading of biographical details, the close reading of a literary text, to arrive at a preferred reading of the autobiographer's final self-portrait as immanently evoked but only solidified by reader interpretation. In this way, the reader transforms the autobiographer's Other back into a self; the reader derives pleasure from the process of reading, and thereby making, another's life.

This process of returning a self becomes problematic when the rhetorical devices employed by the autobiographer efface the distinction between fact and fancy, and make anxious the recognition and reconstitution of the autobiographical self, its making, by its readers. This anxiety can be troubling for those who seek to define autobiography as exclusively nonfictional, and the lack of consistency Grove Press has demonstrated in the marketing of Young Bear's experimental autobiography reflects and exacerbated just this kind of discomfort.[3] The first volume of his narrative, *Black Eagle Child*, is called "an experimental autobiography" by Albert E. Stone in his foreword (1997, x), yet the second volume, *Remnants of the First Earth,* is called Young Bear's "first full-length novel."[4] This, despite the fact that the second volume is a prequel that follows the early lives of the first volume's "biographical" characters. This ambiguity exceeds the generic limits of Native autobiography, which frequently concerns itself with the articulation of a knowable and factual Native self. Both *Black Eagle Child* and *Remnants of the First Earth* are accounts of Young Bear's life as an enrolled member of the Mesquakie (Red Earth) Settlement in Iowa, but the commingling of fictionalized and real events, composite and biographical characters, renders a strictly factual-autobiographical interpretation impossible.

Young Bear himself does little to clear up the ambiguity of genre in his work. Instead, he describes the character of Edgar Bearchild, the protagonist in both volumes, as "mirror[ing] in part my own laborious Journey of

Words" (1997, 256); tellingly, two metaphors, a mirror and a journey, sand-wich the qualifier "in part." While the author is less interested in separating fact from fiction, he characterizes the process of writing the narratives as inherently artistic, akin to the plastic accumulation of detail in visual art: "The creation of *Black Eagle Child* was equivalent to a collage done over a lifetime via the tedious layering upon layering of images by an artist" (255). The collage-effect calls attention to the disparate images in the text, but also to how these images cohere into a meaningful whole. Whether this whole is a "real" life, Young Bear's life, or something else entirely, becomes the fascinating problem.

It would be impossible, I feel, to truly sum up the multiple narrative strategies at play in *Black Eagle Child,* and I have yet to see a critic attempt to do so. In the chapter of *Black Eagle Child* I have chosen to focus upon, "The Supernatural Strobe Light," the main character, Edgar Bearchild, struggles to perfect his talent for storytelling while trying to survive in an isolated cabin on the Black Eagle Child Settlement with his wife Selene. Edgar and Selene arrive home one night and experience an uncanny encounter with a cluster of UFOs. After an aborted attempt to shoot at the cluster, they flee to Edgar's grandmother's house and later return to the scene of the encounter with members of Edgar's family, but the UFOs have disappeared. Two days after the event, Edgar, Selene, and their families watch the UFO cluster cross over the skies of the Black Eagle Child Settlement. Taking inspiration from this volume's overall desire to encourage creative engagements between story and theory, I will follow this particular story through as a spectator/reader. *Theory* and *theater* have the same Greek origin—*thea,* sight, viewing; *theoros,* spectator. Thus, to treat this UFO encounter as a performance will help me remain attentive to moments of reflexivity that evoke theory while contesting (or co-testing) it.

"The Supernatural Strobe Light" begins with a series of descriptions of a "typical Midwestern Sunday" on the Black Eagle Child Settlement. The Settlement has been promoted by the local newscast as an ideal place to watch autumn leaves turn color in the last Indian summer of the season, and Edgar is aware of the political irony of this recommendation: "To be within visual sight of the First North Americans, even if for a moment in an enclosed, air-conditioned car, lent a sense of credibility to earth's physical change" (175). The residents of the Black Eagle Child Settlement take advantage of this intense scrutiny by setting up lawn chairs in front of their homes, "observing the observers" (175). Thus, Young Bear introduces the theme of spectatorship into the narrative, where Native Americans are observed by the tourists who flock to witness a spectacle of authenticity. In similar fashion, readers are reminded how spectatorship can underwrite Native autobiography, where the Native subject is scrutinized by readers who expect a deeper view of culture and identity than a tourist drive-by could ever afford. In his poetry, Young Bear frequently expresses his distaste for this hypocritical spectatorship: "you can't get away from people / who think what they see / is in actuality all they will / ever see / as if all in one moment they can sense / automatically what makes a people" (1980, 171). If readers remain tourists, they have failed to apprehend the "I that speaks." Yet the observation is clearly two-way, and Young Bear lets readers know that he is aware of the expectations of his observers, that his autobiography, in the words of Marlene Kadar, "anticipates the reader's determination of the text" (1992, 10). While he knows we are observing him, he does not refuse to provide a subject for our observation. On the contrary, he takes great pains to provide us, through his proxy Edgar, with intimate details of his life, details that reveal his feelings of inadequacy and failure as a husband, provider, and artist.

Edgar and his wife originally took the secluded cabin on the floodplain to serve as a retreat, where Edgar could live off a modest arts grant and compose "volumes of poetry" (177). But after three years and little to show for his efforts, Edgar acknowledges that the retreat was a literal one, and that "nothing spectacular had happened in terms of our love and commitment to each other—and our work."

He also mourns the lack of children in his life, and sees their pronounced absence as a haunting presence: "The faces and bodies of children assembled themselves from fragmented pieces of our imagination, and they sat down across from us at the supper table" (176). Plagued by writer's block, poverty, constant flooding, and his wife's selling of precious beadwork to tourists,[5] Edgar feels his own failure acutely, and spends his time making a documentary of his decline by turning an old 16mm movie camera on himself: "The physical effects of stress could only be seen on a time-lapse 16mm film in weekly intervals . . . we watched the whirring footage on the drywall" (177). While Young Bear can affirm that "i know for a fact that my people's / ways aren't based on grade-b movies" (1980, 172), Edgar's decline risks becoming just such a production. But like the tourists flocking to witness the death of autumn leaves that becomes conflated with the living Mesquakie people, the film record of his decline can only capture the external objectification of Edgar, an Other to himself, while his narrative emphasizes the magnitude of his pain that constitutes his humanity, a thoroughgoing confession of abjection.

It is at this point that *thea* and *theoros* precipitate in an interpretative solution. Readers, if diligent humanist assemblers, have ample material with which to construct Edgar Bearchild as an "I that speaks." The apparitions of stillborn children, the selling of precious beadwork, and the time-lapse film all can be read as metaphors for Edgar's inability to truly inhabit the present, his self haunted by spectral reminders of his past and future. The ghost children, "Javier, the first child we lost during Selene's sixth month of pregnancy . . . and the other child, the one we didn't even see" (176), mark the grief for the past and the grief for the future, since Edgar and Selene have no parental experiences either to remember or to anticipate.[6] Edgar echoes this theme of future loss even more acutely when lamenting the selling of his wife's beadwork: "I had already seen [the beadwork regalia] as items I would proudly wear at my own funeral in the future." Edgar is a figure haunted by his own demise, and the time-lapse film represents this haunting "as if a carpet needle had been stuck in my ribs, deflating the vibrant self" (177). This entire episode can be read with attention to what anthropologist Clifford Geertz has called "thick description," the "piled-up structures of inference and implication" whose subtlety can reveal culturally constituted (and constitutive) selves to the sensitive observer (1973, 5–6). This mode of analysis furnishes the deferred self-discovery of the subject—the "vibrant self"—that is glimpsed in fragments and must be reclaimed as a gift of return from the reader to the autobiographer. Yet, as the story unfolds, we are made to understand that this gift of return is not necessarily one that we have been authorized to give.

The rest of the story consists of a detailed account of Edgar and Selene's late-night encounter with an otherworldly presence, which first makes itself known as the repeated screeching of an owl in the darkness. Edgar, who fancies himself an accomplished vocalist, chooses to answer the screech in kind, mimicking the changes in the owl's call "with the finesse of an opera singer." But both he and Selene quickly realize that "something extraordinary was pretending to be an owl," whose "childlike wailing" was "unlike any I had ever heard" (180–81), and they quickly take refuge in their cabin. This exchange with the owl, coming on the heels of Edgar's confession, can be read in a way consonant with a humanist redemptive agenda. Having confessed his inadequacy, Edgar can show off as a skilled mimic, able to precisely echo the call of the owl and prove his ability as a vocalist and thus as an artist. In this way, Edgar's statement that "something extraordinary was pretending to be an owl" can be read as self-description by readers who wish to read Edgar's triumphant turn from abjection to mastery, to "something extraordinary." But Edgar also acknowledges that he cannot mimic the "childlike wailing," a detail that both echoes his artistic failures and suggests that the owl's screech could be read as a metaphoric repetition of Edgar's haunting by his nonexistent children, the return of another barely repressed personal failure. As the owl becomes plural, three owls all engaged in "demonic" screeching, Edgar tells us that "my sanity began to splinter into shards of falling glass as the three demonic owls took turns breaking me into pieces" (181). Thus, the duel of mimicry with the owls is easily read within a typical poetics of humanist autobiographical practice as a turning point in the narrative of self-discovery, either towards an ability to know or towards a failure to know one's self.

But the story quickly begins to shatter this neat hermeneutic as surely as the "something extraordinary" shatters Edgar's sanity. Outside their cabin, the unseen owls are joined by hundreds of fireflies in "military jet" formation, a sphere of soft light, a flare-colored oval mass, and finally a supernatural strobe light. Young Bear's humanist autobiographical narrative already presupposes a willing and enforced suspension of disbelief on the part of readers to engineer deferred gratification. Now it is now infused with the narrative of UFO encounters, with its own dynamics of belief and disbelief. The UFOs that Edgar and his wife battle can either be read similarly to the owls, as metaphorical representations of self-estrangement, or as "real," which would force readers to accept the UFO encounter as empirically true and not simply fiction or hallucination. Both interpretative choices yield interesting results.

The UFOs refuse to make their intentions known to the couple in the cabin. They are *theoros,* spectators in the fundamental sense, exaggerated counterparts of the tourists in search of Indian summer who lead off the story. Their veiled but consistent surveillance causes Edgar to confront them with the words: "You, whoever you are, we have done nothing to deserve this, nor have we offended anyone. What is it you want when we live in poverty?" Interestingly, it is at this point, after confessing his abjection openly for the first time in his life, that Edgar comes to the revelation requisite of humanist autobiography: "I had never confessed this verity to anyone, much less to Selene or myself. To realize my own poverty and ineptness as a man—a descendant of a proud people—was painful to me" (182–83). Of course, what is obscured here is the readers' position in relation to this confession. While Edgar hasn't confessed this sense of failure to anyone openly, he *has* confessed it to *us,* only a page before.

What becomes interesting is the construction of the Other in the story, since the humanist model frequently occludes the Self/Other binary in favor of a self-returned-through-the-help-of-another-self dynamic, which is itself a willing fiction. It becomes necessary to see Edgar's relationship with the UFOs, ultimate Others who watch but say nothing, receiving Edgar's pleas without comment, as identical to the relationship between Young Bear and his readers. As readers, *we* are the UFOs, and Edgar's confrontation with the UFOs is also a refigured analogy for autobiographical spectatorship. One of Edgar's strategies to protect himself from the otherworldly visitors is to strip himself naked, based on traditional Mesquakie belief that "night-enemies cannot see a naked human body in their realm . . . you can gain power over them because they, too, are naked" (181). Just as the naked body is at once powerful and abject, so is the "naked" self revealed through humanist autobiography powerful and abject. And we as readers, reading the self's engagement with the absolute Other in the text, are reminded of our own nakedness and Otherness as spectators of this voyeurism. There is no longer the illusion of humanist spectatorial sympathy here, for as Jacques Derrida suggests, "It is the ear of the other that signs. The ear of the other says me to me and constitutes the *autos* of my autobiography" (1985, 51). We as readers can only watch the absolute Other "lend an ear" to Edgar and thereby return the "me" to Edgar, a "me" we might have thought was the readers' to reconstruct and return.

But the UFOs not only lend themselves to being read as a refiguring of the spectatorial relationship; they also impel readers to accept them as real in a material sense. In an interview with Elias Ellefson, Young Bear has affirmed that this story is based on a true experience that happened to himself and his wife Stella: "While it may be visually stunning to watch movies like 'The Exorcist' or 'Close Encounters of the Third Kind,' to be an actual witness or participant in a supernatural manifestation is nightmarish. Steven Spielberg is brilliant, but I doubt if he has ever seen a mega-UFO that fills the sky. We have" (2004). Like any other UFO encounter story, we are confronted with the fundamental issue of belief. If we as readers can choose to believe Young Bear's narrative as "true," we can also choose to accept it as a revealing and important, but nevertheless fictionalized story of self-discovery (a choice closer to the process of literary interpretation of fiction). Young Bear's self-conscious confluence of fiction and autobiography creates both a sophisticated re-presentation of his experience, bringing the readers closer to the process through which subjectivity is limned, and a problematic "escape hatch" for readers, allowing them to dismiss the reality of the fantastic events Young Bear bears witness to, and, by extension, the reality of the "I that speaks" constituted through these fantastic events.

By grounding his revelation of self-discovery in a story that is all about the reality of experience, Young Bear also challenges the expectations of readers who might want a self frontloaded with inherently conservative cultural expectations. When a Native writer attempts to speak a subject through autobiography, the attendant knowledge that is spoken by that subject is often assumed to be strictly framed by the cultural tradition of his or her tribal community, and thus, by the "burden of epistemologies" that Paul Smith identifies in autobiography:

Whenever the "I" speaks, a knowledge is spoken; whenever a knowledge speaks, an "I" is spoken. This is the dialectical mechanism of a certain presumption of the "subject": that is, a "subject" is presumed to exist, indexed as an "I" and loaded with the burden of epistemologies, wittingly or not. (1988, 100)

This burden is not only personal but also ethnically representative, both communal and historical in weight and significance. The Native writer must grapple with indexical knowledges in autobiographical writing that are frequently perceived in dominant discourse as being culturally conservative, non- (or anti-) individualistic, and, if these conditions are met, authentic. And yet Young Bear's experimental autobiography challenges the notion that its "thick description" (Geertz) is meant to make Mesquakie cultural identity transparently knowable for readers.

If subjectivity is neither predicated upon a tightly humanist program of "coherence, progress, and rationality" (Carlisle and Schwarz 1994, 4–5), nor upon a loosely defined (but nevertheless somehow immediately recognizable) index of Native traditions, readers are left without stable signifiers to read or to make readable through reconstitution and recognition. And all so-called ethnic writers of experimental autobiography are caught in a similar double-bind. Shelby Steele, in his discussion of African-American artists, discusses the problematic position of "ethnic" artists, caught between dominant and marginal expectations of how "racial orthodoxy" should be deployed:

> racial orthodoxy is a problem . . . since its goal is to make the individual responsible for the collective political vision. This orthodoxy arbitrates the artist's standing within the group: the artist can be as individual as he or she likes as long as the group view of things is upheld. . . . The effect of this is to pressure the work of art, no matter what inspired it, into a gesture of identification that reunites the artist and the group. (1992, 28)

In this way, the autobiography mobilizes a double return: a self that is returned to "the group" through racial orthodoxy, and a self that is returned to the autobiographer by readers through recognition of this racial orthodoxy. Importantly, the latter return becomes predicated on the former. Edgar desires a gesture of identification with his ethnic group the Mesquakie in order to ground his uncanny experience, as indicated by his solicitation of advice from two Mesquakie elders, Edgar's grandmother and Alfred Pretty-Boy-in-the-Woods (the previous tenant of Edgar and Selene's cabin). What surprises Edgar (and, by extension, anxious readers seeking cultural context to cohere the self) is that "two outstanding elders in whom we had the most trust had no answers. Theories were offered, and all seemed plausible. Each lent the event more mystery and bewilderment" (187). By showing traditional Mesquakie knowledge—such as when Edgar and his wife Selene perform various traditional protective ceremonies that Edgar glosses for the readers—and the limits of this knowledge—Edgar's elders haven't a clue what the UFOs "mean" in a traditional context—Young Bear challenges the readerly expectation that the "I that speaks" will necessarily manifest particular knowledge that can be recognized and accepted as authentic. Because Edgar's experience with the extraterrestrials is outside the conceptual framework of tradition, we are forced to suspend the return of a traditionally revitalized self back to the author.[7] And since the Mesquakie elders are shown offering plausible but unsatisfying "theories" about the encounter, the reader is also reminded that a theory's fit does little to indicate its interpretative use. Once again, the story leaves both Edgar and his readers in limbo.

When one considers how Native identity has been framed in relation to extraterrestrial contact in recent years, Young Bear's narrative strategy makes particular sense. Native peoples and aliens have been connected in both non-Native and Native discourse,[8] and their relationship has been presented as being mutually constitutive of a shared Otherness. On one hand, Native peoples and aliens have been seen to share a common Otherness in relation to dominant culture, a popular example of this connection being *The X-Files'* triptych "Anasazi—The Blessing Way—Paper Clip," first broadcast in 1995.[9] In these episodes, it is suggested that the ancient Southwest people known as the Anasazi ("Ancient Ones," mistranslated in the episodes as "Ancient Aliens") were "taken up" by extraterrestrials hundreds of years ago, and thus, their present-day descendants, the Colorado Navajo, stoically await the visitors' return ("X-Files Scripts Archives" 2005). A more lighthearted take on this scenario is displayed by Native artists such as Mohawk painter

John Kahionhes Fadden and Cherokee writer Thomas King. In Fadden's 1983 painting entitled *Wouldn't It Be Funny?* an alien stands outside of his space craft, having removed his space helmet: his wryly grinning Native face and long black hair tweak the irony of the painting's title (in Ryan 1999, 114). In King's short story "How Corporal Colin Sterling Saved Blossom, Alberta, and Most of the Rest of the World as Well," indigenous peoples all over the world begin to mysteriously stiffen and acquire an iridescent and impenetrable body covering. As "blue coyote-aliens" descend to Earth and begin to stack the Indians like so much living firewood inside their space-ships, one rigid Native is heard to whisper faintly, "What took you so long?" (1993, 53).

There are two underlying premises here concerning the Native-alien re-lationship: the first, that Natives and aliens share an Otherness in relation to dominant discourse, and second, that the Native self is lent consistency in this relationship through the return of the self by the alien Other. In the *X-Files,* the Otherness of the Navajo is linked to the Otherness of the alien visitors. The Navajo become fetishized objects marked by a difference that is both extraterrestrial and terrestrial, un/natural, and therefore always deferred and unknowable. To once again reintroduce the trope of reading into this discus-sion, the floating signifier of "alien" allows readers to read Native peoples as familiar metonyms for a larger Otherness, without ever requiring the fixing of the signifier within material or cultural contexts. As *The X-Files'* series tag-line affirms, "The truth is out there," never here, where Native and non-Native peoples must live. Thus, Native peoples are suspended as Other in dominant discourse through their connection to otherworldly Others; their difference is reinforced rather than explained by the connection, and the Native self is returned through dominant discourse as an Other to itself. In the ironic turn of the trope by Fadden and King, both the Otherness of the Natives and the Otherness of the aliens are shown to be illusory. In one sense, both Fadden and King suggest that neither extraterrestrials nor Native peoples are truly Other, especially to themselves.[10] Fadden and King narrate a return of the Native self made complete and cosmically whole through the intercession of the aliens. Of course, this fabled return is as much a desire as a certainty, and reveals the need for the Native self to dispel the enforced Otherness that dominant discourse has assigned it.[11] Thus, the Native encounter with aliens is either an encounter with absolute alterity or an encounter with the self made readable.

Young Bear's alter ego Edgar Bearchild's uncanny encounter with the UFOs is not only a revision of the typical poetics of humanist autobiography: the UFOs read Edgar, but they also reveal the limits of autobiographical self-discovery when absolute Otherness is confronted. Significantly, the consulted Mesquakie elders agree that despite the unexplainable mystery of the UFOs, their mission was "to get rid of you from the premises by fear." The only advice the elders offer relates as much to the grappling of Edgar with his own self-estrangement as it does to the confrontation with the extraterrestrials: "You will have to go back to the house and resume what you were doing. Which is living and not bothering anyone" (188). If we as readers attempt to discover "meaningful pattern[s] in the flux of past experience" (Neuman), we are forced to trust in experience (no matter how metaphoric, fantastical, or deprived of explication) as productive of the "I that speaks," rather than empirical evidence. As Joan W. Scott suggests, "It is not individuals who have experience, but subjects who are constituted through experience" (1998, 60), and we must accept that Young Bear's "mirror" Edgar Bearchild is as much constituted by popular culture or alien culture as traditional Mesquakie culture.

Perhaps it is Edgar and Selene's final vision of the UFOs outside of Edgar's parents' house that reveals the singular importance of the encounter as a transformative moment in Edgar's life: "After [Selene and I] stopped and signaled one another for confirmation, we looked skyward. Incredibly, we saw the 'lights' again. Lots of them, perhaps hundreds. . . . We ran back into the house and told everyone to come out and observe. With the family as witnesses we felt vindicated. We stood on the driveway and watched the celestial foreground move" (188). It is the "signal of confirmation" between readers and selves, and the "witnessing" of the difficult process of breaking the self into pieces, that eludes the neat teleology underwriting typically humanist autobiography.[12] Perhaps the real gift of return here—a gift facilitated by a theory of reading, or of spectatorship—can never be offered by a reader of this story. In her discussion of Young Bear's book, Maureen

Salzer quotes anthropologist Fredrick O. Gearing, who tells us that for the traditional Mesquakie,

> The natural order was not static. Through the years, according to tradition, individual Fox [Mesquakie] men had, by fasting and other self-mortification, caused supernatural forces to "pity" them and thereby give them special gifts or "blessings," each of which established some slightly new relationship with some part of the natural order. (Qtd. in Salzer 1995, 304)

For Edgar and Selene, the blessing involves a return of self, offered by the alien Other, after the "self-mortification" Edgar narrates in his story. It is a self-mortification we as readers might, in some small way, choose to emulate, as we accept the lesson of interpretative humility Young Bear's bait-and-switch teaches. Edgar Bearchild's "close encounter" with the UFOs in "The Supernatural Strobe Light" presents at least a twofold challenge: a challenge to understanding self-discovery, and a challenge to understanding how readers can or wish to fashion this self-discovery.

NOTES

1. I am using *gift* here in the Maussian sense, where the autobiographer gives the gift of candid self-exposure to the reader, who then must reflect back (and thus reify) the autobiographer's self-image through reconstitutive reading practice. Like Mauss's "total prestation," this exchange of duty is covert, contiguous, yet also expected and reciprocal.

2. While I am most concerned with exploring the literary devices Young Bear employs, Native autobiography has typically been understood as relying on rhetorical devices from anthropology for its effects. These include the registers of participant-observation or the trope of "native informant." Other contemporary Native autobiographers have drawn their rhetorical devices from other types of discourse, such as psychology (see, for example, Beckylane's [Sharon Proulx Turner] use of incest survivor narrative devices in her pseudonymous autobiography *Where the Rivers Join* [1995]).

3. Critics are no less inconsistent on this score: Schmitz calls *Black Eagle Child* "fiction" and "autobiography" (2001, 138, 144), while Salzer calls it "fictionalized verse and prose autobiography" and "novel" (1995, 301).

4. Dust jacket, Young Bear 1996.

5. An interesting reminder of the text's factuality here, since the paperback edition *of Black Eagle Child* (1997) is graced by a photographed example of bandolier-style beadwork, created by Young Bear's wife Stella L. Young Bear.

6. After reading an earlier draft of this essay, Creek-Cherokee critic Craig Womack pointed out to me how doubly (and politically) tragic this childlessness would be, given the dynastic struggle of Edgar Bearchild's family to regain its dominant position in the Red Earth settlement (a struggle described extensively in the book). Even if this ascendancy is reestablished, Edgar is left without heirs to continue the family line (personal correspondence, 19 November 2006).

7. In the 1996 prequel text, Young Bear relates a childhood UFO encounter involving Edgar that echoes Edgar's adult experience in "The Supernatural Strobe Light" ("Unearthly Manifestations," 1996, 35–46). In the prequel's narrative, some attempt is made to connect the aliens with traditional Mesquakie belief, especially malevolent witchcraft and the mythological beings called the Supernaturals, but little traditional framing is applied in "Strobe Light."

8. For examples of how Native authors revise the generic formulas of the "alien" in speculative or fantasy fiction, see William 1994 and Justice 2005.

9. I am indebted to Sara Sutler-Cohen for calling my attention to these episodes.

10. In his discussion of Fadden's painting, Allan J. Ryan observes that "alien beings visiting Earth from their home on the other side of the universe bear a startling resemblance to human beings alienated from their homes here on this side of the galaxy" (1999, 115).

11. For a further discussion of extraterrestrial contact in Native discourse, see Appleford 2002.

12. Kelly Oliver underscores the necessity for the self to be witnessed in order to achieve true subjectivity through the return of the self by others: "Without an external witness, we cannot develop or sustain the internal witness necessary for the ability to interpret and represent our experience, which is necessary for subjectivity and more essentially for both individual and social transformation" (2001, 88).

WORKS CITED

Appleford, Rob. 2002. "'That Almost Present Dream of Tomorrow': Daniel David Moses' *Kyotopolis* as Native Canadian Science Fiction / History Play." In *Crucible of Cultures: Anglophone Drama at the Dawn of a New Millennium*, edited by Marc Maufort and Franca Belarsi, 199–208. Brussels: P.I.E.-Peter Lang.

Beckylane [Sharon Proulx Turner]. 1995. *Where the Rivers Join: A Personal Account of Healing from Ritual Abuse*. Vancouver: Press Gang.

Bhabha, Homi K. 1985. "Signs Taken for Wonders: Questions of Ambivalence and Authority under a Tree Outside Delhi, May 1817." *Critical Inquiry* 12.1 (Autumn): 144–65.

Carlisle, Janice, and Daniel R. Schwarz. 1994. "Introduction." In *Narrative and Culture*, edited by J. Carlisle and D. R. Schwarz, 1–12. Athens: University of Georgia Press.

Derrida, Jacques. 1985. *The Ear of the Other,* translated by Peggy Kamuf, edited by Christie Macdonald. New York: Schocken Books.

Fadden, John Kahionhes. 1999. *Wouldn't It Be Funny?* (1983). In *The Trickster Shift: Humour and Irony in Contemporary Native Art*, by Allan J. Ryan, 114. Vancouver: University of British Columbia Press.

Geertz, Cifford. 1973. "Thick Description: Toward an Interpretative Theory of Culture." In *The Interpretation of Cultures*, 3–30. New York: Basic Books.

Henry, Gordon D., Jr. 2000. "Entries into the Autobiographical I." In *Here First: Autobiographical Essays by Native American Writers*, edited by Arnold Krupat and Brian Swann, 164–81. Berkeley and Los Angeles: University of California Press.

Justice, Daniel Heath. 2005. *Kynship: The Way of Thorn and Thunder (Book One)*. Cape Croker Reserve, Ontario: Kegedonce Press.

Kadar, Marlene. 1992. "Coming to Terms: Life Writing." In *Essays on Life Writing: From Genre to Critical Practice*, edited by Marlene Kadar, 3–16. Toronto: University of Toronto Press.

King, Thomas. 1993. "How Corporal Colin Sterling Saved Blossom, Alberta, and Most of the Rest of the World as Well." In *One Good Story, That One*, 49–66. Toronto: Harper-Collins.

Krupat, Arnold. 1985. "Indian Autobiography: Origins, Type, and Function." In *For Those Who Come After: A Study of Native American Autobiography*, 28–53. Berkeley and Los Angeles: University of California Press.

Krupat, Arnold, and Brian Swann, eds. 2000. *Here First: Autobiographical Essays by Native*

American Writers. New York: Modern Library.

Martin, Biddy. 1988. "Lesbian Identity and Autobiographical Difference(s)." In *Life/Lines: Theorizing Women's Autobiography*, edited by Bella Brodzki and Celeste Schenke, 77–103. Ithaca, N.Y.: Cornell University Press.

Mauss, Marcel. 1990. *The Gift: The Form and Reason for Exchange in Archaic Societies*. Translated by W. D. Halls. 1954; New York: Routledge.

Neuman, Shirley. 1992. "Autobiography: From a Different Poetics to a Poetics of Difference." In *Essays on Life Writing: From Genre to Critical Practice*, edited by Marlene Kadar, 213–30. Toronto: University of Toronto Press.

Oliver, Kelly. 2001. *Witnessing: Beyond Recognition*. Minneapolis: University of Minnesota Press.

Parker, Robert Dale. 1998. "To Be There, No Authority to Anything: Ontological Desire and Cultural and Poetic Authority in the Poetry of Ray A. Young Bear." In *Modern Critical Views: Native-American Writers*, edited by Harold Bloom, 175–94. Philadelphia: Chelsea House.

Ryan, Allan J. 1999. *The Trickster Shift: Humour and Irony in Contemporary Native Art*. Vancouver: University of British Columbia Press.

Salzer, Maureen. 1995. "Ray Young Bear's Cantaloupe Terrorist: Storytelling as a Site of Resistance." *American Indian Quarterly* 19.3 (Summer): 301–17.

Scott, Joan W. 1998. "Experience." In *Women, Autobiography, Theory: A Reader*, edited by Sidonie Smith and Julia Watson, 57–71. Madison: University of Wisconsin Press.

Schmitz, Neil. 2001. *White Robe's Dilemma: Tribal History in American Literature*. Amherst: University of Massachusetts Press.

Smith, Paul. 1988. *Discerning the Subject*. Minneapolis: University of Minnesota Press.

Smith, Sidonie. 1987. *A Poetics of Women's Autobiography: Marginality and the Fictions of Self-Representation*. Bloomington: Indiana University Press.

Steele, Shelby. 1992. "Malcolm Little: The Real Appeal of Malcolm X's Conservatism." *New Republic*, December 21, 27–31.

Stone, Albert E. 1997. "Forward." In *Black Eagle Child: The Facepaint Narratives*, by Ray A. Young Bear, ix–xv. 1992; New York: Grove Press.

"The X-Files Scripts Archives." 2005. In *Inside the X: X-Files*, edited by "Dr. Weesh." 8 January. Http://www.insidethex.co.uk.

William, Gerry. 1994. *The Black Ship*. Penticton, B.C.: Theytus Books.

Young Bear, Ray A. 1980. "For the Rain in March: The Blackened Hearts of Herons." In

Winter of the Salamander: The Keeper of Importance, 163–75. San Francisco: Harper & Row.

———. 1996. *Remnants of the First Earth*. New York: Grove Press.

———. 1997. *Black Eagle Child: The Facepaint Narratives*. 1992; New York: Grove Press.

———. 2002a. "'Reaching Out, Keeping Away'—an Interview with Ray A. Young Bear." In *Modern American Poetry*, edited by Cary Nelson and Robert Dale Parker. 1991; University of Illinois at Urbana-Champaign. Http://www.english.uiuc.edu/maps/poets/s_z/youngbear/interview.htm.

———. 2002b. "A Young Bear Editorial." In *Modern American Poetry*, edited by Cary Nelson and Robert Dale Parker. 1998; University of Illinois at Urbana-Champaign. Http://www.english.uiuc.edu/maps/poets/s_z/youngbear/editorial.htm.

———. 2004. "What It Means to Be a Meskwaki: An Interview with Ray Young Bear." Interview by Elias Ellefson. In *Modern American Poetry*, edited by Cary Nelson and Robert Dale Parker. 1994; University of Illinois at Urbana-Champaign. Http://www.english.uiuc.edu/maps/poets/s_z/youngbear/1994.htm.

Uncomprehended Mysteries: Language and Legend in the Writing of Zitkala-Ša and Mourning Dove

HARRY BROWN

■ Cowauwaúnemun

In 1635 the fathers of the Massachusetts Bay Colony accused Roger Williams of heresy for suggesting that Christian kings had no right to possess Indian lands. Rather, Williams said, they must bargain with the heathens and purchase their lands fairly. In a treatise addressed to John Winthrop, Williams indicted English colonization as "a sinne of unjust usurpation upon others possessions" (1988, 15). Williams fled south to the lands of the Narragansetts, where he established a more equitable settlement at Providence. In 1643, he returned to England, where he received a charter for his new colony and published *A Key into the Language of America*, a practical guide for communicating with the Indians of New England and one of the first efforts to translate Native languages into English. Myra Jehlen argues that Williams's key "is virtually unique in the English literature of colonization in its projection of a developing relationship with the indigenous populations." The few linguistic studies to precede Williams,' Jehlen explains, intended "not to speak with the indigenous people, but to instruct them" (1994, 76).

As a matter of fact, Williams, like his predecessors, proposes not simply to communicate with the Indians but also to convert them. In his preface, Williams declares his intent to help prospective travelers and missionaries to "converse with thousands of Natives all over the Country: and by such converse it may please the Father of Mercies to spread civility, (and in his own most holy season) Christianity" (2002, 338). In his crucial chapter (21) on Narragansett religious belief, Williams begins with the most fundamental translation, placing, as his practice, the Narragansett words on the left side of the page and the English words on the right side:

Manìt-manittó-wock   God, Gods. (344)

The problem, however, is that the English *God* does not match the Narragansett idea of divinity, as Williams concedes: "First they branch their Godhead [*manìt*] into many Gods. Secondly, [they] attribute it to creatures." He concludes, "Herein lies their Misery" (344). Williams then provides a model for religious dialogue, which the prospective missionary might refer to in his attempt to correct the polytheistic, pantheistic Indians:

Tasuóg, Maníttowock.	How many Gods be there?
Maunauûog Mishaúnawock.	Many, great many.
Nétop machàge.	Friend, not so.
Pausuck naúnt manìt.	There is only one God.
Cuppissttone.	You are mistaken.
Cowauwaúnemun.	You are out of the way. (344)

He briefly glosses this last phrase, *Cowauwaúnemun,* an idiomatic expression that likens a wrongheaded person to a traveler lost in the woods, but while he appreciates such subtleties of translation, he seems to disregard the more fundamental disjunction between *manìt* and Judeo-Christian monotheism, insisting in the Narragansetts' own tongue, *Cowauwaúnemun:* "You are out of the way." We find in this exchange not a gesture toward intercultural understanding, as Jehlen claims, but rather a linguistic barrier to understanding, mismatched notions of divinity, and an insistence on each side that the other is mistaken.

■ The Problem of Untranslatabilty

Williams's rudimentary attempt to reflect Indian beliefs in written English represents one of the earliest instances of a theoretical problem that continues to perplex and divide scholars who evaluate strategies for translating and textualizing Indian legends. Scott Vickers asks in *Native American Identities*, "If Indian history since 1492 has been 'written' (authored) by white authority, then how can it attain or retain authentic identities in the present . . . [when] the [white] author of history also assumes the power of author of identity and the arbiter of authenticity?" (1998, 9). In other words, how can translation, perhaps our only means of preserving Indian stories, really preserve them when the act of preservation itself inevitably changes them?

Paula Gunn Allen demonstrates a more acute consciousness of this dilemma in her essay "Kochinnenako in Academe: Three Approaches to Interpreting a Keres Indian Tale." Allen asserts that the "sexist and classist assumptions of the white world" severely compromise interpreters' attempts to understand Indian legends (1986, 224). She cites a Keres story, "Sh-ah-cock and Miochin or the Battle of the Seasons," translated by her uncle, John Gunn, a white man who lived his adult life among the Indians. In Gunn's translation, Miochin, a young hero representing the summer, rescues Kochinnenako, or Yellow Woman, from her unhappy marriage to Sh-ah-cock, a tyrannous old man representing the winter. In his victory over Sh-ah-cock, Miochin returns peace and warmth to the land, but according to their "armistice," the two "combatants" agree to divide the year in half, each ruling in his turn.

Allen emphasizes Gunn's "use of European . . . conflict-centered patriarchal assumptions as plotting devices," such as his framing of the encounter between Sh-ah-cock and Miochin as a battle and his reduction of Kochinennako to a trophy (225). More importantly, Allen argues, Gunn fails to consider the ritual context of the story. His translation does not relate the formal movement of the storyteller, the relationship between the two moieties who traditionally participate in the telling of the story, or the role of Kochinennako as an agent of change and a mediator between the moieties. Allen explains, "The ritual transfers the focus of power . . . held in turn by the two moieties whose constitution reflects the earth's bilateral division between summer and winter, from the winter to the summer people. Each moiety's right to power is confirmed and reflective of the seasons, as it is reflective and supported by the equinoxes" (233). In effect, Gunn transforms a ritual celebration of seasonal change into a Western romance narrative with a dashing hero rushing to rescue a captive maiden from the clutches of an evil overlord. According to Allen, the story of Miochin and Sh-ah-cock does not signify conflict but rather "the change of seasons and . . . the centrality of woman as agent and empowerer of that change" (244).

Conscious of these inevitable hermeneutic distortions of ritual stories, contemporary scholars seem to feel ever more distant from the Native oral tradition, which proves more elusive and more ephemeral the more closely one studies it. In *The Voice in the Margin,* for instance, Arnold Krupat establishes practicable but rigorous criteria: "I think it's reasonable to require that translations of Native American [oral] literature, if they are to be considered approximately accurate, meet two specific conditions. First, they must derive from an actual, taped, or recreative audition of the Native performance. Second, they must be produced in accord with . . . at least a rough working knowledge of the language in question" (1989, 128–29). Finally, Krupat and Allen recognize what Roger Williams did not: even "working knowledge" of Indian languages or long-term immersion in Indian cultures may not yield an authentic understanding of Indian legends.

Other scholars have adopted a different approach to the oral tradition, abandoning to some extent the insistence on cultural purity and an admittedly unattainable standard of authenticity in favor of a more fluid, adaptable hermeneutic model. While these scholars acknowledge the importance of ritual and linguistic context of traditional stories, they also emphasize their performative nature and the role of the storyteller in continuously changing these stories to fit their audience. In this sense, hermeneutic distortion does not represent the corruption of an original, authentic tradition but rather the survival and growth of the tradition in response to new social and historical conditions. Change represents the life, not the death, of the tradition, and untranslatability represents not a barrier to understanding but rather the liberation of the storyteller to make new meanings from old stories.

On these grounds, Barre Toelken defends Barry Lopez's collection of Coyote legends, *Giving Birth to Thunder, Sleeping with His Daughter* (1977). On one hand, Toelken admits that Lopez has given little consideration to the ritual and linguistic sources of his material and affirms Krupat's insistence on knowledge of ethnographic context in the translation of Indian legends: "I should make it clear that to get *beyond* Coyote's fascinating façade we do in fact need to know his local, specific tribal manifestations. And to know these, we need to know the tribal language, the tribal lore about storytelling events, and the local taboos concerning when a story may be told, by whom, to whom, and under what circumstances" (xii). Among the Navajo, for instance, Toelken explains that a Coyote story may only be told during the winter, after the first frost and before the first thunderstorm. Among the Coos, one may tell a Coyote story only in the presence of at least two others who also know the story and then only once in a season. Among other tribes, a Coyote story may be told only by a member of a specific clan who claims ownership of the story. In these cases, Lopez's collection represents not only a violation of ritual practices but also an act of cultural theft. On the other hand, Toelken allows for greater interpretive freedom than Krupat and ultimately finds Lopez's book "defensible" (xiii). He writes, "It does *not* pretend to be an 'Indian book.' It does *not* provide the original language, the ritual detail, the full context; in short, it does not give away or betray the magic of the actual storytelling event" (xiii). Toelken finally appeals to Dennis Tedlock's essay "On the Translation of Style in Oral Narrative," which claims that "we have ways in our own language of representing the *style* of a narrative done in another tongue. The trick consists of finding equivalents rather than direct translations of connotative words or rhetorical strategies" (xiv).

The ethnographic and literary work of Zitkala-Ša (Sioux) and Mourning Dove (Okanogan) during the first three decades of the twentieth century is crucial to understanding this modern theoretical problem of the untranslatability of Indian legends. Both women consciously attempt to reconcile authenticity with adaptability, interpreting traditional stories for an audience they regard as ignorant of Indian culture while maintaining a fidelity to the ritual and linguistic sources of these stories. In this way, their collections of Indian legends offer unique insight into the more recent critical controversy surrounding the problem of untranslatability. For Zitkala-Ša and Mourning Dove, translation represents a means of overcoming cultural misunderstanding and racial difference. Both women, however, remain conscious of the profound contradictions in such a project, the same ones that continue to perplex scholars such as Allen and Krupat. Translating and textualizing Sioux and Okanogan oral narratives inevitably distorted and misrepresented the cultures scholars sought to preserve.

As a way of addressing this problem, both women evolve a new method of translation and storytelling that blends autobiography with collective tribal legends, creating a mixed genre that continues to serve modern Native writers with a way to reconcile their own modern experience with a transformed, elusive, but still deeply felt tradition. While authentic intercultural understanding is impossible, Zitkala-Ša and Mourning Dove suggest, modern readers might achieve some understanding of the oral tradition through contextualization and interpretation by modern storytellers. Both writers foster this approach by altering the meaning of traditional stories to reflect new circumstances, and also by providing clues to the way white audiences should read their stories, interpretive guides that often take the subtle form of their own girlhood memories. These memories do not simply reflect a nostalgic critique of assimilation, as readers of Zitkala-Ša and Mourning Dove most frequently argue, but rather serve to return the stories to their original experiential context, reconnecting story and storyteller and preserving some trace of ritual performance in the textual artifact.

■ The Legends of Zitkala-Ša and Mourning Dove

In their efforts to salvage Indian legends, nineteenth-century ethnographers demonstrate an apparent unconsciousness of the problems that paralyze modern scholars. Early collections like Henry Rowe Schoolcraft's *The Indian Fairy Book* (1856) presented the illusion that the oral tradition emerged in a vacuum and required only an informed amanuensis to convey stories, in their exotic beauty, to the reading public. Reprinted in 1916, while Zitkala-Ša and Mourning Dove themselves were working to adapt Sioux and Okanogan legends, Schoolcraft's book included a foreword that made only a vague, romantic gesture to the spoken origins of the Indian legends: "When the story-tellers sat at the lodge fires in the long evenings to tell of the manitoes and their magic . . . Mr. Schoolcraft listened and wrote the stories down, just as he heard them" (1916, i).

Likewise, Charles Godfrey Leland's 1884 collection, *The Algonquin Legends of New England,* describes the fortuitous discovery of a treasury of legends among the Passamaquoddy in New Brunswick. Assuming that the stories had died with the Indians' conversion to Catholicism, Leland writes:

> What was my amazement, however, at discovering, day by day, that there existed among them, entirely by oral tradition, a far grander mythology than that which has been made known to us either by the Chippewa or Iroquois Hiawatha legends, and that this was illustrated by an incredible number of tales. I soon ascertained that these were very ancient. . . . In fact, I came in time to the opinion that the original stock of all the Algonquin myths, and perhaps many more, still existed, not far away in the West, but at our very doors. (1968, iii–iv)

Leland judges his own achievement to be even greater than Schoolcraft's, re-minding his reader that "there are only forty-two of the Hiawatha legends of Schoolcraft. . . . I have collected more than two hundred" (vii). For Leland, the quantity and apparent antiquity of the stories are more important than the context in which he has heard them or the identities of the storytellers, of whom he says nothing. Both Leland and Schoolcraft approach Indian legends as discovered treasures, not so much to be interpreted or contextualized as polished, displayed, and cherished. Like John Gunn, both Schoolcraft and Leland had a firm understanding of Indian language and culture but none-theless failed to recognize the significance of the stories within the context of performance; nineteenth-century ethnography severed storytelling from storyteller.

This severance of legend from lived experience is the error that both Zitkala-Ša and Mourning Dove work to correct in their own translations. In part, their work is informed by a significant turn in ethnography at the turn of the twentieth century. As the General Allotment Act encouraged assimilation through economic and social interaction between newly propertied Indians and their white neighbors, Indian ethnic identity began to change. Mixed-bloods began to outnumber full-bloods, and conventional definitions of the Indian based on blood quantum lost their relevance. Early twentieth-century writers and legislators required a new definition of racial boundaries, and modern anthropologists like Franz Boas proposed that racial difference consists not in heredity or blood quantum, as Victorian anthropology held, but rather in language and cultural practice. Breaking from previous ethnographers like Schoolcraft and Leland, they insisted on the restoration of Indian legends to their tribal context. In *The Shaping of American Anthropology, 1883–1911,* George W. Stocking Jr. explains that Boas developed an "embracive" anthropology that merged the study of human physical characteristics, human cultures, and linguistics (1974, 14).

With both tribal upbringings and white educations, Zitkala-Ša and Mourning Dove possess advantages that even the most progressive ethnographers did not. Informed both by new ethnographic methods and by their own tribal memories, they restore the legends to their ritual and linguistic contexts, placing a new importance on meanings created through their performance, both in their spoken origins and in their textual form. The challenge for both women, however, is somehow to re-create lived performance in the static, inert medium of text. In order to do so, they merge two genres that evolved separately in the nineteenth century: the Indian autobiography and the collection of tribal legends. While earlier ethnographers like Schoolcraft and Leland studiously transcribe their Ojibwa and Algonquin stories, they preserve them only through a kind of cultural mummification, with the soft, living tissue of the oral tradition dried, hardened, and disfigured. Zitkala-Ša and Mourning Dove restore life to these stories by recounting the circumstances in which they heard them in childhood. As autobiographers, they rely on the reader to identify with their experience; as the stories come to life in the memory of the women, they come to life for the reader.

In *American Indian Stories* (1921), her collection of autobiographical essays and tribal legends, Zitkala-Ša recalls the itinerant storytellers of her childhood. She remembers that they would join her and her mother for evening meals: "I ate my supper in quiet, listening patiently to the talk of the old people, wishing all the time that they would begin the stories I loved best. . . . As each in turn began to tell a legend, I pillowed my head in my mother's lap; and lying flat upon my back, I watched the stars as they peeped down upon me, one by one" (1985, 15). As she recalls her Indian childhood, she remains conscious of her white audience, weaving into her narrative some explanation of the social context of storytelling for readers:

> While one was telling of some heroic deed . . . done by an ancestor, the rest of us listened attentively, and exclaimed in undertones, "Han! Han!" (yes! yes!) whenever the speaker paused for breath, or sometimes for our sympathy. As the discourse became more thrilling, according to our ideas, we raised our voices in these interjections. In these impersonations, our parents were led to say only those things that were in common favor. (22)

Likewise, Mourning Dove introduces her collection of Okanogan legends, *Coyote Stories* (1933), with an autobiographical preface relating her memories of the storytellers of her youth:

> It used to be the custom for story-tellers to go from village to village and relate . . . [the legends] to children. How gladly were those tribal historians welcomed by busy mothers, and how glad were the boys and girls when one came to visit! . . . Vividly I recall old *S'whist-kane* (Lost-Head), also known as Old Narciss, and how, in the course of a narrative, he would jump up and mimic his characters, speaking or singing in a strong or weak voice, just as the Animal Persons were supposed to have done. . . . Another favorite was Broken Nose Abraham. He was old and crippled. He came to our village usually on a white horse, riding double

with his blind wife, who held the reins and guided the horse at his direction. It always thrilled us to see Broken Nose ride into camp; he had a stock of such fascinating stories. Broken Nose could not dance for us. He could not even walk without the support of two canes. But he sang exciting war songs, and we liked to sing with him. (1990, 10–11)

Like Zitkala-Ša, Mourning Dove attempts to reconnect the stories with the living voices, movements, and appearances of the storytellers, re-creating performance as text and effectively regaining that which Allen identifies as lost in Gunn's translation of "Sh-ah-cock and Miochin or the Battle of the Seasons." More specifically, *American Indian Stories* and *Coyote Stories* emphasize the centrality of the feminine in Native storytelling traditions. In both collections, the primary transmission of legends is matrilineal, an exchange between mother and daughter, often in the context of another domestic ritual such as beading or the preparation of food. Just as Zitkala-Ša recalls the participation of her mother in the telling of the stories, Mourning Dove writes in *Coyote Stories*:

> Some of the women were noted story-tellers, but they never made it a business to go from village to village to tell them. We children would go to them. I particularly remember *Ka-at-qhu* (Big Lip), Old Jennie, *Tee-qualt* (Tall), or Long Thresa, and my maternal grandmother, *Soma-how-atqhu* (She-got-her-power-from-the-water). I loved these simple, kindly people, and I think of them often. And in my memory I treasure a picture of my dear mother, who, when I was a very little girl, made the bedtime hours happy for me with the legends she told. She would tell them to me until I fell asleep. Two that are in this collection, "Why Marten's Face Is Wrinkled" and "Why Mosquitoes Bite People," she told over and over again, and I never grew tired of hearing them. (1990, 12)

But even as Mourning Dove maintains this fidelity to her personal and tribal history, she gestures to her white audience with instruction in the Salish language throughout the collection, as she does in her autobiographical preface:

Our name for the Animal People is *Chip-chap-tiqulk* (the "k" barely is sounded), and we use the same word for the stories that are told about the animal people and legendary times. To the younger generations, *chip-chap-tiqulk* are improbable stories; that is the result of the white man's schools. But to the old Indians *chip-chap-tiqulk* are not at all improbable; they are the accounts of what really happened when the world was very young. (7)

By studiously repeating the word, *chip-chap-tiqulk*, Mourning Dove provides guidance for pronunciation and elucidates the variant meaning of the word. Like Roger Williams, she explains Indian language and belief to white readers, but does so without pointing to their error or attempting to convert them. The imagined context for linguistic exchange has shifted profoundly from a missionary's instruction of an ignorant pagan to a pagan's intimate remembrance of her childhood.

In Zitkala-Ša's and Mourning Dove's collections a new figure emerges who remains invisible in Schoolcraft's and Leland's collections: the storyteller, not so much as mystical repository of tribal knowledge as a human being who bears a human relation to those who hear his or her stories, such as a mother who prepares a meal and caresses her daughter's head, an old man who mimics animal voices, and another with a broken nose who sings because he cannot dance. The storyteller figure emerges even more clearly in Mourning Dove's *Cogewea: The Half-Blood* (1927), a novel dramatizing a love triangle on the Horseshoe Bend ranch on the Flathead reservation. Cogewea, or "Little Chipmunk," entertains the affections of two suitors: Jim LaGrinder, a rough but honorable mixed-blood foreman; and Alfred Densmore, a white schemer who tries to seize Cogewea's fortune through false courtship and attempted murder. In the end, Cogewea learns the hard lesson that her centenarian grandmother, Stemteemä, has always preached: Stay away from the *shoyapee*—the white man.

In the novel, Stemteemä embodies the Okanogan oral tradition that Mourning Dove seeks to translate. The personification of these legends in the old woman itself reflects Mourning Dove's effort to restore the stories to a performative context. Stemteemä says: "The story I am telling you is true.

It was given me by my father. . . . He told me the tales that were sacred to his tribe; honored me with them, trusted me. Treasured by my forefathers, I value them, I know that they would want them kept only to their own people, if they were here" (1981, 122). Her words anticipate those that Luther Standing Bear offers in his foreword to Mourning Dove's *Coyote Stories* concerning the importance of legends as an "inheritance" passed from one generation to the next, "memories" of an entire people soon to be forgotten in the wake of the "destruction" brought by the white man. While Standing Bear endorses the reproduction of this inheritance in print, he also reminds readers of their ritual context, the role of storyteller: "The real value of tribal stories lay in the fact that they were closely related to the lives of people" (1990, 5–6).

Throughout the novel, Mourning Dove integrates Salishan language, as she does in *Coyote Stories*. When a rattlesnake crosses her trail, Cogewea declares: "My uncle has told me of your *tahmahnawis* power for doing secret evil to people. Your 'medicine' is strong and my grandmother would not hurt you. But I am *not* my grandmother! I am not a full-blood—only a *breed*—a *sitkum* Injun and that breaks the charm of your magic with me" (1990, 26). But even as Mourning Dove introduces the reader to such tribal words and concepts, the novel maintains the same sense of untranslatability recognized by modernist ethnography, the vague sense of a tribal reality that Western inquiry, barred by language, can never fully contain. Mourning Dove writes:

> The *Stemteemä* knew many interesting tales of the past; legends finer than the myths of the old world; but few of them known to the reading public and none of them understood. . . . Ever suspicious of the whites and guardedly zealous in the secrecy of their ancient lore, seldom do the older tribesmen disclose ancestral erudition, and when they do their mysteries are not comprehended. (40–41)

In her own ethnographic research for *Coyote Stories,* Mourning Dove herself encountered this reluctance among the Indians to share traditional stories. She writes in a letter to her mentor and editor Lucullus Virgil McWhorter in 1918:

They are such a hard people to get anything out from. . . . There are some that are getting suspicious of my wanting folklores and if the Indians find out that their stories will reach print I am sure it will be hard for me to get any more legends without paying the hard cash for them.

She blames white researchers' practice of paying "five dollars a piece for good Indian legends" for the Indians' habit of "cramming" them with inauthentic legends and hopelessly obscuring the very tradition the researchers hoped to illuminate (qtd. in Fisher 1981, viii).

Mourning Dove's difficulty reflects the growing consciousness among ethnographers of the changes they exert on the Native culture through the very act of observation. In attempting to reveal her tribal tradition to outsiders, Mourning Dove herself becomes an outsider.

Leaving the Pine Ridge reservation as a girl, Zitkala-Ša developed a similar sense of estrangement from her own people. In her autobiographical essays "Impressions of an Indian Childhood" and "School Days of an Indian Girl," contained in *American Indian Stories*, she portrays her growing mistrust of the white man, the same lesson so painfully learned by Cogewea in Mourning Dove's novel. As a college student, she won an Indiana state oratory competition, but what should have been a moment of triumph was ruined by hecklers in the audience, other college students who jeered her speech and hoisted a large sign bearing the word *squaw*. The incident, remembered at the conclusion of her essay "The School Days of an Indian Girl," represents the bitter culmination of her educational experience and reveals a deep suspicion of her ability to communicate with the "palefaces" in their own language, let alone hers. Like the tales of Stemteemä, the handful of Sioux legends that Zitkala-Ša collects in *American Indian Stories* consistently emphasize the threat of the palefaces. They contain no language lessons, neither the idiomatic expressions found in *Cogewea* nor the vocabulary found in *Coyote Stories*.

Recognizing, as Krupat would later, the profound difficulty in conveying the meaning of Indian legends to alienated or even hostile white audiences, both Zitkala-Ša and Mourning Dove intervene in the tradition they propose to translate. For them, the stories do not emerge unchanged from a mythical past as they do for Schoolcraft and Leland; they take their meaning from the people who tell them and the present circumstances. In *Cogewea,* the stories told by *Stemteemä* to her romantically deceived granddaughter illustrate the historic abuse of Indian women by white men. In "The Story of Green-Blanket Feet," an Okanogan girl falls in love with a white man and pays for her mistake with a life of slavery among the Blackfeet and the death of her mixed-blood child. Speaking as Green-Blanket Feet, Stemteemä declares, "Much of this hardship, I think, was because I had chosen a *shoyapee* husband instead of one of my own kind; that my child was half white. The great Spirit must have been displeased with me" (1981, 172–73).

Like Mourning Dove's Stemteemä, Zitkala-Ša assumes the role of an interpretive storyteller, revising traditional tales in order to address contemporary circumstances. Jeanne Smith examines the significance of the Sioux trickster Iktomi, the Spider, in Zitkala-Ša's earlier collection, *Old Indian Legends* (1901). Smith argues that "by transplanting trickster tales into written English, telling contemporary trickster stories, and describing her own experience of living between two cultural worlds," Zitkala-Ša engages in "revisionist storytelling," modifying traditional legends to reflect the contemporary reality of cultural assimilation (1994, 47). In "Dance in a Buffalo Skull," for example, the traditional story of Iktomi's intrusion on a party of field mice dancing in a buffalo skull becomes, like "The Story of Green-Blanket Feet," a political allegory. Iktomi represents the overwhelming threat of the white man, and the field mice represent Indian society, precarious and blind to the looming forces of the outside world. For Smith, Zitkala-Ša's genius rests in her blend of autobiography, legend, and political statement: "By grouping these diverse genres together under the label 'stories,' Zitkala-Ša oversteps the traditional boundaries of the short story form and suggests that all of these forms have equal validity. . . . For Zitkala-Ša the personal is inseparable from the political: Her individual story speaks to and comes out of other American Indian stories" (1994, 51).

Alanna Kathleen Brown observes a similar tendency in Mourning Dove's writing: "Caught between being educated to be white and choosing to maintain an indigenous identity, some Indians intuitively incorporated their contemporary experiences into the larger frame of an ongoing Native American oral tradition" (1994, 126). In this respect, *Coyote Stories* is "an important act by a Native American storyteller to preserve some of her cultural heritage in the face of what then appeared to be inevitable cultural genocide" (127). At the same time, Brown recognizes that this preservation depends on the adaptability of the stories and the role of the storyteller in fitting the old legends to new circumstances. In this way, Brown explains, "New stories continually come into being and old stories are altered to incorporate new circumstances. It is the contemporaneity of Mourning Dove's writing that . . . reveals the dynamics not only of lives in flux, but of an oral tradition in the midst of change" (128).

■ Mistrust and Growth

In her novel *Ceremony* (1977) Leslie Silko portrays the mixed-blood medicine man Betonie, in whom Tayo, a troubled Laguna war veteran, recognizes the same hazel eyes as his own, a sign of their shared mixed descent and apparent alienation from tribal tradition. For Silko, however, Betonie is a redemptive figure who represents adaptability and change, using talismans from both the white and Indian worlds in his healing ceremonies and interweaving past and present in the stories he tells. He explains to Tayo:

> At one time, the ceremonies as they had been performed were enough for the way the world was then. But after the white people came, elements in the world began to shift; and it became necessary to create new ceremonies. I have made changes in the rituals. The people mistrust this greatly, but only this growth keeps the ceremonies strong. (126)

Zitkala-Ša and Mourning Dove perform the same function for Indian legends during the difficult assimilation period of the early twentieth century. Recognizing the impossibility of the uncorrupted cultural reproduction prized by nineteenth-century ethnologists, they rely instead on interpretive translations that foster intercultural understanding or depict the ravages and deceits of the *shoyapee*. In their writing, the old stories become more relevant and purposeful, changing to reflect the changed condition of the storytellers and the audiences.

What fundamentally distinguishes the legends of Zitkala-Ša and Mourning Dove from those of earlier ethnologists is their relation of Indian legends within an autobiographical context, a shift that grants new importance to the storytelling act and the role of the performers. Nineteenth-century ethnography effectively severed the stories from the storytellers, mummifying lived experience, performance, breath, gesture, movement, color, and expression in print. Although they predate our theoretical lexicon, Zitkala-Ša's and Mourning Dove's stories represent a pragmatic response to the problem that continues to perplex modern ethnography and literary scholarship. In fusing legend and autobiography, Zitkala-Ša and Mourning Dove reconnect stories with the storytelling act and, to some extent, resolve the perceived dilemma of untranslatability. Both writers, recognizing the impossibility of conveying a full understanding of one culture to another, seek to mediate in their translations an interpretive rather than an authentic understanding of Native culture.

In spite of their common strategy, however, Zitkala-Ša and Mourning Dove nevertheless demonstrate contrasting responses to this problem of untranslatability. The differences in their methods appear most obviously in their use of Indian-language terms. Mourning Dove includes such terms throughout her narratives, along with explanatory footnotes and parenthetical pronunciation guides. She not only wants to convey an understanding of Okanogan stories but also a rudimentary lesson in the Okanogan tongue; legend, for her, is indivisible from language. Zitkala-Ša, on the other hand, divides legend from language, using Sioux terms or Sioux names merely to provide descriptive texture, never serving as a means of linguistic instruction of intercultural communication. While Mourning Dove, whose writing is influenced by McWhorter and thus more informed by contemporary trends in ethnography, emphasizes the importance of Native languages to white audiences, Zitkala-Ša, perhaps more steeled to their resistance by her more direct engagement with them in moments such as the oratory competition, seems to hold her tongue. In the end, this difference seems incidental. For both of them, the fundamental dilemma was that preserving Native lore required its translation, but in this act of translation, the lore was ultimately lost. Their hybrid legends, blends of English and Indian languages, personal history with tribal lore, represent perhaps our best solution to the problem, a practicable means for intercultural connection and the preservation of an oral tradition irreversibly altered by the effects of conquest.

WORKS CITED

Allen, Paula Gunn. 1986. "Kochinnenako in Academe: Three Approaches to Interpreting a Keres Indian Tale." In *The Sacred Hoop: Recovering the Feminine in American Indian Traditions.* Boston: Beacon Press.

Brown, Alanna Kathleen. 1994. "Mourning Dove, Trickster Energy, and Assimilation-Period Native Texts." In *Tricksterism in Turn-of-the-Century American Literature: A Multicultural Perspective,* edited by Elizabeth Ammons and Annette White-Parks, 126–36. Hanover, N.H.: University Press of New England.

Fisher, Dexter. 1916. "Foreword." In *The Indian Fairy Book*, i. 1856; New York: Frederick A. Stokes Company.

———. 1981. "Introduction." In *Cogewea, the Half-Blood: A Depiction of the Great Montana Cattle Range,* edited by Lucullus Virgil McWhorter, v–xxix. 1927; Lincoln: University of Nebraska Press.

Jehlen, Myra. 1994. "The Literature of Colonization." In *The Cambridge History of American Literature,* vol. I: *1590–1820,* edited by Sacvan Bercovitch, 11–168. Cambridge: Cambridge University Press.

Krupat, Arnold. 1989. *The Voice in the Margin: Native American Literature and the Canon.* Berkeley and Los Angeles: University of California Press.

Leland, Charles G. 1968. *The Algonquin Legends of New England: Myths and Folk Lore of the Micmac, Passamaquoddy, and Penobscot Tribes.* 1884; Detroit: Singing Tree Press.

Mourning Dove. 1981. *Cogewea, the Half-Blood: A Depiction of the Great Montana Cattle Range.* 1927; Lincoln: University of Nebraska Press.

———. 1990. *Coyote Stories.* 1933; Lincoln: University of Nebraska Press.

Schoolcraft, Henry Rowe. 1916. *The Indian Fairy Book.* 1856; New York: Frederick A. Stokes Company.

Silko, Leslie Marmon. 1977. *Ceremony.* New York: Penguin.

Smith, Jeanne. 1994. "'A Second Tongue': The Trickster's Voice in the Works of Zitkala-Ša." In *Tricksterism in Turn-of-the-Century American Literature: A Multicultural Perspective,* edited by Elizabeth Ammons and Annette White-Parks, 46–60. Hanover, N.H.: University Press of New England.

Standing Bear. Luther. 1990. "Foreword." In *Coyote Stories,* by Mourning Dove, 5–6. 1933; Lincoln: University of Nebraska Press.

Stocking, George W., Jr., ed. 1974. *The Shaping of American Anthropology, 1883–1911: A Franz Boas Reader.* New York: Basic Books.

Toelken, Barre. 1977. "Introduction." In *Giving Birth to Thunder, Sleeping with His Daughter: Coyote Builds North America,* by Barry Lopez, xi–xiv. New York: Avon.

Vickers, Scott B. 1998. *Native American Identities: From Stereotype to Archetype in Art and Literature.* Albuquerque: University of New Mexico Press.

Williams, Roger. 1988. *The Correspondence of Roger Williams,* edited by Glenn W. LaFantasie. Hanover, N.H.: Brown University Press.

———. 2002. "A Key into the Language of America" (1643). In *The Heath Anthology of American Literature,* 4th ed., vol. 1, edited by Paul Lauter. Boston: Houghton Mifflin.

Zitkala-Ša. 1985. *American Indian Stories.* 1921; Lincoln: University of Nebraska Press.

———. 1985. *Old Indian Legends.* 1901; Lincoln: University of Nebraska Press.

Chances of Survivance: Gerald Vizenor's Autocritical Auto/biographies

ELVIRA PULITANO

Native stories are sound and vision, and both are survivance. My presence is written in stories, and we must come together in the book or be lost to manners and discoveries.

—Vizenor and Lee, *Postindian Conversations*

I have a disease: I *see* language. What I should simply hear, a strange pulsion . . . reveals it to me as a "vision." . . . The primal scene, in which I listen without seeing, is followed by a perverse scene, in which I imagine seeing what I am hearing. Hearing deviates to scopia: I feel myself to be the visionary and voyeur of language.

—Roland Barthes, in *Roland Barthes*

Reading through the 2006 spring issue of the *MLA Newsletter*, I noticed a call for papers on the subject "Theorist Autobiographers," described as "Autobiographical works by writers known as theorists . . . that develop theoretical arguments." I was immediately struck by the list of examples provided as a model of theoretical autobiographies—Augustine's *Confessions,* Montaigne's *Essays,* Wordsworth's *Prelude,* Derrida's *Circumfession* among others—and I wondered what kind of topics would make it to the panel at the 2006 MLA convention in Philadelphia. The text I would have liked to add to such authoritative, established models of Western life-writing is undoubtedly Gerald Vizenor's *Interior Landscapes* (1990), a text that in its blending of "autocritique and everyday life writing" (Smith and Watson 2001, 155) adds to the rich variety of autobiographical practices that in the past decades have visibly expanded and challenged the boundaries prescribed by critics and practitioners of such a vibrant literary genre.[1] While previous critical interpretations of *Interior Landscapes* have focused on the overall significance of the text within the wide range of Vizenor's oeuvre, in what follows I am going to look at Vizenor's autobiography in the context of current debates on autobiographical writing and practices. Specifically, I am going to discuss the interaction between the creative writer and the critic, Vizenor becoming at once both a creator and theorist of the genre of autobiography along the lines of other contemporary and not-so-contemporary theorist-autobiographers. I intend to explore the ways in which a text such as *Interior Landscapes* adds to the current discourse of life writing, while interrogating Vizenor's intriguing ideas on the self in light of his return to the autobiographical motif in his recent poetry.

Subtitled *Autobiographical Myths and Metaphors, Interior Landscapes* challenges all the conventions of Western autobiography and becomes one more narrative in Vizenor's project of writing down oral discourse (Blaeser 1996; Hutson 2000). Employing first- and third-person pronouns and enfolding simultaneously Anishinaabe family history, individual episodes of the author's life, and locales as diverse as city, reservation, America, and Japan, Vizenor seems to follow closely his fellow contemporary Native writers who, along with other major ethnic writers in the United States and postcolonial writers around the world, have in the past few decades significantly redefined the genre of life writing. More important, Vizenor's text testifies to an increasing critical consensus on autobiography as an ambivalent and heterogeneous kind of discourse in stark contrast with Philippe Lejeune's understanding of the genre as a "récit rétrospectif en prose qu'une personne réelle fait de sa propre existence, lorsqu'elle met l'accent sur sa vie individuelle, en particulier l'histoire de sa personnalité" (1996, 14).[2]

In the last chapter of *Interior Landscapes,* Vizenor articulates his ideas on autobiographical theory at the same time as he presents a cogent series of short, interrelated stories of memory that unfold without following a linear course of cause and effect. While such a strategy might unsettle readers looking for "a narrative development of personality" (Evans 1991, 61), I argue that Vizenor's auto/biography becomes a form of auto/criticism, the line between the two discourses constantly blurring in an endless process of transformations and trickster turns. The dialogue with theoretical approaches to the genre of autobiography begins in the very title of Vizenor's text, the myths and metaphors of the subtitle clearly alluding to James Olney's *Metaphors of Self* (1972) and George Gusdorf's definition of autobiography as "the effort of a creator to give the meaning of his own mythic tale" (Olney 1980, 48). Vizenor himself in conversation with Robert Lee acknowledges the influence of Olney's groundbreaking edited collection, *Autobiography: Essays Theoretical and Critical* (1980): "Most of my questions were answered by the essays, or at least my concern and resistance had a critical context that other writers had thought carefully about" (Vizenor and Lee 1999, 58). He adds that by overcoming a certain resistance to a "literary form" in autobiography, to "this idea of absence," he created his own style. "I created myself as one of many characters, in many situations, and gave voices to others who might have something to say about me" (58).

According to Olney, the contemporary study of autobiography begins with Gusdorf's essay "Conditions and Limits of Autobiography" (1956) in which the critic argues that "the individual does not oppose himself to others" (Olney 1980, 29). While Vizenor seems to subscribe to such a view, he does nonetheless insist on "the presence of a voice, and a pose of the self" in life writing, clearly taking a stance on the ongoing debate about Native autobiography as a communal genre. Responding specifically to Arnold Krupat's argument on the synecdochic self in Native autobiography,[3] Vizenor boldly claims that "natives are not as communal as [Krupat] might want them to be in theory" (Vizenor and Lee 1999, 62). While acknowledging that Native autobiographers, including himself, often begin with some reference to a larger community or tribal association, Vizenor argues that "the autobiography does not speak for community, and stories do not represent the self" (61). More precisely, Vizenor suggests that communal practices have a very distinct meaning in Native communities and warns us against "romantic reductions of tradition and community as common sources of native identity" (62). Granting Krupat's originality in his interpretations of Native life stories and autobiographies, Vizenor nonetheless seems to be puzzled by the use of terms that do not translate cultural and epistemological worldviews. Vizenor's autobiography begins with Anishinaabe family history and in that sense might indeed be defined as "synecdochic"; however, his understanding of the self and the way it is expressed through communal and individualistic stories goes beyond literary tropes and restrictive categories. Vizenor's use of pronouns in *Interior Landscapes* testifies to this complex interaction and the difficulties in the translation of memory.

In *Manifest Manners*, Vizenor points out that pronouns are never authentic representations of people, cultures, and environment. He uses the metaphor of translation and Derrida's concept of *différance* to describe the "untranslatable" nature of identities:

> The stories that are heard are the coherent memories of natural reason; the stories that are read are silent landscapes. Pronouns, then, are the pinch hitters in the silence and distance of translation, and at the same time pronouns are the *différance* that would be unheard in translations. The shadows of tribal consciousness, and the shadows of names and natural reason are overheard in tribal stories and autobiographies; in this sense, stories are shadows, shimmers of coincidence, and tribal traceries in translation. (1994, 96)

As "unheard *différance*," pronouns for Vizenor transvaluate and misconstrue memories while elusively inviting us to a sense of presence. His personal dissatisfaction with pronouns reveals a more general dissatisfaction with the English language and with the (im)possibility of conveying in writing the consciousness heard in tribal stories. Discussing the nature of Vizenor's self-authoring in *Interior Landscapes,* Blaeser points out "the degree to which the autobiographical in Vizenor is engaged not with the personal but with the mythic, the metaphorical, the theoretical, particularly the degree to which it is engaged with the mythic Anishinaabe trickster" (1996, 104). Readers of Vizenor's autobiography realize that the "I," "me," and "he" of autocritical stories are part of his ongoing attempt to find "mythic connections" (Vizenor, qtd. in Owens 1992, 239), a strategy Vizenor further articulates in the intriguing concept of "pronounance": "The *pronounance* combines the sense of the words *pronoun* and *pronounce* with the actions and conditions of survivance in tribal memories and stories. The *pronounance* of trickster hermeneutics has a shadow with no person, time, or number. In the absence of the heard the trickster is the shadow of the name, the sound, the noun, the person, the *pronounance*" (1994, 97–98). Vizenor's use of first- and third-person pronouns in *Interior Landscapes* must be seen within this overall artistic scheme of finding new pronouns that would misconstrue essentialist definitions of tribal identities and, more significantly, that would bring to the written page some of the elusiveness of oral discourse.

From the beginning, then, Vizenor's autobiographical gesture is one of resistance and subversion. While starting from Olney and Gusdorf, Vizenor ultimately undermines the latter's sense of autobiography as an essentially Western genre, a genre that, as such, cannot exist among societies that "subscribe to mythic structures" (Olney 1980, 30). Deeply inspired by Anishinaabe "mythic structures" and stories, Vizenor in *Interior Landscapes* gives voice to his "crossblood" remembrances that bring him back to mythic time, to those families of the Crane that are an affirmative presence in the history of the Anishinaabe and that constitute the pre-text of his autobiographical mythic tale.[4]

The last chapter of Vizenor's autobiography bears the title "September 1989: Honor Your Partner." It opens with a quotation from one of Vizenor's earlier autobiographical essays, "Crows Written on the Poplars," an autocritical collage written in the third person: "Gerald Vizenor implies that autobiographies are imaginative histories; a remembrance past the barriers, and wild pastimes over the pronouns" (1987, 262). A few key concepts from this same essay, which cites scholars of autobiography alongside the author's memoir of violently killing a squirrel, are interspersed in this final sequence, and the metaphor of hunting is used to describe the autobiographical act. "My survival is mythical, an imaginative transition, an intellectual predation, deconstructed as masks and metaphors at the water holes in autobiographies" (1990, 265), Vizenor writes, alluding to the power of language and imagination to liberate our minds. The chapter proceeds with an array of quotations from theorists and critical readers of autobiography: Avrom Fleishman (*Figures of Autobiography*), Paul John Eakin (*Fictions in Autobiography*), Vizenor himself (*Growing Up in Minnesota*), but also George Steiner (*After Babel*) and John Berger (*And Our Faces*). As I have discussed elsewhere, elaborating on Kimberly's Blaeser's groundbreaking study, Vizenor's magpie strategy of gathering attractive fragments responds to his overall ideological message of Native survivance as well as to his attempt to convey in writing the liberatory power of oral discourse, a discourse that is open, dynamic, and communal (Pulitano 2003, 154). In *Postindian Conversations* Vizenor argues that "trickster stories, oral or written, and contemporary theories are not developmental ideas . . . [because] the pleasures of tricky language have always been with us and could be more established than manners, in the ironic sense that the earliest uses of language might have been more tricky and deceptive than representational" (Vizenor and Lee 1999, 59). In *Interior Landscapes,* Vizenor refers to Steiner's concept of language as "deception," or more precisely language as "the main instrument of man's refusal to accept the world as it is," unsaying it and speaking it otherwise (1990, 265). In the context of the autobiographical act, Vizenor's discursive strategy forcefully responds to his refusal to accept Native identity as a static, cultural artifact and liberate it from the strictures of anthropological discourse.

Readers might indeed wonder why a book intended to be Vizenor's autobiography, and which begins with Anishinaabe creation and trickster stories, is prefaced with quotations from Eudora Welty, Primo Levi, and Michel Foucault, among others. How do these fragments of lives interact with Vizenor's own life? And how do we make the transition from these literary figures to that trickster consciousness which, according to Blaeser, is such a distinctive signature of Vizenor's work?[5]

An author who has had a significant influence on Vizenor's writing and whose autobiography Vizenor had read when composing the twenty-nine episodes that make up *Interior Landscapes* is the French critic and semiotician Roland Barthes. In *La chambre claire,* translated into English as *Camera Lucida,* Barthes writes of the "uneasiness of being a subject torn between two languages, one expressive, the other critical" (1981, 8).[6] Readers familiar with *Roland Barthes by Roland Barthes* might remember its intriguing mixture of photographs and narrative fragments (the photographs bearing no direct relation to the text itself). This kind of "self-portrait," characterized by a "present-oriented" narrative in which "the self can never be 'fixed,'" would later become a model for postmodern forms of autobiographical writing (Smith and Watson 2001, 202–3).[7] While Vizenor might have had in mind the discursive split enunciated by Barthes and postmodern theories of subjectivity in general, his act of "dispersion" between the critical and the expressive, I argue, takes on a rather different meaning.[8] In the preface to his edited collection, *Narrative Chance,* Vizenor writes that "oral cultures have never been without a postmodern condition that enlivens stories and ceremonies, or without trickster signatures and discourse on narrative chance—a comic utterance and adventure to be heard or read" (1993a, x). He suggests that oral cultures have never been without a critical condition and that the act of telling stories is essentially a theoretical gesture. Regardless of the genre in which he is working, Vizenor's main concern in writing is the primary role of language, which, as in oral discourse, should set people free. Whether we call his fiction metacritical (as critics have done) or his autobiography autocritical (as he has done), we should keep in mind that the blurring of discourses and genres in his work ultimately reflects his ideas on the oral nature of language and, more importantly perhaps, his attempt to mediate between the oral and written expressive modes.

As I am thinking further of that MLA panel on theorist autobiographers and the natural connections between Vizenor's and Derrida's writing,[9] I am nonetheless intrigued by unexplored links and resonances across distances and times. Within the tradition of Western literary autobiography, Vizenor's conception of theoretical autobiographies, I argue, is perhaps closer to Augustine than to postmodern and poststructuralist examples of autobiographical modes, all the more so if we follow recent interpretations of such earlier literary masterpieces. Though considered "the architexte of Western autobiography," *Confessions,* Françoise Lionnet argues, is the literary expression of a man living on cultural and linguistic borderlines (1989, 18–20). Born in North Africa, speaking Numidian (a Berber language) at home—in the town of Thagaste, near Carthage, a colony of the Roman Empire—learning Latin at school, the language that he would later use as a writer, Augustine would for the rest of his life strive for a state of metaphysical communion in the attempt to reach a form of discourse that would transcend language itself. The nonnarrative quality of the last four books of *Confessions,* which abruptly shift to the sphere of interpretation and theoretical practices—a subject of controversy for many critics and editors of Augustine's text—might ultimately convey echoes of the struggle between orality and literacy that Augustine lived in his own experience. In adopting a "relational" approach, one that would resist a Manichaean worldview in favor of a Neoplatonic Christian theology, Augustine, according to Lionnet, ironically becomes the predecessor of contemporary autobiographical women writing and their strategies of *métissage* (1989, 36–37). Departing from a crucial episode in Book 13, a passage in which the converted Augustine criticizes Manichaeans, whom he called *insani* or madmen, for failing to see God's harmonious creation of the world,[10] Lionnet detects distinctively "feminine elements" in the poetics of the *Confessions.* She writes: "It is thus extremely appropriate to begin my book with a detailed analysis of the *Confessions* . . . and to attempt to reread it in light of my own contemporary feminist commitment to eliminating the artificial boundaries that century of Manichean—indeed phallogocentric—thinking have helped to erect. . . . My approach to Augustine seeks to free the *Confessions* from the philosophical and theological traditions that have appropriated it" (36–37). Augustine's "poetics of harmony," Lionnet maintains, ultimately relies on "valorizing aural forms of knowledge" (59) confiding in the power of God's word to unify and transform the human aspect of his life narrative.

From Carthage to Anishinaabe country the road is indeed far, and any attempt to link Neoplatonism with Vizenor's reenacting of Anishinaabe myths and metaphors might seem pretentious to say the least. Lionnet's rereading of Augustine's text nonetheless strikes an important chord in the context of my rereading of Vizenor's autobiography. "These critical ideas," Vizenor comments in response to a question on the nature of orality in his autobiography, "are in the very play of oral and written language. The sound of the word, and the image of the sound of the word, does not play, at times, rightly on the page, and must be teased by a wider gesture, or season of meaning. . . . My interest, always, has been in the story. And the problem, almost always, has been that gesture of the oral turned over on the written page. How do the words transform the images of memory" (personal correspondence, 8 May 2006).[11]

Transformation and re-expression are at the center of the Anishinaabe oral experience. In *Earthdivers,* Vizenor reminds us that Wenebojo (the trickster figure also known as Naanabozho) brings up five grains of sands from the water, lets them dry up to the sun, and starts throwing earth around to create "a little island" (1981, xiii–xiv). For Vizenor, contemporary mixedblood trickster writers are the new mythic earthdivers. Like Wenebojo, they must create a new space, a new "turtle island" on the written page in the attempt to translate the elusive but liberatory power of the spoken word into the written text. Perhaps Vizenor's most effective attempt to articulate the harmonious nature of the oral and the written is to be found in his use of the metaphor of the shadow. "The shadow is that sense of intransitive motion to the referent; the silence in memories. Shadows are neither the absence of entities nor the burden of conceptual references. The shadows are the prenarrative silence that inherits the words; shadows are the motions that mean the silence, but not the presence over absence of entities," Vizenor writes in *Manifest Manners* (1994, 64), clearly resisting a tradition of Western literary discourse based on mutually exclusive categories—most notably the split between voice and silence, word and text. Such resistance, critics today maintain, might indeed have been a crucial concern, albeit for significantly different reasons, in the work of one of the founding fathers of the genre of autobiography, Augustine of Hippo.

At the same time as he engages in conversation with theorists and critical readers from the contemporary cultural and intellectual scene, Vizenor,

however, always reassures us that he is indeed writing autobiographical stories, stories reflecting the performance of everyday practices and that his multifaceted self ultimately establishes a presence in the telling: "I am a storier,
and my stories enfold the creation of a voice, a time, and a place that is always
in motion, or visionary transmotion. And the stories create me" (Vizenor and
Lee 1999, 61).

Interior Landscapes ends with eight autobiographical stories marked by
locales as diverse as California, South Dakota, Minnesota, and Wisconsin and
by events that in some cases would make a reader wonder whether these experiences are indeed believable. Vizenor himself writes that a professor at Ma-
calester College in Saint Paul once told him that his stories "were not true"
(266). In eight autobiographical episodes Vizenor tells how, upon meeting
James Baldwin at UC Berkeley, he was mistaken for the black author by a boy
eager to deliver his practiced speech to the great writer. He writes about his
editorial essays on the American Indian Movement, his role in James White
Hawk's case (a photograph of White Hawk is included among other personal
and family photographs in *Interior Landscapes*), and his experience with a
young Native American student suffering from terminal cancer whose life
Vizenor almost ended up making even more miserable. This cycle of ordinary
life occurrences closes with a story set in Bena, Minnesota, a story linked to
the genealogies of his Anishinaabe family, and with two additional episodes
related to his experiences as a university student and later a writer. The man,
the journalist, the writer, the university professor nicely converge in these
narratives that create a character in a communal scene while reflecting some
of the split intentionality (the "I" becoming a "he") that Louis A. Renza
has outlined in his reflections on the theory of autobiography ("The Veto of
the Imagination," qtd. in Olney 1980, 279). Within the context of contemporary theorization of performativity, these stories also reveal that the autobiographical speaker, far from expressing an inner self that is "ontologically
whole, seamless and 'true'" (Smith 1998, 108, paraphrasing Judith Butler), is
constantly engaged in a performative act, in a theatrical recitation of the self
that is the essential aspect of living a life.

A life lived performatively inevitably gets narrated in a "purely fragmen-
tary, incomplete literary project," and such life narrative becomes "an endless

prelude, a beginning without middle . . . or without end" (Renza, qtd. in Olney 1980, 295). *Interior Landscapes* is not Vizenor's last book, one that would give us a sense of closure. On the contrary, its final stories testify to future narratives, a proliferation of stories to come. More importantly perhaps, the final stories affirm the ubiquitous presence of the trickster elsewhere defined by Vizenor as "a comic holotrope in a language game" (1993b, 200). Elements of trickster humor permeate the final story about Melvin McCosh, the owner of a bookstore near the University of Minnesota at the time when Vizenor was a sophomore there, in the late fifties. Students would frequently wander into this bookstore asking for required textbooks:

> "Do you have psych one?"
> "Would you be asking for a book?"
> "Yes, for my class."
> "Would you happen to know the title?"
> "Intro to psych," the student would answer.
> "Never heard of that book."
> "It's on the list," the students would plead.
> "Did someone write this book?"
> "I don't know."
> "What is the book about?"
> "Psych one."
> "Never heard of that book."
> "But it's on my list."
> "The University bookstore has introductions," he would announce
> and then touch his wild white beard." (278)

In perfectly trickster fashion, McCosh (alias trickster Vizenor) would tease students challenging their imagination with the liberatory power of language. "The University of Minnesota was a new world to some students from rural communities where there were no bookstores. McCosh might have been their first humane encounter with a trickster at the university" (278), Vizenor writes in visibly self-referential mode. McCosh (alias trickster) would challenge aspiring writers as well. Commenting on Vizenor's first collection of poems, *South of the Painted Stones,* McCosh urged young Vizenor to protect those poems with copyright.

> "Indeed, you must copyright these poems."
> "Thank you, McCosh."
> "Do you want to know why?"
> "Well, yes of course."
> "These poems are bad, so bad, that one day, when you are a better writer, you'll need the copyright to protect your reputation, to keep these poems out of circulation," said McCosh." (279).

Again and again in his work Vizenor has pointed out that the trickster cannot be confined within the strictures of anthropological discourse. Against static definitions of the trickster as an amoral, individual figure, one who, in the words of Paul Radin, "knows neither good nor evil yet is responsible for both" (qtd. in Vizenor 1981, xii), Vizenor affirms that the trickster is not representational. As Blaeser points out, Vizenor's trickster consciousness "arises from a certain state of mind, an anarchical energy, a liberating humor" (1996, 137). When translated into Vizenor's writing, such trickster energy results in a style that refuses the logic of cause and effect. It's a style that embraces chance, celebrates play, relishes ambiguity, breaks rules, confounds expectations, and invites involvement. "The most active readers," Vizenor writes, "become obverse tricksters" (1988, x).

According to Richard Hutson, Vizenor's trickster signature "sounds like the very muse of autobiography" if we consider the genre as marked by contradictions and ambiguity (2000, 112). More importantly, perhaps, within the context of a theoretical approach to autobiography, as I have attempted to outline so far in this essay, a text such as *Interior Landscapes* contributes original insights to this fascinating topic that since Augustine's *Confessions* has generated critical investigation. For the purpose of my discussion, I focus on the last chapter of Vizenor's autobiography, for in it we see the most effective strategies of autocritical life writing. And yet almost any chapter of *Interior Landscapes* can be approached in such a dialogic mode, with its stories that read as simply self-enclosed narratives or "as tales with extensive ramifications and resonances" (Hutson 2000, 112) in Vizenor's complex mythic universe. One such story is the mystery surrounding the death of his father, Clement William Vizenor. Given the central role this story occupies in Vizenor's text, I deem it appropriate, at this point, to include it in my discussion on autocritical autocritique.

• • •

The mixedblood wavers in autobiographies; he moves between mythic reservations where tricksters roamed and the cities where his father was murdered

—"Crows Written on the Poplars"

Already in his early autobiographical essay Vizenor refers to his father's tragic death in urban Minneapolis and to the legacy of mixedblood memories that Clement William Vizenor left to his son. "Tricksters," Vizenor writes in the section of *Interior Landscapes* titled "The Trickster and Libertina," "eased the pain in stories" (1990, 74), alluding to his refusal to act as a victim despite the severe desolation, violence, and trauma that characterized his childhood. "Clement William Vizenor lost the game with the evil gambler and did not return from the cities. He was a house painter who told trickster stories, pursued women, and laughed most of his time on earth. He was murdered on a narrow street in downtown Minneapolis" (27), Vizenor writes in the opening sections of *Interior Landscapes,* a section interspersed with quotations from the journalistic account of his father's murder on 27 June 1936. Vizenor was not even two years old when his father died by "accident," as his family used to say throughout his childhood. It was more than twenty years after the fact that Vizenor discovered, by chance, that his father had actually been murdered, "a case of unsolved homicide." If autobiographies are, in Vizenor's terms, "imaginative histories; a remembrance past the barriers" (1990, 262), the episode of his father's death reimagined in trickster fashion allows Vizenor to go past the barriers of absence, illegitimacy associated with the mixedblood status, and confusion surrounding his father's mysterious death and the difficult times that would follow.

"Measuring My Blood," the section in *Interior Landscapes* devoted to

Vizenor's father, contains a poem titled "The Last Photograph," a clear articulation of the photograph of father and son reproduced on the book cover and following the table of contents.[12] According to Jack Foley (Vizenor 1996), the poem conveys the feeling of the presence of Vizenor's father, "even in absence," a feeling, he suggests, that we find at the core of all of Vizenor's work.

> clement vizenor would be a spruce
> on his wise return to the trees
>
> corded on the reservation side
> he overturned the line
> colonial genealogies
> white earth remembrance
> removed to the cities at twenty three
>
> my father lived on stories
> over the rough rims on mason jars
> danced with the wounded shaman
> low over the stumps on the fourth of july
>
> my father lied to be an Indian
> he laughed downtown
> the trickster signature to the lights
>
>   • • •
>
> clement posed in a crowded tenement
> the new immigrant
> painted new house pure white
> outback in saint louis park
>
>   • • •
>
> my father holds me in the last photograph
> the new spruce
> with a wide smile
> half white

half immigrant
he took up the cities and lost at cards (29–31)

Written in a style reminiscent of Vizenor's haiku, which in turns combine the
tradition of Ojibway dream song and Japanese poetic form (Blaeser 1996,
108), the poem offers vivid images with very little interpretation. The ambivalence set in motion by the term "spruce"[13] immediately establishes the
idea of "presence" despite Clement's tragic death. The poem moves back
and forth between the third-person "clement" and the much warmer and
personal "my father," as Clement himself moved back and forth between city
and reservation. The prototype of what social scientists would label as "an
urban Indian," Clement nevertheless, Vizenor writes, "overturned the line /
colonial genealogies" (1990, 30) with his Anishinaabe memories and trickster
stories. His is not a story of the tragic mixedblood caught up in two worlds
and unable to relate to either of them. Clement would dance with the shaman at the same time that he would pose as a new immigrant in a "crowded
tenement," informing and transforming his life within a trickster story that
would allow him to survive until the final game with the evil gambler, when
"he took up the cities and lost at cards."[14]

Through the photograph picturing father and son a few weeks before
Clement's death, Vizenor attempts to remember that moment, or rather
re-member the shadows of that moment, the last time together before the
abrupt separation. He writes: "I hear my father in that photograph and
imagine his touch, the turn of his hand on my shoulder, his warm breath
on my check, his word trickeries, and my grandmother behind the camera"
(1990, 32) as if attempting to bring to life the "suchness" of the moment,
something that "the interimage simulation" of the camera cannot do. Even
though it has been argued that photographs are a confirmation of an existence, cultural artifacts that allow us to get closer to the subject, Barthes
promptly reminds us that in photography the body "never finds its zero
degree" (1981, 12). In *Camera Lucida,* written shortly after the death of his
beloved mother, Barthes describes the painful moment of going through
his mother's pictures in the attempt to find a photograph of her in which he
could *find her,* and find a mark of a past presence: "Photography therefore

compelled me to perform a painful labor; straining toward the essence of her identity, I was struggling among images partially true, and therefore totally false" (1981, 66). Whereas in *Roland Barthes by Roland Barthes,* the move to photography and to the autobiographical—the two cannot be considered apart from each other in Barthes's experimental text—is clearly announced before the title page, through a picture of his mother, and immediately following the opening narrative, through a picture of his mother holding him (and captured under "the demand for love"), *Camera Lucida,* a meditation on the absence inherent in photography but also a personal account about Barthes's recent loss, deliberately omits any picture of the author's mother. Although photographs, as approached by sociologists, are "nothing but the trace of a social protocol of integration, intended to reassert the Family" (1981, 7), Barthes is painfully aware that *what has been* cannot be called up: "In short, I found myself at an impasse and, so to speak, 'scientifically' alone and disarmed" (7).

If we follow Vizenor's commentary on photography in *Fugitive Poses,* which weaves statements by Jean Baudrillard, Susan Sontag, John Berger, and Barthes himself, among others, we might wonder about Vizenor's decision to make "the last photograph" such an important thematic and structural component of his autobiography. "The notion that a photograph is worth a thousand words is untrue in any language. Native stories create a sense of presence, a tease of memories, and a resistance to pictures of victimry" (1998, 154), Vizenor writes in "Occidental Surveillance," a section exploring how photographic representations of Natives became evidence of a vanishing race and the ultimate affirmation of theories of dominance and racialism. Vizenor's reflections on "portraiture" allow him to elaborate his notions of presence and absence and the contradictions and ironies inherent in trickster stories. Vizenor's last photograph in *Interior Landscapes* undoubtedly reveals some of these contradictions. Despite a postmodern tendency to consider the use of photographs in autobiography a confirmation of the central role of "visibility" in contemporary life (Luri 1998, 2) and with all the influence that postmodern writing has on Vizenor's work, his "pictorial turn" in *Interior Landscapes* goes beyond mere postmodernism and celebrations of visibility in the culture of simulacra.

At the end of "Occidental Surveillance," Vizenor writes: "Watch the eyes and hands in fugitive poses to see the motion of natives, and hear the apophatic narratives of a continuous presence" (1998, 165). What did Vizenor see in those eyes and hands holding him as a twenty-month-old infant in that last photograph reproduced in his autobiography? What narrative did he hear in his father's "wide smile"? "Photographs in themselves do not write," John Berger claims in *About Looking*, "they preserve instant appearances" (qtd. in Vizenor 1998, 158). Clement's instant appearance in the photograph cannot give the narrative and presence of his life. But the poem "The Last Photograph," the only one of its kind in Vizenor's entire autobiography, and the story it narrates most certainly can. It could be argued that the poem "stories" into the photograph to make us hear the continuous presence of the persona in the picture. As a "half white," "half immigrant," urban mixed-blood removed to the cities at twenty-three, Clement William Vizenor was imprisoned in the simulation of Indianness, a misnomer, Vizenor has pointed out, that erases a Native presence while affirming a logocentric absence. Employing Derridean terminology, Vizenor in *Fugitive Poses* discusses how in colonial discourse Natives have become the absent Others, simulations of racialism serving the scientific discourse of modernity. Writing specifically about his father, Vizenor argues that Clement William Vizenor "was *anishinaabe* by reservation ancestors and *indian* by simulation" since "the census counted him as an *indian,* the absence of a native presence in the city" (1998, 50). Nevertheless, Vizenor concludes, "Clement, his brothers, and other natives in urban areas were *indians* by simulation, transethnic by separation, but natives in their stories of survivance" (51). The persona honored in "The Last Photograph" is a storier, and his stories are stories of survivance. As much as *Interior Landscape*s is a book about Vizenor and his life, it is also the autobiography of his father, Clement William Vizenor, who did not write but whose life stories remain within the memory of his Anishinaabe family. An absent other in official colonial discourse, Clement becomes an enduring *presence* through his son's imaginative powers and autobiographical gestures.

In the last chapter of *Interior Landscapes*, Vizenor quotes Paul John Eakin: "When we settle into the theatre of autobiography . . . what we are ready to believe . . . is that the play we witness is a historical one, a largely faithful and unmediated reconstruction of events that took place long ago, whereas in reality the play is that of the autobiographical act itself, in which the materials of the past are shaped by memory and imagination to serve the needs of present consciousness" (1990, 263). In creating his autobiographical "myths and metaphors," Vizenor *unsettles* the theater of autobiography, apparently playing the role of the faithful reconstructor of salient events of his life but ultimately and inevitably *playing* with the autobiographical act itself. His crossblood remembrances take the form of differing discourses, pronouns, and voices, and much like a trickster, they remain ultimately and inevitably untamed. As a creative and theoretical text, *Interior Landscapes* offers an additional example of the essential ambiguity and open nature of the autobiographical act as it has been elucidated in the criticism of autobiographical narratives, particularly in the last two decades. More importantly, perhaps, *Interior Landscapes* offers an example of autocritical writing through which the author continues to wage his cultural word wars on restricted views of mixedblood identity while confirming his dedication to stories and narratives of survivance.

NOTES

This essay grew out of a paper delivered at the international two-day symposium "Gerald Vizenor: Litterateur at Large," Université Paul-Valéry, Montpellier III, France, May 2006. The original version appears in *Gerald Vizenor,* edited by Simone Pellerin. *Profils américains* 20, 2007. Montpellier, France: Presses universitaires de l'Université Paul-Valéry—Montpellier III. I am grateful to Simone Pellerin and the editors of Presses universitaires de l'Université Paul-Valéry—Montpellier III for permission to reprint.

1. The rich and diverse history of self-referential writing has inevitably resulted in animated discussions concerning the validity of the term *autobiography*, which in its original Greek meaning—*autos, bios,* and *graphe*—still privileges the act of *writing* vis-à-vis other means of self-expression. According to Sidonie Smith and Julia Watson, the term *autobiography* still evokes a genre focusing on the lives of Western great men—Augustine, Rousseau, Franklin, Goethe, Adams, among others, "whose

accomplished lives and literary tomes assured their value as cultural capital" (1998, 5). While *life writing* has become a commonly accepted substitute for autobiography, *life narrative,* Smith and Watson suggest, seems to be "a wide-ranging term for exploring diverse modes around the autobiographical" (2001, 223) today. Working at the intersection of various discourses, first and foremost the oral and the written, Gerald Vizenor's autobiographical mode seems to me to respond perfectly to the notion of life narrative as conceived by Smith and Watson.

2. While Lejeune's ideas of autobiography as voiced in *l'Autobiographie en France* (1971) and in a more comprehensive form in *Le Pacte autobiographique* (1975) are still widely quoted by practitioners of the genre, it should be pointed out that the critic has been revising his formulations about life stories and autobiography since the original publications. Lejeune's own discussion on the limitations of some of his earlier terminology clearly suggests an understanding of autobiography as a genre in constant transformation and reinvention. For some of Lejeune's revised ideas on autobiography, see *On Autobiography* (1989).

3. Upon considering oral techniques of transmitting knowledge among Native cultures, Krupat envisions Native American autobiography as essentially synecdochic in orientation, one in which part-whole relations stand in stark contrast with part-part relations (metonymy) typical of modern Western autobiography (1992, 216).

4. Theoretical studies of women's autobiographies in particular in the last two decades have devoted a significant amount of attention to diasporic, cross-cultural subjectivities emerging from formerly colonized countries, forcefully disputing the notion of autobiography as an expression of the (male) Enlightenment subject. For a historical overview, see Smith and Watson 2001. At the same time, non-written forms of personal narratives such as storytelling performances and pictographic stories have been increasingly considered in studies of Native American autobiography. See Wong 1992.

5. See especially the chapter "Trickster Signature" in her *Gerald Vizenor* (Blaeser 1996).

6. My references from Barthes's texts are from the English translations: *Camera Lucida* (1981) and *Roland Barthes by Roland Barthes* (1977).

7. Though often referred to as an autobiography (especially in the United States), it should be pointed out that Barthes's text is one in a famous collection of monographs of major French authors, and a few other authors, a collection featuring 106 volumes in total. Exceptionally, Barthes was in charge of the issue on himself. The use of text, pictures, and other documents applies to the entire collection, not only to Barthe's

issue. In French intellectual circles, *Roland Barthes by Roland Barthes* is not discussed as an autobiography. I would like to thank Simone Pellerin for bringing to my attention such an interesting issue. For additional discussion see the website created by the research group of the Ecole normale supérieure in Paris, http://www.fabula. org/forum/barthes.php. See also Smith and Watson's discussion of Barthes's text as "autofiction" (2001, 186).

8. Asked specifically about Barthes's influence on his autobiography, Vizenor commented: "I had certainly read *Roland Barthes by Roland Barthes* ("Autocritical Autobiographies" was published in 1987) but his ideas in other critical essays seem now to be more memorable. . . . I resisted his literary manner, which, of course, was in translation, and his tease in the native sense of communal stories. His direction, as words oversee the literary creation of an autocharacter, was more image than the tricky native gestures of stories" (personal correspondence, 8 May 2006). Readers might also recall Vizenor's overall dissatisfaction with the category of postmodernism, humorously articulated in his introduction to *Narrative Chance* (1993a, 3–16).

9. Critics such as Ruoff, Krupat, Owens, Blaeser, and myself have discussed Vizenor's indebtedness to Derrida. And yet Elaine Jahner's critical analyses, especially her unpublished essay, "Heading 'Em Off at the Impasse," which I refer to in my *Toward a Native American Critical Theory*, remains, in my view, the most limpid interpretations of Vizenor's convergence and divergence from poststructuralist and deconstructivist theories. Jahner's essay is also mentioned in Blaeser, 1996.

10. "They say you did not produce the creation from your own matter, but that its elements were already created elsewhere by another power, and that you gathered them together and assembled and organized them. . . . They claim that in the lower places of the world those things are generated and formed by a hostile mind and an alien nature, *not created by you but opposed to you*. This is the utterance of *madmen*. They do not see your works with the help of your Spirit and do not recognize you in them" (Augustine 1991, 13:30; my emphasis).

11. Interestingly enough, *memoria*, which in Augustine's view is infused with Platonic doctrines of *anamnesis*, and therefore has a deeper and wider meaning than our *memory*, is the subject of Book 10 of *Confessions*, the first of the so-called nonnarrative books in his autobiography.

12. Originally published as "Family Photograph" in 1975, in a collection edited by Kenneth Rosen, the poem has recently been revised to appear, with the original titled, in

Vizenor's volume of poetry *Almost Ashore* (2006). Similarly, "Measuring my Blood" first appeared with the title "1936: Measuring Blood" in "In Know What You Mean, Erdrupps MacChurbbs," in *Growing Up in Minnesota: Ten Writers Remember Their Childhood* (Anderson 1976). For a comprehensive bibliography of Vizenor's work see Blaeser 1996.

13. As a noun, *spruce*, according to the OED, refers to "a species or a single tree of spruce fir," whereas as an adjective it means "brisk, smart, lively."

14. This sense of motion or, as Vizenor puts it, "Native transmotion," is vividly conveyed in the revision of the original poem, included in *Almost Ashore* (2006). Here both the terms "immigrant" (repeated twice) and "exile" are used to describe Clement's relocation from White Earth to Minneapolis.

WORKS CITED

Anderson, Chester G., ed. 1976. *Growing Up in Minnesota: Ten Writers Remember Their Childhood*. Minneapolis: University of Minnesota Press.

Augustine, Saint. 1991. *Confessions*. Translated by Henry Chadwick. Oxford: Oxford University Press.

Barthes, Roland. 1981. *Camera Lucida*. Translated by Richard Howard. New York: Farrar, Straus, and Giroux.

———. 1994. *Roland Barthes by Roland Barthes*. Translated by Richard Howard. 1977; Berkeley and Los Angeles: University of California Press.

Blaeser, Kimberly. 1996. *Gerald Vizenor: Writing in the Oral Tradition*. Norman: University of Oklahoma Press.

Evans, Robley. 1991. Review of *Interior Landscapes: Autobiographical Myths and Metaphors*, by Gerald Vizenor. *Studies in American Indian Literature* 3.4: 57–61.

Gusdorf, George. 1980. "Conditions and Limits of Autobiography." In *Autobiography: Essays Theoretical and Critical*, edited by James Olney, 28–48. Princeton, N.J.: Princeton University Press.

Hutson, Richard. 2000. "A Crossblood at the Scratch Line: *Interior Landscapes*." In *Loosening the Seams: Interpretations of Gerald Vizenor*, edited by A. Robert Lee, 10–25. Bowling Green, Ohio: Bowling Green State Popular Press.

Jahner, Elaine. 1996. "Heading 'Em Off at the Impasse: Native American Authors Meet the Poststructuralists." Unpublished essay, Dartmouth College.

Krupat, Arnold. 1992. *Ethnocriticism: Ethnography, History, Literature.* Berkeley and Los Angeles: University of California Press.

Lejeune, Philippe. 1989. *On Autobiography.* Edited by Paul John Eakin. Translated by Katherine Leary. Minneapolis: University of Minnesota Press.

———. 1996. *Le pacte autobiographique.* Nouvelle édition augmentée. Collection Essais-Points, 1975. Paris: Le Seuil.

Lionnet, Françoise. 1989. "Augustine's *Confessions:* Poetics of Harmony, or the Ideal Reader in the Text." In *Autobiographical Voices: Race, Gender, Self-Portraiture,* 36–66. Ithaca, N.Y.: Cornell University Press.

Luri, Celia. 1998. *Prosthetic Culture: Photography, Memory, Identity.* New York: Routledge.

Olney, James. 1972. *Metaphors of Self: The Meaning of Autobiography.* Princeton, N.J.: Princeton University Press.

———, ed. 1980. *Autobiography: Essays Theoretical and Critical.* Princeton, N.J.: Princeton University Press.

Owens, Louis. 1992. *Other Destinies: Understanding American the American Indian Novel.* Norman, Oklahoma: University of Oklahoma Press.

Pulitano, Elvira. 2003. *Toward a Native American Critical Theory.* Lincoln: University of Nebraska Press.

Renza, Louis A. 1980. "The Veto of the Imagination: A Theory of Autobiography." In *Autobiography: Essays Theoretical and Critical,* edited by James Olney, 268–95. Princeton, N.J.: Princeton University Press.

Smith, Sidonie. 1998. "Performativity, Autobiographical Practice, Resistance." In *Women, Autobiography, Theory,* edited by Sidonie Smith and Julia Watson, 108–15. Madison: University of Wisconsin Press.

Smith, Sidonie, and Julia Watson, eds. 1998. *Women, Autobiography, Theory.* Madison: University of Wisconsin Press.

———. 2001. *Reading Autobiography: A Guide for Interpreting Life Narratives.* Madison: University of Wisconsin Press.

Vizenor, Gerald. 1981. *Earthdivers: Tribal Narratives on Mixed Descent.* Minneapolis: University of Minnesota Press.

———. 1987. "Crows Written at the Poplars: Autocritical Autobiographies." In *I Tell You Now: Autobiographical Essays by Native American Writers,* edited by Brian Swann and Arnold Krupat, 101–9. Lincoln: University of Nebraska Press.

———. 1988. *The Trickster of Liberty: Native Heirs to a Wild Baronage.* Minneapolis: University of Minnesota Press.

———. 1990. *Interior Landscapes: Autobiographical Myths and Metaphors.* Minneapolis: University of Minnesota Press.

———, ed. 1993a. *Narrative Chance: Postmodern Discourse on Native American Indian Literatures.* Norman: University of Oklahoma Press.

———. 1993b. "Trickster Discourse: Comic Holotropes and Language Games." In *Narrative Chance: Postmodern Discourse on Native American Indian Literatures,* edited by Gerald Vizenor, 187–211. Norman: University of Oklahoma Press.

———. 1994. *Manifest Manners: Postindian Warriors of Survivance.* Hanover, N.H.: University Press of New England.

———. 1996. "A Chance of Survivance: An Interview with Gerald Vizenor." Interview by Jack Foley. Part I broadcast on *Cover to Cover,* KPFA-FM, 26 August.

———. 1998. *Fugitive Poses: Native American Indian Scenes of Absence and Presence.* Lincoln: University of Nebraska Press.

———. 2006. *Almost Ashore: Selected Poems.* Cambridge: Salt.

Vizenor, Gerald, and A. Robert Lee. 1999. *Postindian Conversations.* Lincoln: University of Nebraska Press.

Wong, Hertha Dawn. 1992. *Sending My Heart Back across the Years: Tradition and Innovation in Native American Autobiography.* Oxford: Oxford University Press.

Ignatia Broker's Lived Feminism: Toward a Native Women's Theory

MOLLY MCGLENNEN

A story begins by pulling back the layers
and then putting new ones on.
Simultaneously. A palimpsest made of voices.

This essay examines the shortcomings of Western feminisms' appli-cations to Native American women's texts by addressing the com-plexities of what I term a Native women's theory. Utilizing Ignatia Broker's *Night Flying Woman: An Ojibway Narrative* and its charac-ters Oona and Awasasi as models of "lived feminisms," I problematize the application of "isms" to Native texts because of the manner in which they direct themselves; Western theoretical frames mainly work from the outside in, whereas Native texts like *Night Flying Woman,* I argue, facilitate theory to arise from within the text itself, from the inside out. *Night Flying Woman* with its powerful female figures is a text that resists complementarity with linear and hierarchical constructs of Western sociopolitical frames that do not mirror a more three-dimensional theoretical lens that is needed to examine Native texts. Oona's teachings and Awasasi's wisdom serve as navigation for survival and growth and show the need to reclaim traditions that have sustained Native people for generations. The effect within the text, a *spiral evolution,* innately exists as an implicit gauge for comprehending ideas of multiple narrators/narratees, listening, and community. The narrative in *Night Flying Woman* illustrates a "lived feminism," which is a re-calling of tradition-based definitions of womanhood that ultimately defy fixed or specified doctrines of female conditions while continually responding to both modernity and erasure.

In order to understand how this essay examines Native stories' familiarity with the concerns of Western theory, it is important to consider the history of colonization in North America as it intersects with gender and violence. Much of the West's understanding about Native Americans has been heavily influenced by the writing of European chroniclers and early ethnographers. Prevalent within these documents is the colonialist mentality that upholds gender inequity and the necessarily subordinate position of women in society. In their pursuit to tame and secure land and resources, colonists regarded nature as "gifts from God," believing they had both divine and civil rights to American virgin land and its creatures. What stood in the colonizer's way were nature's "inhabitants," the *savage* Indian—heathens in the untamed environment. As Andrea Smith (Cherokee) documents in *Conquest: Sexual Violence and American Indian Genocide,* the image of Native peoples, like the vanishing wilderness, reinforced an "absence" in the U.S. colonial imagination that "effected a metaphorical transformation of Native bodies into a pollution of which the colonial body must constantly purify itself" (2005, 9). Stemming from this mythology, the demonization and oppression of Native women grew because of their perceived dirtiness; this provided, moreover, the basis for the strategies of Euro-American men to maintain control over Euro-American women. Thus, as Smith argues, racism and colonial oppression served the purposes of patriarchy. While white women were subdued but "protected" by white men, Native women were dehumanized and hypersexualized as a means to implement gendered and racist hierarchical structures of power.[1]

The practitioners of colonization and the Christian conquest of the Americas, in efforts to subjugate indigenous nations, recognized the implicit need to subdue Native women through rape and murder in order to maintain their hierarchy of gender and power; this was necessary to eradicate Native people's traditional egalitarian societies and uphold the colonizer's imperialist (as well as misogynistic, racist, and sexist) agenda. According to Smith,

> The egalitarian nature of Native societies was threatening the legitimacy of the abusive nature of European societies; it was imperative that Native societies be exterminated and demonized in order to legitimize the European social structure. (1995, 381)

Smith states further,

> Colonizers realized that in order to subjugate indigenous nations, they would have to subjugate women within these nations. Native peoples needed to learn the value of hierarchy, the role of physical abuse in maintaining that hierarchy, and the importance of women remaining submissive to their men. (378)

Needless to say, Native women's stories and histories have, with few exceptions, been inaccurately portrayed, often tainted with sentimentality and delivered through a lens of Western patriarchy and domination. In addition, what is historicized in ethnographic literature about Native societies is predominantly male-oriented or viewed through a framework that is imperialistic and paternal. However, Native texts—oral and written—show that Native women have been and are responding to five hundred years of colonization, both in their traditional homelands and in urban areas, employing strategies of survival and continuance.

These Native women's stories, because of their dialogical, interrogative, and flexible structures, inherently contest the utility of Western feminist theories. In general, Western feminisms, when applied to these narratives, often do not incorporate anticolonial indigenous perspectives, which necessarily require consideration of issues like sovereignty, assimilation, traditionalism, balance, spirituality, oral tradition, and *relationship* with (not *ownership* of) the land. Native women's "anticolonial" standpoints, on the whole, stem directly from their autochthonous roots in specific North American landscapes based on their complex relationship to oral narratives. While Native women most certainly engage in Western feminist dialogues, and Western feminists most certainly can contribute to decolonizing and indigenous dialogues, the two traditions have distinct theoretical trajectories in relation to land(scape) and community. Indeed, there is a continuum of feminist viewpoints, but these interstices have to do with lived experiences based upon more than social constructions of race, class, and sexuality. What Native women's narratives like *Night Flying Woman* suggest is that retaining traditional meanings of balance from and toward one's community is a form of combat and resistance to women's oppression, and these systems have always been encoded in the stories. Thus, I believe Western feminisms—when not attentive to these significant differences—fail to advance a Native woman's idea of selfhood in its entirety, a holistic and adaptable positioning that keeps her in balance with respect to her history, land, spirituality, culture, and language. In other words, for Native women it has never been about *liberation;* it has always been about *reclamation.*[2]

In their introduction to a *Feminist Theory Reader: Local and Global Perspectives*—a collection the publisher boasts of as offering "a multiplicity of feminist standpoints" and "a challenge to the hegemony of white, Western feminism"—the editors, Carole McCann and Seung-Kyung Kim, commence by saying,

> The term "feminism" usually refers in its most general sense to political activism by women on behalf of women. Widely used in the "second wave" of the US women's movement beginning in the 1970's, it seems to have originated in France in the 1880's. (2003, 1)

While the 1970s feminist movement might very well have roots in French political philosophy, it seems amiss that a collection that prides itself on the flexibility and ambiguity of defining feminism includes not one Native North American–authored essay and totally leaves out (consciously or not) the unmistakable influence of the Iroquois clan mothers on early U.S.

suffragists, as documented by Sally Roesch Wagner (2001). In all fairness, essays within McCann and Kim's collection demonstrate the need for multiple definitions of feminist ideology. Women of color, especially, assert analyses of the intersections of race, class, and gender. For example, bell hooks makes the distinction between "feminism-as-choice to *form* a community" and "feminism-as-a-political-commitment *to* one's community":

> Certainly many black women as well as women from other ethnic groups do not feel an absence of community among women in their lives despite exploitation and oppression. The focus of feminism as a way to develop shared identity and community has little appeal to women who experience community, who seek ways to end exploitation and oppression in the context of their lives. (2003, 54)

Contemporary Native women, as their stories express, find ways to heal and mend from oppression and exploitation, usually through reclaiming traditions that regularly sustained their particular communities. Contemporary Native women have built into their identities their traditional communities through living stories, and these stories are models for existing without oppression, without exploitation, without sexism.

But these assertions, as well, deserve clarification and justification. Native women writers have analyzed how indigenous stories (manifested in many different forms—oral and written, prose and poetry, etc.) are incompatible with the way in which Western feminist approaches seem to extract meaning from narratives, pulling it out, instead of understanding the "theory" within, and simultaneous with, the experience of the story—presupposing theory itself. Marilou Awiakta (Cherokee) tells the lesson an elder related to her: "Look at everything three times: Once with the right eye. Once with the left eye. And once from the corners of the eyes to see the spirit of what you're looking at" (2003, 56). To see these edges, this roundness, is to raze Western dichotomous structures that pit against each other humanity and nature, women and men, reality and spirituality. She argues that it has always been Native people's way to sing, dance, and live "poetry as a habit of being," as the movement of her own essay reflects:

Having taken its measure from the corners of the eyes, we must use the right and the left eye to take clear bearings: our point of departure, the lay of the trail from beginning to end, the experiences we should anticipate. We are going from contemporary space to primal space, from life on the square to life in the round, and from the line to the curve of time. . . . The language is intimate, for the primal mind there is *no psychic distance* between the singer and the song; listeners share the web of context and experience. Also, instead of following Western linear progression (A, B, C, etc.) and reasoning from the outside in, the essay begins with the center, Part I, and moves in a widening spiral to the conclusion, developing the thought from the inside out. This is the traditional American Indian mode that originated in primal space, where everything is connected. (57)

Because indigenous stories work in this way, ought not the frames of inter-pretation mirror this movement? Moreover, have the mirrors been embedded in the stories all along?

Similarly, Kimberly Blaeser (Ojibwe) questions if contemporary theory gives an incomplete reading of Native American literature; she notices an overwhelming amount of Native women's writing demonstrating that the story "both theorizes and enacts a Native aesthetic of literature and culture" where "the creative and the critical coexist" (1998, 266). Blaeser asserts,

The work of Native women writers especially carries a new vision as it re-fuses to separate the literary and academic from the sacred and the daily, as it brings to the text the unpaginated experiences of contemporary tribal reality. Writing by Native women remains infused with supraliter-ary intentions. (266)

While several models of interpretation of Native stories exist, the frequent and recognizable pattern of the web and circularity can run the risk of oversimplification. Blaeser is quick to point out that the notion of the web—permeating many aspects of many diverse tribal backgrounds—not only il-lustrates the complex "interweaving of both 'radial' and 'lateral' strands," but also, in its function, "involves the relationship between the various elements of construction, *the vibration of the web in response to contact*—that is, motion" (267; emphasis mine). Here, Blaeser recognizes the three-dimensionality of such Native literary frames, the necessity of building into models of interpretation the space for a listener, a receiver of knowledge, a community. Likewise, Ignatia Broker's narrative generates its own indigenous model of interpretation.

In *Night Flying Woman*,[3] the female characters propel the text and illustrate how womanhood was and is understood for the Ojibwe, defined in ways that assert a framework for a Native women's theory. This framework is specifically constructed in three respects: the idea of balance or the circle, the power of dreaming, and the reverence for land and spirit. In her prologue, Broker highlights the philosophy of the narrative that will follow:

> They have said there will be five generations of Ojibway who will make a circle. The first people will start the circle and the others will move from the Ojibway ways. There will be those who will ask questions and those who remember, and the last generation will act again as the Ojibway have acted in years before. Then the circle will be closed. (1983, 8)

Broker knows she is responsible in continuing the motion of the circle, and this is because her own children and grandchildren, now in urban areas, urge her to recall the old ways for them: "These children," she says, "who could hum the songs on the radio but did not know the songs of the drum" (xiii), "are again honoring the Old People by asking them to speak, and I—like other older people—will search my memory and tell what I know" (7). Implicit in these remarks, before Broker begins to speak Oona's (her great-great-grandmother's) story, is that there must be listeners if balance is to return, if the circle is to be complete. There must be an honoring, a respect, and a desire for the stories to be told again. Also, the circle—because it is a metaphor for reclamation—becomes, I argue, a *spiral evolution*, where through language and story, through listening (people completing the story through the exchange) the motion heals. Pieces from the past are incorporated into the present to maintain the balance needed to move the community into the future.

The connections between the narrator and narratees are formulated because of this motion. Broker begins her narrative by saying, "When the forest weeps, the Anishinaabe who listen will look back at the years. In each generation of Ojibway, there will be a person who will hear the si-si-gwad, who will listen and remember and pass it on to the children" (1). Memory and speaking-that-memory is always preceded by listening, and in this case, it is specifically listening to the land, the forest (*si-si-gwad*) that is so vital to the Ojibwe. What initiates the healing, then, is the memory of that which had always sustained them: the oral tradition, the language, and the land. I do not mention these terms lightly or generically. In the narrative, Oona is born not only during a change of seasons, but also an eclipse. Throughout the text there are references to Oona's birth, and ultimately her strength and vision, centered around the half-light of the forest, the darkness in day (the eclipse), the interchange of seasons (Ojibwe culture is based upon the seasons).[4] These are important markers because they signify the complexity and the power of Oona as an Ojibwe woman in relation to the earth. Each indicates a threshold and openness where change is about to come, but all the while Oona is firmly grounded in that fluidity. This is not a position of weakness, nor a position of victimization, nor a position of nostalgia. Broker takes note of these natural markers and imbeds them into her narrative to illustrate the reverence for and power of women in traditional Ojibwe society.

This is also reflected in how Oona is named. Oona's namer, chosen by her parents and grandparents, is Awasasi, a wise storyteller and healer in their community. When Awasasi is asked by Oona's family to seek out a name for her, the pipe is lit and an offering of *kin-nik-a-nik* is presented to the Great Spirit, and from there Awasasi goes into the forest with medicine to meditate and to choose an animal and a song.

> Awasasi had chosen the name Ni-bo-wi-se-gwe, which means Night Flying Woman, because Tiny Girl [the baby] had been born during the darkness of the day. Awasasi said that the shadows when the sun left the earth and the shadows when the day began would be the best time for her. (16)

Throughout the text, this divination turns out to be true. Not only does this illustrate the reverence for intellect and vision in the women—showing Awasasi as a profound leader of her community's ways—but also the confidence invested in young women to grow up to be the intellectual and visionary leaders of their communities, as Oona indeed does. Her power as a woman, her visions, dreams, and so on, come through *being* a source of balance, being a link between worlds and ideas. This negates rigid or fixed constraints of linearity or hierarchy upon her communal worldview. Broker says, "[Oona's] life followed the pattern the Ojibway had followed for many years. It was a pleasant cycle and she learned all that young Ojibway girls must know. It seemed to Oona as if this place had always been her home" (49). In Broker's memory of this cycle, in telling Oona's story, she relays what traditional Ojibwe lifeways brought the people and how relearning them can restore that sense of home. It is as if Broker is equipping her listeners with the tools to return.

This homecoming, however, is not the nostalgic "returning to the days before the white man" (the "Garden of Eden" stereotype); Native peoples throughout history have proven to be syncretistic in nature. Ojibwe epistemology and gender roles are intricate and sophisticated, and Broker exemplifies their rich variations in several ways. As Oona grows older, and the Ojibwe are forced to the reservation, when the children are coerced into schools that are meant to assimilate them, "kill the Indian" inside them, Christianize and Anglicize them, Oona seeks the advice and knowledge of her elders because she is confused by the contradictions she sees within the teachings of the church and in her school and the teachings of her elders that had kept her family happy. Now Oona, with the onset of Europeans, sees her mother in great despair and her community starving and distressed. Still, Oona prompts the wisdom her grandparents ultimately relay:

> Our way of life is changing, and there is much we must accept. But let it be only the good. And we must always remember the old ways. We must pass them on to our children and grandchildren so they too will recognize the good in the new ways. (94)

Not only does this underscore the fundamental tenets of balance and the *evolutionary spiral* motion of living for the Ojibwe ("recognizing the good in new ways"), but it also highlights the fact that they honor and rely on the past in a way that is essential to helping them in the future. And it is from this pivotal moment in Oona's life that she initiates her puberty ritual:

> It is a belief among the Ojibway that when a girl changes into a woman she has a great power for good or evil. So it is the custom that at the very first time—and only the first time—a young girl has the physical signs of change, she must go into the forest, build a ba-ca-ne-ge, a small lodge for herself, and fast. She will stay there for a period of ten days, or as long as she can. . . . The longer she fasts, the clearer her dreams will be of what she will do in life. If she is a Dreamer or a Medicine Person, her visions will confirm this. (95)

This illustrates the power that women traditionally held: They had the power to initiate rites, to honor their bodies, to celebrate their bodies, to fend for themselves, to be by themselves, to be the seekers and purveyors of higher knowledge, to determine their route in life, to be decision makers—but all in the name of their community's survival. This is the type of lifeway the Ojibwe honored and perpetuated for millennia. This is the vision that Broker, at the time she is writing the book, relays to the young Ojibwe who are desperately seeking solace and restoration.

Because traditional Native societies are generally not based upon women's oppressed states, Native women's lives do not follow the same trajectory that Western women's lives have followed. That said, it is also fair to claim that contemporary Western women, no matter their race, class, or sexual preference, do endure *some* of the same forms of oppression and exploitation through the patriarchal structures implicit in the fabric of Western nation-states. Nevertheless, as Paula Gunn Allen (Laguna Pueblo / Sioux) explores in a good portion of her pioneering text *The Sacred Hoop: Recovering the Feminine in American Indian Traditions,* patriarchal socialization among all Americans, Native and non-Native alike, allowed and still allows the justification of genocide, the resistance to clan-structured societies and noncorporatized societies, and, most imminently, the breakup of "gynecentric" systems that "distribute power evenly among men, women, and berdaches as well as among all age groups" (1992, 41). These gynocracies uphold subsistence and egalitarian economic and sociopolitical networks that necessarily honor the place of women. Within the West's colonial structure, however, Euro-American women are mainly the profiteers and Native women are mainly the defeated.[5] Acknowledging this difference in experience, the editors of *Feminist Theory Reader* recognize

> the exclusions created by the initial definitions of feminist theory's early core concepts. [Contemporary feminist theorists] point to the false universalism and essentialism of those concepts and examine *lived differences* among women, focusing on international structures of class, the social construction of race, ethnicity, nationality, and sexuality . . . [and point out] that one's *location* within the intersecting systems of oppression shapes knowledge and experience. (McCann and Kim 2003, 7; emphasis mine)

While this two-dimensionally addresses the need for (re)consideration of Native women's and other women of color's positionality in feminist ideology, the claims still lie flat in linear constructs of *individual* categorizations that occlude tradition, spiritualism, and the viability of stories' contributions to theory. In addressing the hegemonic dominance of white academic women and the class and racial hierarchies naturalized in the feminist movement, bell hooks says in her essay "Feminism" that "personal experiences are important to the feminist movement but they cannot take the place of theory" (2003, 56). She views experiential work as the only allowable (and subordinate) entrée by women of color into the domain directed by white intellectuals. I believe, however, that Broker negates this presumption. In critically analyzing Ojibwe womanhood in Broker's text, we observe that Oona's story is a progenitor of a theory—a unique, three-dimensional, and palimpsestic method that originates in the women's lived experience and spoken lessons.

If theories are to help us create models that will in turn help us understand confusing issues or ideas, how are Western feminisms appropriate paradigms for unpacking concepts outlined in my discussion of Broker's text, including the cycle of five generations, the concept of *spiral evolution,* ideas of reclamation, spirituality, homelands, racial oppression? Does feminist theory have the potential to heal (as Oona and Awasasi's stories do)? Do Western feminisms honor "listening" as a potential critical frame, or maintain an approach through an interrogative perspective rather than a prescriptive one (as Oona's teachings are entirely based upon a listener's initial question)? Phrasing the question another way, Devon Mihesuah (Choctaw) asks: how do we interpret the term *feminism* to mean that the use of female power is to aid her tribe or community (2003)? Lastly, can a Native women's theory help redefine the nature of theory itself, as many Native women scholars have begun to articulate? When I present it that way (a Native women's theory as a self-reflexive model for reading texts), does it make the center uncomfortable that the very face of theory might be disrupted? These are questions essential to the struggle for significant inclusivity and flexibility in the development of "theory."

Feminism can mean that self-love and putting community first are not necessarily mutually exclusive. A Native women's theory acknowledges the reclamation of that which sustained communities and its re-implementation in individuals' lives, all the while taking into consideration realms that aren't worldly in the Western sense and honoring a *roundness* in women—something that has always been there, and does not need to be constructed, invented, dictated, or performed. Norma Alarcón scrutinizes the utility of Western feminisms that popularize femaleness as "an autonomous, self-making, self-determining subject who first proceeds according to the *logic of identification* with regard to the subject of consciousness, a notion usually viewed as the purview of man, but now claimed for women" (1990, 357). While this comment runs the risk of essentialization, it still stands as a reminder that "alternative" structures of identity exist. Native people's distinct but balanced view of gender roles were and are fundamental to the maintenance of societies in which women first and foremost identify by clan, by familial associations, by community.

Much of contemporary feminist theory highlights the need and the space for women of color to enter into the dominant center's discourse on their own cultural, gendered, and sociopolitical terms. But this is not what Broker's text is telling us to do. What her text prompts, I believe, is to seek out our communal knowledge—like Oona, to remember what our female elders have taught us, to remember and retell how we have been shaped. *To listen.* Through Broker's and other Native women's words, we learn that creative expression creates the critical models, models that teach women how to heal, how to live in the right way, how to keep in balance. Native literature has within it "women's theory." It draws the maps that define who we are and what can heal us, not so much didactically but holistically, spiritually, and with reverence for what came before and what is to come ahead, as Janice Gould (Maidu) says: "Poetic cartography provides a way to imagine and claim those landscapes we know or remember in order to assert what we belong to, what is tied in at the deepest place to our psyches" (2003, 24–25). These maps are the theoretical frames; Native women's stories are the route home. By continually completing the circle of five generations, being a part of that *evolutionary spiral*—eternally forming a series of constantly changing planes, Broker's *Night Flying Woman* brings present the heartbeat that will course the blood of generations to come. As Inés Hernández-Ávila (Nez Perce) says, "To be a revolutionary is to be original, to know where we came from, to validate what is ours and help it flourish, the best of what is ours, of our beginnings, our principles, and to leave behind what no longer serves us" (1997, 246).

NOTES

1. In particular, I focus a Native *women's* theory in this essay because of the specific targeting of Native women for sexual violence as a colonial tool of genocide against Native people. As Andrea Smith analyzes, Native women were and are seen as "the bearers of a counter-imperial order and pose a supreme threat to the dominant culture. [Thus], symbolic and literal control over their bodies is important in the war against Native people" (2005, 15). Contrary to this conception, Native communities see Native women as the carriers of culture, the progenitors of the generations to come that ensure the survival of the nation. Many traditional stories accord respect to

Native women and women's ability to preserve that power within themselves. *Night Flying Woman* is no different.

2. Some might argue that such pressing contemporary issues as abuse and sexual violence against women *within* tribal communities seems antithetical to the idea of "reclamation over liberation." However, pioneering texts such as Kim Anderson's (Cree/Métis) *A Recognition of Being: Reconstructing Native Womanhood* (2000), Inés Hernández-Avila's (Nez Perce) edited *Reading Native American Women: Critical/Creative Representations* (2005), and Lee Maracle's (Stoh:lo) *I Am Woman: A Native Perspective on Sociology and Feminism* (1996) (not to mention the words of dozens of Native women creative writers) each demonstrate the devastating effects of the "dismantling" of gender balance and equity of traditional cultures through colonization as well as the importance history holds in the reinterpretation of Native women's identity. The "lateral violence" (Maracle's concept) Native women experience from Native men "results from the accumulation of hurt by our people over a long period of time" (ix), the sexism, racism, and genocidal policies endured over the centuries. "Re-feminizing our original being" as Maracle says, and to which each of the women above refer, is about understanding the power Native women are harnessing in order to alter the oppressive environment around them on behalf of their communities. This sense of "reclamation" is primarily based upon *healing*.

3. Broker was born in 1919 on the White Earth Reservation in northern Minnesota, attended boarding schools for all but twelfth grade, and began a career with the Minneapolis Public Schools in 1966—where she was very involved in developing Native curriculum and serving as a member of a number of Indian organizations. In 1969 she began working on her only novel, *Night Flying Woman: An Ojibway Narrative,* but it was not published until 1983 (by the Minnesota Historical Society Press). The text is the story that was told to her by her great-great-grandmother, Ni-bo-wi-se-gwe, also known as Oona, and the many significant changes that happened to her and the Ojibwe people with the coming of white settlers, the timbering industry, missionization and assimilation, and the deterioration of Ojibwe language and culture.

4. The Ojibwe lived traditionally according to the four seasons. For a thorough illustration of this lived philosophy, see Jim Northrup's *With Reservations* (1996), a documentary depicting how the landscape of the woodlands, the earth and its cycles, determine how one lives in the world, one's cultural ties, one's place in community, and one's relationship to Creator.

5. See Zinn and Dill 2003 for analysis of racial and cultural distinctions as they interlock with notions of gender.

WORKS CITED

Alarcón, Norma. 1990. "The Theoretical Subject(s) of This Bridge Called My Back and Anglo-American Feminism." In *Making Face, Making Soul. Haciendo Caras: Creative and Critical Perspective by Feminists of Color,* edited by Gloria Anzaldúa, 356–69. San Francisco: Aunt Lute Books.

Allen, Paula Gunn. 1992. *The Sacred Hoop: Recovering the Feminine in American Indian Traditions.* 1986; Boston: Beacon Press.

Anderson, Kim. 2000. *A Recognition of Being: Reconstructing Native Womanhood.* Toronto: Second Story Press.

Awiakta, Marilou. 2003. "Daydreaming Primal Space: Cherokee Aesthetics as Habits of Being." In *Speak to Me Words: Essays on Contemporary Indian Poetry,* edited by Dean Rader and Janice Gould, 56–57. Tucson: University of Arizona Press.

Blaeser, Kimberly. 1998. "Like Reeds through the Ribs of a Basket." In *Other Sisterhoods: Literary Theory and U.S. Women of Color,* edited by Sandra Kumamoto Stanley, 265–76. Urbana: University of Illinois Press.

Broker, Ignatia. 1983. *Night Flying Woman: An Ojibway Narrative.* St. Paul: Minnesota Historical Society Press.

Gould, Janice. 2003. "Poems as Maps in American Indian Women's Writing." In *Speak to Me Words: Essays on Contemporary American Indian Poetry,* edited by Dean Rader and Janice Gould, 21–33. Tucson: University of Arizona Press.

Hernández-Ávila, Inés. 1997. "An Open Letter to Chicanas: On the Power and Politics of Origins." In *Reinventing the Enemy's Language: Contemporary Native Women's Writings of North America,* edited by Joy Harjo and Gloria Bird, 237–46. New York: W. W. Norton.

———, ed. 2005. *Reading Native American Women: Critical/Creative Representations.* Lanham, Md.: AltaMira Press.

hooks, bell. 2003. "Feminism: A Movement to End Sexist Oppression." In *Feminist Theory Reader: Local and Global Perspectives,* edited by Carole R. McCann and Seung-Kyung Kim, 50–56. New York: Routledge.

Maracle, Lee. 1996. *I Am Woman: A Native Perspective on Sociology and Feminism.* Vancouver: Press Gang.

McCann, Carole R., and Seung-Kyung Kim, eds. 2003. *Feminist Theory Reader: Local and Global Perspectives.* New York: Routledge.

Mihesuah, Devon. 2003. *Indigenous American Women: Decolonization, Empowerment, Activism.* Lincoln: University of Nebraska Press.

Northrup, Jim. 1996. *With Reservations.* Documentary. Dir. Mike Rivard. Native Arts Circle.

Smith, Andrea. 1995. "Christian Conquest and the Sexual Colonization of Native Women." In *Violence against Women and Children: A Christian Theological Sourcebook,* edited by Carol J. Adams and Marie M. Fortune, 377–403. New York: Continuum.

———. 2005. *Conquest: Sexual Violence and American Indian Genocide.* Cambridge, Mass.: South End Press.

Wagner, Sally Roesch. 2001. *Sisters in Spirit: Haudenosaunee (Iroquois) Influence on Early American Feminists.* Summertown, Tenn.: Native Voices.

Zinn, Maxine Baca, and Bonnie Thornton Dill. 2003. "Theorizing Difference from Multiracial Feminism." In *Feminist Theory Reader: Local and Global Perspectives,* edited by Carole R. McCann and Seung-Kyung Kim, 353–62. New York: Routledge.

Critical Traces

A Sovereignty of Transmotion: Imagination and the "Real," Gerald Vizenor, and Native Literary Nationalism

NIIGONWEDOM JAMES SINCLAIR

Perhaps . . . it is best not to think that one understands [Vizenor] too easily. He is a contrarion, the crossblood trickster he celebrates in his fiction. His stories are comic acts of survivance, helping crossbloods imagine themselves and negotiate their world the same way their ancestors imaginatively found their way through their own world via story. His works contain truth, but truth that transcends mere fact.

—Jace Weaver, *Other Words: American Indian Literature, Law, and Culture*

Boozhoo. I begin with a story that I frequently teach from, called "Wenabojo and the Cranberries," taken from anthropologist Victor Barnouw's 1977 book *Wisconsin Chippewa Myths and Tales and Their Relation to Chippewa Life*. Collected in 1944 at the Lac du Flambeau reservation from an Anishinaabe storyteller Barnouw calls "Tom Badger" (a pseudonym), it goes like this:

As Wenabojo was traveling one day, he went along the edge of a lake and saw some highbush cranberries lying in the bottom of the shallow water. He tried to fish them out time and time again, but every time he tried, they just stayed on the bottom. Well, he finally gave up. But he tried to grab them with his mouth by sticking his head into the water. Then he dove down into the water. The little rocks in the bottom hurt his face. While he was holding his face, Wenabojo happened to look up and saw the berries hanging up there. But he was so angry that he just tore the berries off the tree and wouldn't eat any, and he walked away. (46)[1]

I use this *aadizookaan* ("sacred," "traditional," or "classical" story)—of which countless other versions (across centuries and communities) are available—for several purposes in my teaching. One instance is to discuss the history of anthropology and Anishinaabeg communities, the ethics of collecting and translating stories, and specifically Lac de Flambeau experiences with Barnouw. Combining these aims with the sparse contextual details Barnouw mentions, with historical particulars, and with scholarship, I encourage students to examine the way "Tom Badger" and Anishinaabeg literatures are constructed in the text.[2] Delving into the story itself, I propose scientific and philosophical lenses through which the story can be examined, and show how Anishinaabeg storytellers engage interdisciplinary interests.[3]

In literature courses I draw out theoretical possibilities in the story and often make comparisons to literary "high" theory.[4] Sometimes I compare this narrative to others like it, and bring in what other critics have to say about those versions.[5] In addition—following many trajectories of ethnocriticism—I examine what tenets of orality, morality, and ceremony can be ascertained from the story, and attempt to pinpoint aesthetics of "oral traditions" in Indigenous cultures (as well as address the effects that "writing" has on such traditions). Students, coming to the story with a wealth of reading and experience in literary criticism, mention many of these considerations before I do.

In my personal and professional work on Anishinaabeg literature and literary criticism I take up the task of uncovering what Cape Croker Ojibway storyteller Basil Johnston calls the three interconnected meanings of Anishinaabeg "traditional" stories: a "surface meaning" (derived from the basic words), a "fundamental meaning" (derived from contextual analysis), and a "philosophical meaning" (derived from identifying the beliefs inherent to the worldview, or epistemology, being expressed) (1998, 100). It is here, I assert, where some Anishinaabeg-specific theories embedded in *aadizookaanag* can be uncovered. There are other ways this exposure can be done, but I employ this important theory here to make a few points.

I start with the "surface meaning." As he regularly desires, Wenabojo wants to eat. Whether he is hungry or starving or a glutton we don't know for sure, but we know he eats to live, to continue, to assert presence. Of course, as things usually go, the journey Wenabojo takes to fulfill his "need" does not result in success but a failure (a "hurt face," in fact). Whether he knows it's going to end this way or not (Wenabojo does "give up" and yet tries again), he acts, discovering that his mistake is in his perception, reasoning, and trust of his own faculties. What he thinks are *real* berries are reflections, mirror images, simulations of actual ones. By the time he realizes his error it is too late, and he is already "so angry that he just tore the berries off the tree and wouldn't eat any."

What's most upsetting for Wenabojo is his inability to recognize the trickery embedded in the images on the water. While appearing to give a promise of sustenance, what they really hold are absences as unsatisfying, empty, and ultimately inedible "fakes." By disconnecting the reflections from their "real" counterparts, Wenabojo has discovered that there are unsettling disjunctions between perception and reality, and he should be careful (perhaps suspicious) of what he imagines he sees. While this is an educational moment and one full of possibilities, it is also a reminder that "reality" not only exists but comes with responsibilities and consequences (like carefully thinking, looking, and considering before acting—or else one may be the recipient of a "hurt face"). If he is going to avoid bruises, satisfy his needs, and assert presence, Wenabojo had better consider the intricate and important connections between acts of imagination and material realities.

An analysis of Johnston's "fundamental meaning" considers the many constituent parts that make up a story, its surrounding universe, and the web of relationships actualized by its telling. While this discussion could take up hundreds of pages, here I explore one fascinating possibility, invoking the work of the late Lac du Flambeau Anishinaabe scholar Gail Guthrie Valaskakis.

Valaskakis in *Indian Country: Essays on Contemporary Native Culture* discusses the specific contexts of her community's history, entry into the Treaty of 1854 with the United States government, creation of their reserve, and the cultural, economic, and social evolution of the Lac du Flambeau band of Lake Superior Chippewa.[6] As other tribes experienced in the late nineteenth century, federal Indian policy resulted in the sale of land allotments and resources at Lac du Flambeau, settlers flooding the area (specifically for logging), and wide introduction of educational, social, and religious influences and institutions (2005, 14–16). By the 1930s, after years of exploitation, massive deforestation (resulting in the end of the sawmill industry), and the onset of the Great Depression, settlers and Lac du Flambeau members needed new economic opportunities.

With beautiful lakes, plenty of opportunities to hunt and fish, and a culturally rich population, most Lac du Flambeau citizens turned to tourism. As a result, for decades tourists flocked to the region—exponentially increasing demands for land and rapidly changing (often for the worse) Lac du Flambeau life.[7] "By then," Valaskakis asserts, "almost half of our reserved lands were privately owned, mostly by non-Indians," and community life had been radically undermined and altered (2005, 16).[8] Specifically, she cites a 1937 survey of the lands at Lac du Flambeau, where "the most desirable and valuable portions of lands along the lake shores have practically all been alienated [from Indians] by white owners and much of the remaining land, owned by Indians, is swamp lands, cut over or burned over timberlands and for the most part is of little value" (McKinsey, as qtd. in Valaskakis 2005, 16). Of course, resistance and activism took place during and before these years, and Valaskakis cites her ancestors' political subversions, traditional practices, and ceremonial activities. Reflecting on this time, Valaskakis describes the past seventy years as a process of moving "from silence, through the rosary of resentments, to decisions on housing and working, to controlling and living our lives in Lac du Flambeau, all in the shadow of the government of Others, and always angry. We are still often angry, with imposed policy and decided practice, with non-Indians and other Indians and with one another" (18).

Placing this knowledge in the context of Barnouw's seventy-year-old Lac

du Flambeau informant (who undoubtedly witnessed the impact of colonialism on his community), telling this story to an anthropologist (a colonial
microcosm of cultural "tourism")[9] that speaks of empty and unsatisfying illusions on lakeshore water (which by then would signify "white owned" land)
and describing the infuriating disjunctions between perceptions and realities
(surely evidenced by the original hopes and devastating results of the Treaty
of 1854 for Lac du Flambeau members), one can see an activist narrative at
work. Wenabojo's "hurt face" certainly rings of the pain felt by failed prom-
ises and constant barrages on Lac du Flambeau sovereignty, while the anger
in realizing such trickery resounds of community discontentment regarding
legacies of landownership, impacts of industries, and colonial exploitation.
And Wenabojo's tearing of the berries "off the tree," refusal to eat them, and
ultimate departure certainly reminds of the resistance, activism, and moves
Lac du Flambeau members took in the interests of "controlling and living
our lives in Lac du Flambeau."

This brief view of context uncovers some of the "philosophical meaning"
in the story and parts of Anishinaabeg "worldviews" or "epistemologies."
These, naturally, are several. The first is that *aadizookaanag* have specific
spatial and historical relations, based in individual and collective Indigenous
subjectivities that are complex and political. The second is that both the
physical and psychological realms of the universe are made up of intercon-
nectivities and relationships. In terms of this story, ties are demonstrated
between history and storytelling, politics and expression, mind and body, and
imagination and reality. The third is that Anishinaabeg stories of Wenabojo
(also called Wenabozho, Naanaboozhoo, Nanabush) are considerable not
only as mythic vehicles and vessels for Anishinaabeg spirituality, philosophy,
and "traditional" teachings (as they are most often posited), but as historical,
subjective, and political Anishinaabeg-centered creative, critical, and activist
acts. And while scholars have tended to laud "tricksters" like Wenabojo as
representations of Native re-creation in narrative worlds (and figures used
to enforce, tease, and test the boundaries and possibilities of existence), they
are also methodologies Indigenous storytellers and audiences use to assert,
interrogate, and continue individual and collective existences as members of
nations—community spaces with diverse conceptual and corporeal relationships, rights, and responsibilities. While "trickster" stories are definitively

about imagination, possibility, and transgression, they are also—proven by the mere fact that they are told by human beings—tied as much to complex histories, politics, and experiences as anything else. It is put best by Anishinaabe critic and author Gerald Vizenor:

> Naanabozho, the compassionate woodland trickster, wanders in mythic time and transformational space between tribal experiences and dreams. The trickster is related to plants and animals and trees; he is a teacher and healer in various personalities who, as numerous stories reveal, explains the values of healing plants, wild rice, maple sugar, basswood, and birch bark to woodland tribal people. More than a magnanimous teacher and transformer, the trickster is capable of violence, deceptions, and cruelties: the realities of human imperfections. (1984, 3–4)

As in "Wenabojo and the Cranberries" these stories explain some of the diverse values embedded in Anishinaabeg conceptions, understandings, and experiences of treaty rights, land claims, and history too.

I turn now to the important critical and creative contributions of Vizenor—whose creative and critical work has much to say on these issues. While much (and deservedly so) has been written on Vizenor,[10] most critics are satisfied with emphasizing single aspects of his work and limit their criticisms along political lines and tastes (not to mention romanticization and demonization). While right to varying degrees, most critics unfortunately sell his writings short, using them for somewhat polemical assertions on the makeup of Native identities. Mindful of this danger (and Weaver's ominous advice in the epigraph to this chapter), I do not want to rehash tired and banal theories on Vizenor's work but suggest something few have: that Vizenor's imaginative ideas can be applied to current material struggles of Indigenous (and specifically Anishinaabeg) sovereignty and self-determination.

In particular this essay will argue that Vizenor's writing is deeply applicable to one of the most important processes happening in Anishinaabeg communities: the redefining, reestablishment, and reassertion of practices and processes necessary for Anishinaabeg notions of nationhood to be reactualized. Vizenor's work, I will posit, points to necessary evolutions in the application of Anishinaabeg structures necessary for modern-day continuance on Turtle Island, and critics interested in grassroots struggles, governance, and political activism may be well served in taking up his contributions. One strand is his vision of a sovereignty of "transmotion," a complex, powerful message based in Anishinaabeg consciousness and intellectualism. It is a hopeful, useful, and inspiring idea of how Anishinaabeg survivance is actualized and assured.

For years critics of all stripes and interests have declared Vizenor to be a writer focused primarily on struggles of the imagination, and have described his legacy in these terms. In the most wide-ranging and extensive study of his work, *Gerald Vizenor: Writing in the Oral Tradition*, fellow Anishinaabe academic Kimberly Blaeser notes that Vizenor's "primary goal, in fact, seems to center on preserving or creating a space of survival [for Natives] . . . more imaginative than physical" (1996, 39). He does this by "upsetting the status quo, . . . deconstructing the term 'Indian,' . . . re-defining the mixed-blood, and . . . liberating the contemporary Native peoples he identifies as postindian" (2005, 257). In other words, the articulation of Native identities is the primary method by which the imagination is "freed." One would be hard pressed to find a critic who doesn't rely on these primary tenets in making claims about Vizenor.

For the most part, these criticisms can be broken down into two veins of thought, with accompanying conclusions emerging continuously. The first posits that Vizenor is a virtual cultural relativist engaged in the process of undermining, subverting, and exploding almost all parts of Native identities. The second is that Vizenor is overly distanced from most real-life Native contexts, struggles, and discourses, and this makes his articulations of Native identities vague and dubious at best, and fraught with assimilationist rhetoric and Eurocentrism at worst.

In terms of the former, most critics have focused on Vizenor's subversion of problematic, static discourses on "Indianness" (what he calls "terminal creeds"), particularly as they are embedded in imperial, oppressive, and domineering colonial intellectual legacies (what he calls the "manifest manners" of dominance). Although Natives have complex and ever-changing lives, cultures, and histories, David Murray writes,

this most ambiguous and paradoxical group has been subject to an essentializing rhetoric, in which Indianness is constantly associated with
purity or simplicity, rather than the complexities and ambiguities of
change and history. . . . Vizenor's writing, with its emphasis on the
crossing of races, genres, conventions and boundaries of all kinds[,]
offers one of the most powerful and extended demystifications of this
rhetoric of Indianness, wherever it is found. (2000, 20)

These are activist moves, remarks the late critic Louis Owens:

All of Vizenor's work represents . . . a liberation, a brilliant attempt to
free us from romantic entrapments—especially victimage—and to liberate the imagination. The principal targets of his writing are the signs
"Indian" and "mixedblood," with their predetermined and well-worn
paths between signifier and signified. Vizenor's aim is to free the play
between these two elements, to liberate "Indianness" in all of its manifestations. (1998, 86)

For Elvira Pulitano, everyone is implicated in this "liberatory" effort, as
"at the heart of Vizenor's writing lies the intent to discard the institutional
and academic stereotypes 'invented' for Native Americans by Euroamerican
culture, to liberate his characters and readers and win for all the freedom of
realistic growth and continual becoming" (2001, 242). Hundreds of similar
claims exist.

According to these critics, Vizenor advocates that Indigenous peoples
cast off all imposed subjectivities and, with the help of poststructuralist
theories, adopt a fluid, mediated, "crossblood," cosmopolitan space existent
in the contact zone between cultures—similar to what Owens has named
the "frontier" (1998, 52). After centuries of colonial discourses, policies,
and practices on Native peoples (most embodied in the misnomer *Indian*),
the need always and continually to forge "new" identities in the interests
of resistance and survival is an idea commonly attributed to Vizenor. Most
claim that his vision of the "postindian," most articulated in his 1994 book
Manifest Manners: Postindian Warriors of Survivance, recognizes Native

Americans as "mirror selves yet also actual selves," and residents of modern, inter-subjective realities (Lee 2000a, 6). Lee, in fact, calls Vizenor's writing that of a "textual shape-shifter . . . a 'postindian' authoriality ingeniously at one with 'postindian' Native life and experience" (16).[11]

For the most part, these theories posit that Vizenor's focus on the liberative abilities of language will free Native individuals to constantly make and remake themselves using "trickster discourse," a theory that combines notions of Native "trickster stories" with postmodern moves toward fragmentation, the destabilization of signifiers, and wordplay. This is all to avoid cultural ossification and stasis in the interests of continual reproduction of individualistic and infinitely refractable identities. According to Karl Kroeber, "Vizenor turns for recourse to the trickster . . . [to] manifest the creative force within individuals that allows them to escape from crippling burdens of the traditions they depend on for their sense of personal and communal identity. Vizenor dramatizes natives' skill in individual visionariness to resist becoming victims *even of their own culture*" (2008, 29, original emphasis). Existing in a world where only Baudrillardian simulation is possible, Native identities must be multiply constructed and deconstructed in a continual linguistic performance of identity—remade in every dialogic negotiation, every utterance, every re-creation of the real. According to these critics, Vizenor offers chance, language games, and eternal transgression as some of the keys to the liberation of Native identities. Mirroring Kroeber's description, Deborah Madsen argues that Vizenor reminds that "the self is always multiple and subject to liberating transformation" (2008, 69). Even the notion of any unified Indigenous subjective position (especially those based on notions of tradition and history) is destabilized in favor of multiplicities based in cultural relativism, humanism, and hybridity. Many additionally argue that these are "tribal" values.

Even several theorists who have taken up Indigenous-centered and nationalist approaches to Indigenous literatures are occupied with the kinds of Indigenous identities Vizenor describes in his writing. This has led to the second most popular conclusion on Native identities in Vizenor's work: that they have little to no relation to Native political movements because of his rhetoric and style, close relationship to poststructuralist theories, and privileging of postmodern individualism. Osage critic Robert Warrior, for example, in an early essay entitled "Intellectual Sovereignty and the Struggle for an American Indian Future," accuses Vizenor (at that time) of not putting most Indigenous interests at the center of his work as he "replicates the conclusions and praxes of French theory." On his applicability to Indigenous struggles for "intellectual sovereignty," Warrior claims, "while he opens tremendous avenues at the level of creativity and critical reflections, at the level of program, Vizenor offers us little" (1992, 17).[12] Although pointing out that Vizenor is "a writer I personally admire" for wide-ranging contributions and "heterodoxy," Muskogee Creek nationalist writer Craig Womack writes that Vizenor's discourses distance him from most Native readers who could benefit from his work and are removed from tribal realities (particularly in his use of "trickster consciousness") (2008, 64). Womack also critiques the implications of his overly open theories and "grab-bag relationship with theory" (70–72).[13] Anishinaabe critic Joanne DiNova takes these claims a step further, asserting that Vizenor's notions of Native identity are naive, empty, and self-serving, using "some Native terminology and some mild (but not disturbing) allusions to Native issues within a distinctly Western and elite discourse," concluding that, in terms of Indigenous interests, his work is meaningless (2005, 75–84). Vizenor's writing and theories, to these critics, is not in the interests of tribal "sovereignty," distanced from Native contexts, and—in the opinion of DiNova—assimilationist.

All of this (none of which I am saying is wrong or without merit, but certainly shows more evidence of politics and tastes than of anything else) has resulted in some very limited notions of Vizenor's ideas. One such displacement occurs in Arnold Krupat's essay entitled "'Stories in the Blood': Ratio- and Natio- in Gerald Vizenor's *The Heirs of Columbus*," where Krupat runs into a familiar Vizenorian phrase—an assertion that Native peoples (in the case of the novel, Christopher Columbus and his genealogical "heirs") carry "their stories in the blood." Krupat laments that this "troubling locution" "occurs some 53 times in a novel of 189 pages": "I don't . . . believe that there is any gene for narrative orientation or preference, nor that stories can be inherited 'naturally,' remembered, listened to, heard 'in the blood'" (2000, 168). Krupat concludes (employing the work of Frederic Jameson and

Kwame Anthony Appiah) that Vizenor must be playing with racist discourse, in turn healing tribal cultures by "rattling the bars of nationalism" and insisting that national and tribal identities, as well as the nation-state concept, be abandoned (172–73). Everyone in the novel, Krupat concludes, would be better off if they thought themselves as hybrid, crossblood "mongrels" (170).

As Jace Weaver has rightly pointed out, although he refers to his characters most times as "postindians," and "crossbloods," Vizenor "nonetheless champions them as *Natives* rather than 'hybrids'" (2001, 22, original emphasis). If Krupat considered this nomenclature, he might see that a concept such as "stories in the blood" is not so troubling. If we think of the characters in *The Heirs of Columbus* as like their real-life counterparts—historical Indigenous subjects with spiritual, cultural, and political claims and members of still-existent Native communities—the fact that they have maintained their identities in the face of colonial invasion, genocide, and subjugation proves that they are living a narrative of Indigenous survivance. Their continual genealogical line of strong, tribally based, Native "heirs" from Christopher Columbus's bloodline—withstanding the legacy of the architect of the most genocidal narrative in Indigenous history—is a testament to the resiliency, political savvy, and innovative cultural abilities of Indigenous peoples. Vizenor writes that "the presence of natives on this continent is an obvious narrative on sovereignty" (2000, 182). The ongoing presence, lives, and blood that runs through the veins of the tribal heirs is a true story, facilitating the possibility of Indigenous continuance.[14]

Krupat's conclusion about *Heirs*—that we need to abandon national identities—stands in marked contrast to the end of the novel, where a "new tribal nation," which the heirs name "Point Assinika," is founded. Krupat, in this instance, seems to be conflating Indigenous "nationhood" with the historically European, progressivistic, and patriotic "nation-state," while Vizenor is doing something quite different.

Point Assinika is a tribal utopia that holds the power to heal the world.[15] It is a place where few insipid discursive structures, what Louis Althusser (1971) identifies as "ideological state apparatuses" (the police, courts, schools, government, media, and the church), exist—at least in the patriotic and historical nation-state sense. In addition, erased at Assinika are all of the institutions brought to North America by colonialists to affirm, entrench, and carry out their power over Indigenous peoples. It is a place where colonial discursive mechanisms, such as blood quantum, can be overcome. It is also a beautiful place of resilience, resistance, and power based on values such as chance, "postindian" creativity, and survivance (which, in other work, Vizenor cites as Native-centered narrative practices) that tie citizens to one another. And, perhaps most interestingly, it is also a place where sovereign and referential Indigenous identities (and arguably others) can be forged and continued through these linguistic and community practices. It is Indigenous survivance in action.

What's most interesting to me is how much Assinika recalls the kinds of tribal nations envisioned by certain Native literary nationalist critics. Although Assinika is an imaginary construct, compare it to the visions of Indigenous nationhood in Jace Weaver, Robert Warrior, and Craig Womack's collaboratively written 2006 book *American Indian Literary Nationalism*. In the text's afterword, written by Abenaki critic Lisa Brooks, her notions of Indigenous nationhood are of healing, of "a nationalism that is not based on the theoretical and physical models of the nation-state; a nationalism that is not based on notions of nativism or binary oppositions between insider and outsider, self and other; a nationalism that does not root itself in an idealization of any pre-Contact past, but rather relies on the multifaceted, lived experience of families who gather in particular places" (2006, 244). In these ways it resembles Assinika. As described by Womack, Indigenous nations are definitively cosmopolitan but have "strong roots" at their bases, define relations, responsibilities, and rights between family, relatives, and kin, and have citizens that tell stories grounded in specific histories, politics, and perspectives (Weaver, Warrior, and Womack 2006, 168–69). And while Indigenous stories take up resistance to colonialism, states Weaver, they are equally about sovereignty, "about the ability of Natives and their communities to be self-determining rather than being selves determined" (Weaver, Warrior, and Womack 2006, 41). Virtually echoing *Heirs*, Robert Warrior points out that Indigenous intellectual practices emerging from complex Indigenous national experiences and perspectives not only ensure the continuance of tribal subjectivities, but benefit others and the world as a whole (Weaver, Warrior, and Womack 2006,

198–99). And—as if describing Assinika itself—Cherokee literary nationalist critic Daniel Heath Justice notes that "Indigenous nationhood is more than simple political independence or the exercise of a distinctive cultural identity; it's also an understanding of a common social interdependence within the community, the tribal web of kinship rights and responsibilities that link the People, the land, and the cosmos together in an ongoing and dynamic system of mutually affecting relationships" (2006, 151).[16]

Although Krupat calls Assinika a "post-tribal utopian community" (2000, 173), one cannot ignore the intriguing vision of Indigenous nationhood offered in the text, and the interesting similarities between Vizenor's vision and what Indigenous literary nationalist critics are seeking.[17] Additionally, equally utopist endings also occur in Vizenor's novels *Bearheart: The Heirship Chronicles* and *The Trickster of Liberty: Tribal Heirs to a Wild Baronage* (although admittedly none use the notion of "nation" as vividly as does *Heirs*). And although Krupat identifies all of these texts as positing "post-tribal utopian communities," critics have argued that these texts posit Anishinaabeg-specific endings[18]—which inevitably has relations to Anishinaabeg nationhood.

At this point it's crucial to identify Vizenor's skepticism of nationalist movements. It was the monolithic and Western drive to build nations, he points out in *Fugitive Poses: Native American Indian Scenes of Absence and Presence*, that dominated and sought to erase Native perspectives from the landscape. Any forms of pride that unify a community, such as "colonialism, nationalism, and theocentrism," can be "variations on narratives of dominance" (2000, 181). Vizenor also holds great suspicion of "concurrent native literary nationalists [who] construct an apparent rarefied nostalgia for the sentiments and structures of tradition and the inventions of culture by a reductive reading of creative literature" (2008, 17).[19] I propose that this skepticism is healthy, important, and valid, but more on this in a moment.

While admittedly useful, most criticisms of Vizenor have obscured the fact that although he has written widely on Native identity, he has most often used Anishinaabeg-centered discourses in which to do so. From his description of what drives his writing in the introduction to *Escorts to White Earth, 1868–1968: 100 Year Reservation* (where "The fine spirit of the Ojibway song has been held in the heart") (1968, 2), to his recent poetic retelling of Anishinaabeg history in *Bear Island: The War at Sugar Point* (which calls the Leech Lake defeat of the Third Infantry "a continental shimmer / of native liberty") (2006, 82), Vizenor consistently employs Anishinaabeg cultural expressions, historical events, and political practices as his primary methodology. Most often, his main characters are Anishinaabeg, they come from Anishinaabeg communities, and they engage (or reference) some aspect of Anishinaabeg traditions. In particular, Vizenor most interests himself in how Anishinaabeg discourses resist, confirm, or coalesce with Western theories, colonial practices, and rhetorical imperialisms, but as I intend to show, he also explores them on their own terms.

Although Vizenor is definitely interested in individualistic identities, he does not abandon Native-specific community processes as a crucial defining feature of Native identities. Take, for example, his virtual call to action in the final sentences of *Fugitive Poses*. Vizenor opens up the term "We, the people" in the Constitution ("not a foremost pronoun of native presence on this continent" because of its historical enabling of domination and exclusion of Indigenous peoples):

> The promise of that plural pronoun is not passive, but an active obligation to be *the* people of this nation; the *we*, as natives of this continent, are the presence, transmotion, and stories of survivance.
>
> We, the natives of this continent, are the storiers of presence, and we actuate the observance of natural reason and transmotion in this constitutional democracy. (2000, 197, 199)

If Americans recognized that "the presence of natives on this continent is obvious, a natural right of motion, or transmotion, and continuous sovereignty; in other words, natives are neither exiles nor separatists from other nations or territories. The presence of natives on this continent is an obvious narrative on sovereignty—that is, natural reason and sovenance of motion, and survivance" (181–82), this turns "We, the people" into words of presence, words of inclusion, and an American nation where *all are native*. While tricky, Vizenor's use of the pronoun *we* is both specific and multiple.

For American identities (where individualism is a primary tenet) to have legitimacy, Native sovereignties (forged through their own "we" practices) must be recognized.

As he does in virtually all of his work, Vizenor employs what he posits as evidence of sovereign Indigenous principles today ("natural reason and sovenance of motion, and survivance"), bases them in historical evidence (namely that Indigenous presences are "obvious" and "natives are neither exiles nor separatists from other nations or territories"), and makes an argument that a "narrative on sovereignty" exists. Then he asserts that all can learn and benefit from this. And in typical Vizenorian fashion, he invents a neologism to convey how this "natural right of motion" and "continuous sovereignty" exists: *transmotion*.

While I also affirm that he may have some grounding in certain post-structuralist and other "nativist" discourses, I want to argue that in making this claim Vizenor is grounded in an Anishinaabeg intellectual tradition, and that transmotion is, in fact, a cultural, political, and historical Anishinaabeg method of continuance. This shows evidence of an Anishinaabeg-specific way of studying Vizenor's texts, and a tribally specific application that evades most studies of his work. Using a traditional and historical sense of motion, grounded in Anishinaabeg politics and intellectualism, Vizenor invents and didactically describes the struggles Anishinaabeg should take up to articulate concepts of nationhood and assert sovereignty. And although perhaps repulsed by certain attachments to "tradition" as a formative claim for identity, Vizenor himself writes, "Natives have been on the move since the creation of motion in stories; motion is the originary" (2000, 55).

To understand transmotion, one must engage survivance, for the two are interrelated. Most explored in *Manifest Manners*, "survivance" (a neologism that combines the words *survival* and *endurance*) is the state where Indigenous continuance is imaginatively and creatively conceived of, and then advocated, by Indigenous thinkers in real-life contexts and circumstances. For Vizenor, this is particularly salient in the work of Native writers such as Luther Standing Bear, who encounter, overturn, and rewrite the "manifest manners of domination"—those narratives and actions that subjugate, simulate, and ultimately seek to replace Indigenous presences in real and literary landscapes (1999, 3–5). In *Fugitive Poses,* Vizenor expands on the activist nature of the term: "Survivance, in the sense of native survivance, is more than survival, more than endurance or mere response; the stories of survivance are an active presence. . . . The native stories of survivance are successive and natural estates; survivance is an active repudiation of dominance, tragedy, and victimry" (2000, 15). In his recent introduction to *Survivance: Narratives of Native Presence,* Vizenor describes the idea as "a practice, not an ideology, dissimulation, or a theory" and mentions (without always critiquing) alternative spaces where it asserts difference in certain nationalist, global, and linguistic contexts (2008, 11, 18–22). And while not describing it as exclusively an Indigenous "practice," Vizenor does argue that "the nature of survivance is unmistakable in native stories, natural reason, remembrance, traditions, and customs and is clearly observable in narrative resistance and personal attributes, such as the native humanistic tease, vital irony, spirit, cast of mind, and moral courage" (1).[20]

For Vizenor, survivance begins in creative and active imaginations. While many critics (and often rightfully so) have turned primarily to poststructuralist theories to understand Vizenor's advocacy of the imagination, I'd like to join the few who suggest that to do so exclusively is overly limiting.[21] His determination to maintain "native" specificities here is equally worth considering. The strongest case for this allegiance is in A. LaVonne Brown Ruoff's important early essay "Woodland Word Warrior: An Introduction to the Works of Gerald Vizenor," which documents Vizenor's writings in the context of his "commitment to his own Ojibwe heritage" (1986, 23). Like many scholars, Ruoff explains that for Vizenor the imagination is the battleground Native peoples must take up if they seek to sustain themselves, their sovereignties, and their cultures against colonialism:

> It is in the imagination of tribal people, not in the documents of historians and anthropologists, that their culture is recorded and transmitted. Vizenor stresses that "traditional tribal people imagine their social patterns and places on the earth, whereas anthropologists and historians invent tribal cultures and end mythic time." For Vizenor, "to imagine the world is to be in the world; to invent the world with academic

predications is to separate human experience from the world, a secular transcendence and denial of chance and mortalities." (1986, 24)

As Griever de Hocus (whom Ruoff claims is Vizenor himself) pronounces in *Griever: An American Monkey King in China*, "Imagination is the real world, all the rest is bad television" (Vizenor 1987, 28). For "tribal people" (like Vizenor himself) to continue, they must imagine themselves into reality.

Creative and imaginative tribal knowledges, experiences, and sovereignties do not end when they encounter others.[22] Even postmodernity, what critics point to as Vizenor's "transculturalism," can be made tribal. As he writes in his preface to *Narrative Chance*, "The postmodern opened in tribal imagination; oral cultures have never been without a postmodern condition that enlivens stories and ceremonies, or without trickster signatures and discourse on narrative chance—a comic utterance to be heard and read" (1993a, x). Vizenor is right—certain postmodern theories such as polyvocality, "open-ended" texts, deconstruction, and subversion of monolithic didacticism are arguably a part of tribal knowledges. Notions such as hybridity, multiplicity, and wordplay could be posited too. Yet he cites the misdirection of most literary criticism: "Native American Indian literatures have been overburdened with critical interpretations based on structuralism and other social science theories that value incoherent foundational representations of tribal experiences. . . . Foundational theories have overburdened tribal imagination, memories, and the coherence of natural reason with simulations and cruelties of paracolonial historicism" (1999, 75). Postmodernity, Vizenor reminds us, "is the discourse of histories over metanarratives," an action that, when adopted by Native peoples, results in "the advance of survivance hermeneutics" (167).[23] Like English, Christianity, and computers, Native peoples can use postmodernity on their own terms. And, they can decide which parts are useable, and which parts are not.

Blaeser posits in *Gerald Vizenor: Writing in the Oral Tradition* that Vizenor's employment of the imagination is both tribal and political. Building on Ruoff, Blaeser reviews Vizenor's tribal, pan-tribal, and postmodern traditions, strategies, and tropes, all employed in the interest of Indigenous survivance. In particular, she shows that Vizenor models his writing after stories he heard as a young man and grassroots activist in Anishinaabeg communities, uses Midéwiwin song structures, "word cinemas" available in Anishinaabemowin, and cites events in Anishinaabeg history, all of which substantiates her theory that Vizenor achieves "a sense of cultural continuity in his writing" (1996, 11).

In the book's strongest chapter, "Intersections with the Oral Tradition," Blaeser explains that Vizenor "attempt[s] to invest the written form and his own creative works with the qualities and the power of the oral" (1996, 16). As she mentions, Vizenor draws on a long history of tribal beliefs about the necessity of combining thought and language to create the world. One of his central methods is celebrating "the power of words to affect their reality, to bring about change, to create" (17). Words are vessels of thought, formulated by the creative impulse of the imagination, and the way tribal existence is conceived, understood, and lived. According to the preface to *Wordarrows: Indians and Whites in the New Fur Trade*, "We are touched into tribal being with words, made whole in the world with words and oratorical gestures. Tribal families created the earth, birds and animals, shadows and smoke, time and dreams, with their words and sacred memories" (Vizenor 1978, vii). Joining with several other tribal writers such as N. Scott Momaday, Simon Ortiz, and Leslie Marmon Silko, Vizenor maintains that words predate humanity, and that "storytellers (and, by extension, writers) are merely vehicles or voices for the words that have always existed" (Blaeser 1996, 18). Embodying this vein of thought, Vizenor's character Almost Browne states,

> Listen, there are words almost everywhere. I realized that in a chance moment. Words are in the air, in our blood, words were always there. . . . Words are in the snow, trees, leaves, wind, birds, beaver, the sound of ice cracking, words are in the fish and mongrels, where they've been since we came to this place with the animals. My winter breath is a word, we are words, real words, and the mongrels are their own words. (1991b, 8)

For all human beings to reside in relationships with each other, the earth, the universe, and ascertain the meanings of all of this—in other words, *to live*—they must creatively engage in the act of perceiving and expressing the world, giving back gifts that existence has given them. The processes of this experience are the words that become narratives that explore a living, creative, and active universe. Vizenor takes part in a tribal principle (that thought and expression are intrinsically tied together), whereby creativity and narrative invoke real-life change (Blaeser 1996, 18).

This process carries with it great responsibility, however, for words can also bring forth death if the imagination is limited, as it does for the "terminal believers" who speak the "last lecture on the edge" in *The Trickster of Liberty*, or Belladonna Darwin-Winter Catcher in *Bearheart*. Language has the ability to create, to remake, and to change the world, but it also has the ability to constrain, to hurt, and to cause death if not understood appropriately (Blaeser 1996, 19–20). And, of course, linguistic acts are distinctly tied to human experiences, politics, and history.

This is why part of the powerful ability and responsibility of articulating the imagination is to maintain ties to referential realities, even if this unfolding is fraught with difficulties. If we turn back to "Wenabojo and the Cranberries" for a moment, we notice that Wenabojo's words are in his actions, directed from his "incorrect" perceptions of the images on the water. His failure to understand the expansiveness of his creativity, conceptions, and contemplations makes his "words" empty, frustrating, and ultimately self-defeating. In connecting his sign to illusory referents instead of life-giving ones, he goes hungry. His only way to assure his presence, *his survivance*, is to learn, move on, and try again. If sovereignty is the ability to fail, grow, and learn on one's own terms, Wenabojo's actions suggest just that independence.

Many Anishinaabeg authors have also spoken and written about the beginning of sovereignty in thought. As Basil Johnston recounts in *Ojibway Heritage*, the world began in a creative act of imagination when

Kitchie Manitou beheld a vision. In this dream he saw a vast sky filled with stars, sun, moon, and earth. He saw an earth filled with stars, sun, moon, and earth. He saw an earth made of mountains and valleys, islands and lakes, plains and forests. He saw trees and flowers, grasses and vegetables. He saw walking, flying, swimming, and crawling beings. He witnessed the birth, growth, and the end of things. At the same time he saw other things live on. Amidst change there was constancy. Kitchie

Manitou heard songs, wailings, stories. He touched wind and rain. He felt love and hate, fear and courage, joy and sadness. Kitchie Manitou meditated to understand his vision. In his wisdom Kitchie Manitou understood that his vision had to be fulfilled. Kitchie Manitou was to bring into being and existence what he had seen, heard, and felt. (1976, 12)

Important to note is the power of imaginative perception, the vision, which brings forth expression, action. After creating all things, Kitchie Manitou then created humankind, and "Though last in the order of dependence, and weakest in bodily powers, man had the greatest gift—the power to dream" (13). This gift of dreaming, as stated by the White Earth elder Odingun, gave human beings purpose (as they had "no minds of their own" previously), and "they learned how to heal the sick . . . how to teach the children and do everything" (qtd. in Vizenor 1984, 3). The imaginative power to dream is a part of an Anishinaabeg "life principle," the way *Manidoo-waabiwin*, "revealed spiritual knowledge," is attained from all of creation. This also uncovers how one maintains a meaningful relationship with the world and within the universe (Johnston 1976, 13, 15–16; Rheault 1999, 88–90). The imagination is multifaceted, existing in all parts of Anishinaabeg life: consciousness (in intuition), unconsciousness (in dreams), and spiritual existences (in visions) (Benton-Benai 1988, 78; Rheault 1999, 88–92; Johnston 1976, 119–33).

Each imaginative process holds meaning only if action is taken. Language is the best, clearest, and strongest form of bringing thought into motion (although not the only way). As an example, one could cite naming ceremonies, a time-honored tradition of most Anishinaabeg communities. A person who has been given the gift of naming is someone who can access the spiritual existence where knowledge is revealed, the space where Anishinaabeg relatives of the past and future reside, and where spirits visit humans when they are sleeping. Many elders believe, in fact, that this is a world that operates primarily in the Anishinaabemowin, invoking the belief that all Anishinaabeg are able to speak our traditional language on this plane of being. It is a crucial part, these elders argue, of how Anishinaabeg can travel to and understand that spiritual world. Name givers can see, hear, and comprehend Anishinaabeg existences on that plane of being and in turn reveal the stories embedded in names there. When named, an Anishinaabe makes a real-life connection between this existence and the spiritual realm. As Eddie Benton-Benai explains, spirits can then see the face of the individual and recognize him or her completely (1988, 9). A name giver assumes an important responsibility in this imaginative ability to harness the movement between these two worlds.

While Vizenor's modus operandi is the liberation of Native American identity, Indigenous values must be at the heart of such a revolution and Indigenous cultural and political sovereignty must continue. The attack on Indigenous identity has always been political to Vizenor, and therefore necessarily requires a subjective response. Blaeser writes, "If there is a single note intoned more loudly throughout Vizenor's work than any other, that note is survival" for Indigenous people. "Survival, in Vizenor's view, is keenly dependent on identity; identity is formed through language and literature; language and literature is driven by money and politics. . . . His primary goal, in fact, seems to center on preserving or creating a space of survival. Oddly, that space of survival may be more imaginative than physical" (1996, 38–39).

With all due respect to Blaeser, I maintain that Vizenor is embedded and interested in a physical, real-life activist space too. As she herself demonstrates, Vizenor's use of tribally based references to language, the same method that achieves "a sense of cultural continuity in his writing" (1996, 11), is evidence of this interest. Language is the manifestation of imagination, while the power of language is to reveal knowledge and "bring about change, to create" existence in reality. This process of perception and expression in fact interconnects humanity and all of creation. If we turn for a moment to Vizenor's engagement with an Anishinaabeg understanding of the role of imagination, however, more knowledge reveals itself.

As Vizenor writes in *The People Named the Chippewa*:

Traditional tribal people imagine their social patterns and places on the earth, whereas anthropologists and historians invent tribal cultures and end mythic time. The differences between tribal imagination and social scientific invention are determined in world views: imagination is a state of being, a measure of personal courage; the invention of cultures is a material achievement through objective methodologies. To imagine the

world is to be in the world; to invent the world with academic predications is to separate human experiences from the world, a secular transcendence and denial of chance and mortalities. (1984, 27)

For Vizenor, as I have stated often throughout this essay, there are such
things as tribal cultures, tribal histories, and tribal imaginations, and they have
been under attack for over five hundred years. The remedy is "to imagine the
world"—to maintain that courageous realm of creation where "anthropologists and historians" and their "objective methodologies" cannot overcome
all discourse—and to "be in the world"—partake in the active process of
bringing forth this vision.[24]

But it's crucial that this participation be done responsibly, ethically, and
communally. In "Wenabojo on the Cranberries," Wenabojo's mistake is his
own perceptions. Trends towards nationalism and nationhood should be
treated similarly, and not be immediately accepted but scrutinized, engaged,
and enacted after careful consideration. Anishinaabeg peoplehood, sovereignty, and nationhood, if they are to exist, must be carefully and responsibly
conceived, defined, and imagined by Anishinaabeg. To not do so would be to
accept the empty reflections on the water as truth, when they are intended to
be provocations and possibilities, what Vizenor often calls "narrative chance."

If one conceives of Vizenor's sense of the imagination as Anishinaabeg-
centered, apothegms such as "Native survivance is a sense of presence, but
the true self is visionary" and "Nature, shamanic visions, oneiric presence,
and the simulations of culture are true in the imagination, not discourse;
one is survivance, the other is commodity" take on decidedly Anishinaabeg
referents (2000, 20, 26). One starts to believe that Vizenor is advocating
the kinds of action where spiritual knowledges affect Anishinaabeg politics.
Personally, Vizenor has seen this movement in action, in the activist nature of
his *Anishinaabe-gokomis*, who defined her "reservation in words" and "created a homeland in the memories of native humor" in her stories (2000, 54).
So, if Vizenor is articulating a sovereign Anishinaabeg "homeland" in the
imagination, can it be brought into reality?

In the final thirty pages of *Fugitive Poses*, entitled "Native Transmotion,"
Vizenor weighs in on Indigenous sovereignty. What is remarkable is not that

he engages sovereignty but how he does so, weaving in traditional Anishinaabeg ideas of motion with contemporary struggles for nationhood. Vizenor opens with a discussion of the differences between Anishinaabeg and Euro-western senses of mapping. Citing a thirty-year-old court battle over wild rice paddies pitting members of the East Lake Reservation in Minnesota and the U.S. government, Vizenor shows that traditional concepts signifying Indigenous relationships to land and history, embedded in the oral tradition, are seen as nothing more than "hearsay" in court struggles. Treaties, he argues, are the only languages of value the courts recognize. Although treaties may be valuable, Native senses of sovereignty are more valuable than these paper contracts. As Charles Aubid, an eighty-six-year old member of the East Lake Reserve who testified at the trial, says, Native senses of sovereignty live in "four distinct creases of native reason": language (specifically Anishinaabemowin), courage and the seizure of an opportunity to speak honestly (what Vizenor calls "the mien of a chancer"), "stories of survivance," and "presence."

In a way similar to that by which Momaday imagines, and thus invokes, his grandmother and his people in this world and reality in "The Man Made of Words," Aubid tells a story that brings people into being from a tribal imagination. Both planes of reality, the imaginative and the physical, are connected through his story. Vizenor, by narrating a story about Charles Aubid, who tells his own narrative about other elders who were present at the original treaty signing between U.S. government officers and Anishinaabeg leaders, literally brings all of them and their histories into being. Through language, Vizenor, like Aubid (and in turn like me), has brought the national homeland of the Anishinaabeg into being in this world. This embodiment of the oral tradition, in fact, is the practical combination of perception and expression, thought and action, imagination and motion. It is this movement between imaginative and "real" worlds that brings sovereignty into being.

Transmotion is not about giving up tribal identities, knowledges, and beliefs when you leave the imaginative world, but bringing them into being. By *evoking* them, Anishinaabeg can *invoke* them to assert experiences, ideas, and knowledges as families, relatives, kin. These invocations can also become complex expressions of collectivity, interconnectivity, and nationhood. These creative and critical processes also fulfill the responsibilities Anishinaabeg undertook when receiving the gift of dreaming, to engage with each other and the universe respectfully and holistically. As Vizenor claims, other Native writers perform this task in their writing, defining a "transmotion of native consciousness" and a "literary giveaway" that defines other sovereignties too (2000, 55).

Although critics like to cite Vizenor's point that "native transmotion is survivance, a reciprocal use of nature, not a monotheistic, territorial sovereignty" (2000, 15), this does not mean that he envisions land claims, borders, and tribal citizenship as irrelevant. These are necessary aspects of transmotion and survivance too. As Vizenor claims, Aubid's testimony "mapped a visual representation" through his words. Mapping, one might recall, is a critical aspect of nationhood and a crucial way nations recognize each other's sovereignty. Mapping, Vizenor notes, is an Anishinaabeg tradition too. As he points out, "Maps are pictures, and some native pictures are stories, visual memories, the source of directions, and a virtual sense of presence" (2000, 170). Maps are narratives devised by the imagination, placed onto land, enforced by belief, maintained through struggle. Just as colonial agents in the West have created maps of lands using principles of individualism, capitalism, and colonialism, so too must Anishinaabeg create maps of lands using tribal values (note: "a reciprocal use of nature").

According to Vizenor, in fact, for Anishinaabeg these maps have already been created, and are available through pictographs kept in Midéwiwin scrolls. In one important scroll teaching, the Midéwiwin "path of life," Anishinaabeg people are instructed on how to live. It is one of the primary teachings of *bimaadiziwin*, or "living the sacred life." Citing Frances Densmore's version from her book *Chippewa Music*, Vizenor interprets the scroll:

> The tangent lines at the turn of each angle are representations of the seven temptations, a virtual cartography. Densmore pointed out that the sense of temptation in this connection "implies primarily a trial of strength and motive." The first and second tangent lines are resistance and the chance for life; the third, a spiritual initiation of the *midewiwin*; fourth, the temptation of middle age; fifth, the temptation and reflection

of old age; and sixth, a return to a spiritual presence, the temptations of
the visionary. The seventh and last temptation is the endurance of old
age, at a time when *maji manidoo*, or ·the evil spirit, comes to mind.
(2000, 172)

This is a map of life, a story that shows the life process of birth to death,
explaining how an Anishinaabe person upholds his or her responsibility as
member of Anishinaabeg society. It is a narrative about age, time, life, and
most importantly, motion. It goes from right to left, which on a map (depending on where one was standing) would often signify from east to west,
the same path the sun takes, which ends up at the same ending point where
the "path of souls," the place where passed-on and future kin reside, exists
(Johnston 1976, 103–8). It has several divergent points, places along the path,
where one could stop if one wanted to without straying too far to continue.

This map also holds a teaching about Anishinaabeg history and relationship with land. As Benton-Benai narrates, the Anishinaabeg received
a prophetic vision many years ago (around A.D. 900) to move from their
traditional home on the eastern shores, near what is now New Brunswick,
Canada, and the state of Maine in the United States. They had seven places to
pause on the way, where many peoples stopped and split off from the group,
residing in those areas. Many Anishinaabeg continued, however, looking for
the "food that grew on water"—a signal that they were to cease moving west.
This, the Anishinaabeg discovered, was wild rice, found near Madeline Island
in Minnesota. As Benton-Benai notes, this journey took over five hundred
years (1988, 94–113).

The migration path teaches Anishinaabeg that motion is the way geographical, social, and spiritual relationships have been forged, maintained,
grown, and fortified. And while the Anishinaabeg nation's borders, citizens,
and cultures have shifted and moved as others were met and warred with, and
knowledge was traded, the nation as a whole has continued. Some peoples of
the Anishinaabeg nation have even moved in other directions, splintering off
like the Pottawotomi or the Odawa, while some stayed behind to guard the
Eastern Doorway, such the Abenaki. All have always maintained that they are
members of a living and continuing Anishinaabeg nation.

As Vizenor states, "Motion is the originary." The idea that Anishinaabeg peoples have always been on the move, on their own imaginative and narrative terms, is a sovereign concept. It is a principle inherent in Anishinaabeg notions of lands, maps, histories. It is the way material existence is perceived and the way bodies travel, live, and die in this life. It is also the way change is provoked and tribal selves and communities are maintained, as well as how both are brought bring forth into reality. As Vizenor reminds us, Native transmotion is not only lines on a map, it is a tribally sovereign worldview, a way of life.

This way of life, of course, has been disrupted by colonial advancement and domination, signified in land struggles and court battles. In fact, many Anishinaabeg have continued their westward expansion as a result of colonial displacement—some by choice, some not. So how does thinking through a lens of transmotion help sovereignty debates today? Critics who claim that Vizenor is not interested in these discussions quote lines like "The native sense of motion and use of land in the northern woodlands does not embrace inheritance or tenure of territory" (2000, 178). Critics should not think, though, that Vizenor is saying claims to land are not important (why would he cite Aubid's important points about wild rice paddies, for example), but that they are not the only struggles sovereignty should take up. As he writes,

> Colonialism, nationalism, and theocentrism are variations on narratives of dominance; these political, economic, and causal powers are not obvious historical instances of natural reason, rights of motion, or entitlements of native sovereignty. At the same time, the establishment of constitutional democracies in the past two centuries has secured new and diverse narratives of governance: the diplomatic narratives of treaties, executive documents, and court decisions that acknowledge the rights and distinctive sovereignty of native communities. (2000, 181)

Crucially, Vizenor is not saying that tribal nations should give up claims to land, but that tribal peoples must think of land in *tribal ways, through tribal traditions, according to tribal beliefs and community-derived decision-making methods.* Tribal peoples must carefully think of land beyond reservations and speak to others about it, perhaps in the same way Leslie Marmon Silko imagines it—without colonial vestiges—in her important novel *Almanac of the Dead*. Tribal peoples must think of sovereignty as

> mythic, material, and visionary, not mere territoriality, in the sense of colonialism and nationalism. Native transmotion is an original natural union in the stories of emergence and migration that relate humans to an environment and to the spiritual and political significance of animals and other creations. (Vizenor 2000, 183)

Individual and community diversity, creativity, and uniqueness is what Anishinaabeg bring to the table of creation. As teachings and stories suggest, Anishinaabeg have a responsibility to think and speak, no different than engaging with the earth creatively and respectfully. Anishinaabeg should not, and must not, destroy either imagination or earth by introducing methods of destruction, erasure, and domination but keep them thriving through values that celebrate ethical communities, growth, and continuance. As one of hundreds of tribal examples, this requirement is demonstrated in the Anishinaabeg Seven Sacred Teachings.[25] This celebration is how Anishinaabeg foster meaningful relationships with the earth (while encouraging and supporting others in similar ways) that keep it, most of all, living. This is the way Anishinaabeg keep it Anishinaabeg.

Thinking of the Anishinaabeg nation in this way also imaginatively expands notions of peoplehood. One starts to include Anishinaabeg people in cities, for example. One starts to imagine economic methods where money, capitalism, and environmental degradation do not have to be the central tenets of economic self-sustainability. One can even imagine a space where legacies of colonialism, violence, alcoholism, racism, romanticism, and war can be overcome. Tribal "heirs" can tell stories of these imaginings, and even, perhaps, change the world. They might create a new nation, name it Point Assinika, invite children, and inject them with healing "stories in the blood" too.

Perhaps literary critics can draw on this idea next time they see another essay on Vizenor, or mainstream Americans when they tune in to *Dances with Wolves* or *Apocalypto*. Most importantly, though, Vizenor's transmotion is something Anishinaabeg can take to their next encounter at the negotiation table, session in the conference boardroom, or sight of berries on the water. By drawing on collective knowledges embedded in history, language, and land, Anishinaabeg can learn from mistakes, devise notions of nationhood, and assert presence. By looking up, grabbing a handful of cranberries and eating them, not only will the images change—but so will futures. Many Anishinaabeg, like myself, can draw from these life-giving possibilities. Miigwetch.

NOTES

Since the writing of this article, Gerald Vizenor's continued interest and commitments to Indigenous nationhood and sovereignty through writing and narrative can be seen in his work as the principal writer of the White Earth Nation Constitution ("Ogimaawiwin Enaakonigaadeg Gaa-waababiganikaag"), printed in full in *Anishinaabeg Today* (14:6), 6 May 2009, and available at www.whiteearth.com/.

1. Barnouw also claims that this "story of oral frustration" appears alternatively in works collected by E. R. Young and Paul Radin (1977, 46–47).
2. For example, Alan Velie (1993, 126) posits that Barnouw constructs Badger as "a Chippewa Hemingway," particularly in his representation of female Anishinaabeg speech.
3. Some of the most interesting discussions have been in considering how this story explores scientific concepts such as physics, botany, and refraction and philosophical notions such as cause and effect, logic, and reason. Inevitably these discussions have led to debates over Indigenous and non-Indigenous notions of natural and common law as well.
4. "High" literary approaches I have personally taken up in my teaching of this story is Plato's allegory of the cave, Baudrillard's simulacra and simulation, Lacan's "three orders," and certain notions in semiotics as pursued by Saussure, Jakobson, and others.
5. An example is Cherokee critic Sean Teuton's essay "The Callout: Writing American Indian Politics," where he employs a version found in Stith Thompson's 1929 anthology *Tales of the North American Indians* (citing Paul Radin as the collector). According to Teuton, the story "reminds us through [Naanabozho's] hasty and unself-aware behavior that we should reflect before diving in for our desires, for what we truly need

might be right in front of us" (2008, 115–16).

6. See specifically Valaskakis's chapter entitled "Living the Heritage of Lac du Flambeau: Traditionalism and Treaty Rights" (2005, 9–34).

7. According to Valaskakis, "By the late 1940s, there were one hundred resorts installed next to one thousand summer homes on the reservation, and summer came to mean tourists. Chippewa spearers were transformed into fishing guides, specialists of the storm warning, the brush pile, and the shore lunch. And women, the hearth of our culture pursued for their bodies or their souls, now sold beadwork and domestic service" (2005, 16–17).

8. Valaskakis compares the devastating and fracturing legacies of boarding schools, alcohol, churches, diseases, and capitalism on her community to "confronting a mythical, flesh-eating Windigo" (2005, 14–15).

9. A close reading of Barnouw's work certainly indicates exploitative, objectifying, and consumptive interests. Vizenor has done an excellent close analysis, examining the anthropologist's recording of, and commentary on, Chippewa "trickster stories," concluding that "Barnouw delivered his interpretations in isolation, as an anthropologist; he rendered a tribal language game into power theories, linear social structures, and carried on an autistic monologue with science" (1993b, 198).

10. Entire book-length studies and interviews are published on Vizenor's wide-ranging contributions, while hundreds of discussions are conducted in anthologies, at conferences, and in university classes. Even this book adds a few more. All of this attention, though, is unquestionably well deserved. Vizenor's award-winning skill is complex, diverse, and multidimensional while his talent is immense. His interests are expansive, and his writerly résumé is "one of Native America's most prolific and protean" (Weaver 2001, 54). His theoretical work has been included in such notable anthologies as *The Norton Anthology of Theory and Criticism*, and he has authored, edited, or collaborated on over thirty-five books, novels, collections of poetry, anthologies of literary criticism, and one screenplay. Kimberly Blaeser, in her entry on his work in *The Cambridge Companion to Native American Literature*, rightfully calls Vizenor "one of the most prolific and one of the most versatile of contemporary Native writers" (2005, 257).

11. Lee argues that through his interweaving of postmodern theory, "simulations" of Native America, and experiences of Native histories and issues, Vizenor's writing reflects "chameleonism," "a crossblood signature in textuality to match that in life" and a

"call to remedy and, at the same time, the very embodiment of remedy" in approaches to Native identities in literatures (2000b, 265, 266, 274).

12. In defense of Warrior, he did not include this passage in the final, edited chapter of *Tribal Secrets* (1995), perhaps signifying a change of heart.

13. Womack's criticisms should also be considered in the context of this section in his essay "A Single Decade: Book-Length Native Literary Criticism between 1986 and 1997," which directs equal attention to Kimberly Blaeser's analysis of Vizenor's writings and to Vizenor's work itself. Womack also admits that "Vizenor's oeuvre is so varied that a generalized critique is almost always reductive" (2008, 72).

14. This is not to mention the endurance of the "heirs" through community principles based in kinship and in ceremonial and political histories, but that is an argument for another essay.

15. Declared sovereign on October 12, 1992, and situated "in the Strait of Georgia between Semiahmoo, Washington, and Vancouver Island, Canada," Assinika becomes the place where "the wild estate of tribal memories and the genes of survivance in the New World" are celebrated and fostered (Vizenor 1991a, 119). Using profits from three "tribal" business ventures destroyed in a thunderstorm—the Santa Maria Casino, the Niña (a restaurant), and the Pinta (a tax-free market)—at their old, destroyed "moored reservation," the heirs announce that Assinika will be a "a free state with no prisons, no passports, no public schools, no missionaries, no television, and no public taxation," while "genetic therapies, natural medicine, bingo cards, and entertainment [will be] free to those who came to be healed and those who lived on the point" (11, 124). Its trickster spokesman, Stone Columbus, pronounces that because Indians are "forever divided by the racist arithmetic measures of tribal blood" he "would accept anyone who wanted to be tribal, 'no blood attached or scratched,'" as citizens, preferring instead to "make the world tribal" (162). As "the first nation in the histories of the modern world dedicated to protean humor and the genes that would heal," Assinika invites all wounded, lonesome, and abused children to come and be liberated through shared stories and injections of "genetic signatures of survivance" (119). These signatures are taken from the genes of the heirs who "carried an unbroken radiance, a genetic chain from the first hand talkers of creation" (132–33). Thousands of children come and are healed, "with no conditions" (146). In response, threatened governments, lawyers, and tribal politicians denounce Point Assinika, fabricate claims regarding its illegitimacy, and attempt to annihilate it by releasing a thawed *wiindigo*.

Defending their community, the heirs cleverly outwit the cannibal beast by showing it the beautiful possibilities of humanity (embodied in the chance of a moccasin game, the liberative creativity in laser show stories, and the visionary narrative of Black Elk's war herb) and as a result the nation, its citizens, and the heirs of Columbus persist.

16. Justice (2006, 25) envisions Indigenous nationhood as "the political extension" of "peoplehood," a concept first put forth by Cherokee anthropologist Robert K. Thomas.

17. I don't perform this reading to focus specifically on Krupat, a fairly careful and considerate reader, but to show evidence of how politically motivated are his conclusions about Vizenor's work (as are those of several critics—including my own). It's also not to show that Krupat's ideas are the same throughout his career. In fact, in Krupat's *Red Matters: Native American Studies*, he alters his opinion, arguing that "the identity Vizenor has elaborately been defining and redefining has at base the deep and unmistakable roots of 'tribal' values—which can and indeed must be taken along wherever one may go—to the cities, to Europe, to China, anywhere. . . . In these regards, Vizenor may well have provided *Indian* versions of cosmopolitan patriotism" (2002, 112). This statement is slightly displaced by Krupat's refusal to align Vizenor with "nationalist" Indigenous writers interested in maintaining Indigenous communities through political movements such as nationhood and sovereignty. In a footnote he writes, "Vizenor on occasion constructs an argument for sovereignty that I have found to be 'cultural nationalist' [but this] should not be taken to contradict his basically cosmopolitan or cosmopolitan patriot position" (141 n. 28).

18. For further critical studies on Anishinaabeg-specific conclusions of *Heirs, Bearheart*, and *The Trickster of Liberty*, see Ruoff 1986; Blaeser 1996; Barry 2002; and Burgess 2006.

19. Interestingly, Vizenor does not name whichever "concurrent native literary nationalist" he is describing (2008, 17).

20. Vizenor (2008, 14–16) also critiques certain Native writers, such as David Treuer, for their lack of imaginative methods of survivance.

21. In an excellent essay entitled "Trickster Discourse and Postmodern Strategies," the late Elaine Jahner explores how Vizenor employs postmodern theories on political engagement, deconstruction, the destabilization of the object/subject binary, and representation, all of which enriches understandings of Vizenor's work as well as his use of tribal traditions such as dreams, storytelling, and trickster stories. In addition to

showing these powerful possibilities, Jahner also importantly identifies the shortcomings of such an approach, showing that "the postmodern condition . . . is still being choreographed with intent to exclude tribal dances. Postmodern theorists need some time to mediate on an intertribal pow-wow" (2000, 56).

22. This also problematizes a popular notion: that Vizenor's use of tricksters fragments any sense of unified tribal subjectivities. While unable to expound the problem thoroughly here, I propose that, to Vizenor, Indigenous subjectivities can be both multiplicitous and unifying—much in the same way that Anishinaabeg are U.S./Canadian citizens, citizens of one or more tribal nations, and members of the human race. While they are all of these things, none of their Anishinaabeg centrality is lost. For examples, I draw upon Vizenor's trickster characters, who travel the world but constantly emerge from Naanaboozhoo myths or come from, return to, or stay close to Anishinaabeg peoples or communities. One important instance in which one of Vizenor's major trickster characters, Griever de Hocus (in *Griever: An American Monkey King in China*, 1987) leaves Anishinaabeg communities behind, he importantly draws on knowledge from his White Earth Anishinaabeg home throughout. Vizenor's tricksters seem to be very interested in maintaining their Anishinaabeg specificity, so much so that scholars frequently draw on Anishinaabeg writers and thinkers such as Basil Johnston, Eddie Benton-Benai, and Patronella Johnston to illuminate Vizenor's works. Several notable scholars, in fact, have pointed out that Vizenor's tricksters differ from their tribal conceptions, including Cree scholar Neal McLeod, who notes that in his tradition there are more kinship ties embedded in *wîsahkêcâhk* stories (2007, 97) and Sto:lo Salish writer Lee Maracle (as qtd. in DiNova, 2005, 82), who suggests that Raven is more invested in holistic change. In an intriguing essay Daniel Morley Johnson (n.d.) explores game playing as a sacred practice where balance and contradiction is sought, meaning that as much as transgression is celebrated, so are boundaries and morality. For Vizenor, even Naanaboozhoo lives within the frames of tribal histories and politics.

23. I also maintain that part of this "survivance hermeneutic" is a model of cultural continuance (and perhaps even a nationalist one) that Vizenor employs in the act of utilizing postmodern theory as well. By privileging postmodern theories in relation to tribal knowledges and traditions, Vizenor engages in a process of survivance by recognizing tribal, current, and community-forged discourses as crucial in any process of knowledge creation. This is a cultural method also articulated by Simon Ortiz in which knowledges, objects, and practices can become authentically "Indian

because of the creative development that the native people applied to them. Present-day Native American or Indian literature is evidence of this in the very same way. And because in every case where European culture was cast upon Indian people of this nation there was similar creative response and development, it can be observed that this was the primary element of a nationalistic impulse to make use of foreign ritual, ideas, and material in their own—Indian—terms. Today's writing by Indian authors is a continuation of that elemental impulse" (Ortiz 1981, 8).

24. A constant influence on Vizenor has been N. Scott Momaday's famous "Man Made of Words," the keynote address to the First Convocation of American Indian Scholars in 1970, which Vizenor cites regularly throughout his critical and creative work. As Momaday states, and we can certainly see evident in Vizenor, Native peoples have an imaginative agency and power to define themselves and their realities: "We are what we imagine. Our very existence consists in our imagination of ourselves. Our best destiny is to imagine, at least, completely, who and what, and *that* we are. The greatest tragedy that can befall us is to go unimagined" (1975, 103).

25. The Seven Sacred Anishinaabeg Teachings are wisdom, love, respect, bravery, honesty, humility, and truth. These teachings are cited in several sources, but I am using *The Mishomis Book: The Voice of the Ojibway* (Benton-Benai 1988, 64) in this instance.

WORKS CITED

Althusser, Louis. 1971. "Ideology and Ideological State Apparatuses (Notes towards an Investigation)." In *Lenin and Philosophy and Other Essays*, translated by Ben Brewster, 121–76. London: New Left Books.

Barnouw, Victor. 1977. *Wisconsin Chippewa Myths and Tales and Their Relation to Chippewa Life*. Madison: University of Wisconsin Press.

Barry. Nora Baker. 2002. "Postmodern Bears in the Texts of Gerald Vizenor." *MELUS* 27.3: 93–112.

Benton-Benai, Edward. 1988. *The Mishomis Book: The Voice of the Ojibway*. Hayward, Wis.: Indian Country Communications.

Blaeser, Kimberly. 1996. *Gerald Vizenor: Writing in the Oral Tradition*. Norman: University of Oklahoma Press.

———. 2005. "Gerald Vizenor: Postindian Liberation." In *The Cambridge Companion to*

Native American Literature, edited by Joy Porter and Kenneth M. Roemer, 257–70. Cambridge: Cambridge University Press.

Brooks, Lisa. 2006. "Afterword: At the Gathering Place." In Jace Weaver, Robert Warrior, and Craig S. Womack, *American Indian Literary Nationalism*, 225–52. Albuquerque: University of New Mexico Press.

Burgess, Benjamin. 2006. "Elaboration Therapy in the Midewiwin and Gerald Vizenor's *The Heirs of Columbus*." *Studies of American Indian Literatures* 18.1: 22–36.

DiNova, Joanne R. 2005. *Spiraling Webs of Relation: Movements toward an Indigenist Criticism.* New York: Routledge.

Jahner, Elaine A. 2000. "Trickster Discourse and Postmodern Strategies." In *Loosening the Seams: Interpretations of Gerald Vizenor*, edited by A. Robert Lee, 38–58. Bowling Green, Ohio: Bowling Green State University Popular Press.

Daniel Morley Johnson. N.d. "(Re)Nationalizing Naanabush: Anishinaabe Sacred Stories, Nationalist Criticism and Scholarly Responsibilities." In *Troubling Tricksters: Revisiting Critical Conversations*, edited by Deanna Reder and Linda Morra. Wilfrid Laurier University Press, forthcoming.

Johnston, Basil. 1976. *Ojibway Heritage.* Toronto: McClelland and Stewart.

———. 1998. "Is That All There Is? Tribal Literature." In *An Anthology of Canadian Native Literature in English*, 2nd ed., edited by Daniel David Moses and Terry Goldie, 105–12. Toronto: Oxford University Press.

Justice, Daniel. 2006. *Our Fire Survives the Storm: A Cherokee Literary History.* Minneapolis: University of Minnesota Press.

Kroeber, Karl. 2008. "Why It's a Good Thing Gerald Vizenor Is Not an Indian." In *Survivance: Narratives of Native Presence*, edited by Gerald Vizenor, 25–38. Lincoln: University of Nebraska Press.

Krupat, Arnold. 2000. "'Stories in the Blood': Ratio- and Natio- in Gerald Vizenor's The Heirs of Columbus." In *Loosening the Seams: Interpretations of Gerald Vizenor*, edited by A. Robert Lee, 166–77. Bowling Green, Ohio: Bowling Green State University Popular Press.

———. 2002. *Red Matters: Native American Studies.* Philadelphia: University of Pennsylvania Press.

Lee, A. Robert, ed. 2000. *Loosening the Seams: Interpretations of Gerald Vizenor.* Bowling Green, Ohio: Bowling Green State University Popular Press.

———. 2000. "The Only Good Indian Is a Postindian? Controversialist Vizenor and Manifest Manners." In *Loosening the Seams: Interpretations of Gerald Vizenor*, edited by A. Robert Lee, 263–78. Bowling Green, Ohio: Bowling Green State University Popular Press.

Madsen, Deborah. 2008. "On Subjectivity and Survivance: Rereading Trauma through *The Heirs of Columbus* and *The Crown of Columbus*." In *Survivance: Narratives of Native Presence*, edited by Gerald Vizenor, 61–88. Lincoln: University of Nebraska Press.

McLeod, Neal. 2007. *Cree Narrative Memory: From Treaties to Contemporary Times*. Saskatoon, Saskatchewan: Purich.

Momaday, N. Scott. 1975. "The Man Made of Words." In *Literature of the American Indians: Views and Interpretations*, edited by Abraham Chapman, 96–110. New York: Meridian.

Murray, David. 2000. "Crossblood Strategies in the Writings of Gerald Vizenor." In *Loosening the Seams: Interpretations of Gerald Vizenor*, edited by A. Robert Lee, 20–37. Bowling Green, Ohio: Bowling Green State University Popular Press.

Ortiz, Simon J. 1981. "Towards a National Indian Literature: Cultural Authenticity in Nationalism." *MELUS* 8.2: 7–12.

Owens, Louis. 1998. *Mixedblood Messages: Literature, Film, Family, Place*. Norman: University of Oklahoma Press.

Pulitano, Elvira. 2001. "Travelling the Hyperreality of Indian Simulations: Gerald Vizenor's Darkness in Saint Louis Bearheart." *Paradoxa* 15:241–62.

Rheault, D'Arcy Ishpeming'Enzaabid. 1999. *Anishnaabe Mino-Bimaadiziwin: The Way of a Good Life*. Peterborough, Ontario: Debwewin Press.

Ruoff, A. LaVonne Brown. 1986. "Woodland Word Warrior: An Introduction to the Works of Gerald Vizenor." *MELUS* 13.2: 13–43.

Teuton, Sean. 2008. "The Callout: Writing American Indian Politics." In *Reasoning Together: The Native Critics Collective*, edited by Craig S. Womack et al., 105–25. Norman: University of Oklahoma Press.

Valaskakis, Gail Guthrie. 2005. *Indian Country: Essays on Contemporary Native Culture*. Waterloo, Ont.: Wilfrid Laurier University Press.

Velie, Alan. 1993. "The Trickster Novel." In *Narrative Chance: Postmodern Discourse on Native American Indian Literatures*, edited by Gerald Vizenor, 121–40. Norman: University of Oklahoma Press.

Vizenor, Gerald, ed. 1968. *Escorts to White Earth, 1868–1968: 100 Year Reservation*. Minneapolis: The Four Winds.

———. 1978. *Wordarrows: Indians and Whites in the New Fur Trade*. Minneapolis: University of Minnesota Press.

———. 1984. *The People Named the Chippewa: Narrative Histories.* Minneapolis: University of Minnesota Press.

———. 1987. *Griever: An American Monkey King in China.* Minneapolis: University of Minnesota Press.

———. 1988. *The Trickster of Liberty: Tribal Heirs to a Wild Baronage.* Minneapolis: University of Minnesota Press.

———. 1991a. *The Heirs of Columbus.* Hanover, N.H.: Wesleyan University Press.

———. 1991b. *Landfill Meditation: Crossblood Stories.* Hanover, N.H.: Wesleyan University Press.

———, ed. 1993a. *Narrative Chance: Postmodern Discourse on Native American Indian Literatures.* 1989; Norman: University of Oklahoma Press.

———. 1993b. "Trickster Discourse: Comic Holotropes and Language Games." In *Narrative Chance: Postmodern Discourse on Native American Indian Literatures,* edited by Gerald Vizenor, 187–212. Norman: University of Oklahoma Press.

———. 1999. *Manifest Manners: Narratives on Postindian Survivance.* 1994; Lincoln, Nebr.: Bison Books.

———. 2000. *Fugitive Poses: Native American Indian Scenes of Absence and Presence.* 1998; Lincoln, Nebr.: Bison Books.

———. 2006. *Bear Island: The War at Sugar Point.* Minneapolis: University of Minnesota Press.

———, ed. 2008. *Survivance: Narratives of Native Presence.* Lincoln: University of Nebraska Press.

Warrior, Robert. 1992. "Intellectual Sovereignty and the Struggle for an American Indian Future." *Wicazo Sa Review* 8.1: 1–20.

———. 1995. *Tribal Secrets: Recovering American Indian Intellectual Traditions.* Minneapolis: University of Minnesota Press.

Weaver, Jace. 2001. *Other Words: American Indian Literature, Law, and Culture.* Norman: University of Oklahoma Press.

Weaver, Jace, Robert Warrior, and Craig S. Womack. 2006. *American Indian Literary Nationalism.* Albuquerque: University of New Mexico Press.

Womack, Craig. 2008. "A Single Decade: Book-Length Native Literary Criticism between 1986 and 1997." In *Reasoning Together: The Native Critics Collective,* edited by Craig S. Womack et al., 3–104. Norman: University of Oklahoma Press.

Writing the Intertwined Global Histories of Indigeneity and Diasporization: An Ecocritical Articulation of Place, Relationality, and Storytelling in the Poetry of Simon J. Ortiz

SUSAN BERRY BRILL DE RAMÍREZ

ontemporary scholars of Native American literatures are pushing theoretical debate to consider the appropriateness of Western critical theory and criticism in accessing and opening up Native American and global Indigenous literatures. The crucial issues of tribalism and sovereignty bespeak these scholars' concerns regarding the extent to which nonIndigenous critical methodologies represent colonialist discourse and ideology. By using indigeneity and tribal sovereignty as pivots in their responses to Native American literatures, scholars emphasize the particular historicity of the Americas, which demands a fitting critical lens. Scholars of Native literatures grapple with the limits of Western literary criticism's apparent inability to reach the depths and truths that Indigenous literary voices speak. In the 1990s, a number of scholars of Native literatures produced monographs that directly engaged the tribal voices in the literatures. Kimberly Blaeser's pioneering study of fellow Anishinaabe writer Gerald Vizenor elucidates oral storytelling aspects of his work that were informed by his tribal, regional, and urban background and experience. My 1999

■ 159

volume, *Contemporary American Indian Literatures and the Oral Tradition,* turns to traditionally conversive and co-creative tribal oral storytelling and story-listening practices as models for the analogously conversive process of listening-reading—as a means of accessing the wealth of stories behind and within the written literary texts. Vizenor's own *Fugitive Poses: Native American Indian Scenes of Absence and Presence* asserts a powerful Indigenous lens towards the Americas, arguing that such history and literature cannot be understood outside of the centrality of Native American Indian presence. Robert Warrior's comprehensive *Tribal Secrets: Recovering American Indian Intellectual Traditions* articulates the larger context of the tribal and Indigenous intellectual traditions that surrounded the development of contemporary Native American literatures, and Craig Womack's trenchant *Red on Red: Native American Literary Separatism* directly critiques an outsider non-Native American literary criticism as distanced from, and often irrelevant to, the realities that inform American Indian writing and storytelling. Using his own literary and storytelling voice, Womack demonstrates the distinct insights that come from a tribally relational approach. More recently, meetings around the turn of the century in California and Mexico addressed the larger interdisciplinary fields of Native studies in terms of hemispheric perspectives and concerns (Hernandez-Avila and Varese 1999). Building on the earlier work in Native literatures and moving beyond the more limited scope of tribalism (without abandoning specific commitments to tribal sovereignty), scholars of Native literatures (many of whom are Indigenous) are working to describe and articulate distinctively Indigenous criticisms and theories by incorporating a broad view of a twenty-first-century indigeneity that recognizes common global Indigenous realities.[1]

While affirming the geocentric boundaries of indigeneity, this essay suggests ways by which Native American literatures shed light on contemporary theories of diaspora, which, in turn, can open up new directions for critical interpretations and understandings of Indigenous literary works. To this end, a number of questions present themselves as elucidating the underlying conditions that come together in experiences of diasporized indigeneity and indigenized diaspora:

- What does it mean to live in a condition of alienation even though one's bodily presence is within or near one's ancestral homelands (e.g., the condition and sense of a diasporized indigeneity)?

- What are the elements that coalesce to facilitate a lived and perceived sense of belonging and "home" even when one is geographically distanced from one's ancestral homelands (e.g., the condition and sense of an indigenized diaspora)?

- What are the processes that enable a person to ascribe meaning to a place?

- How is it that a place becomes deeply meaningful to a person, even without a tribally ancestral affiliative relationship; and how might such interconnective geographies of place, not only not diminish, but actually strengthen tribal and other geopolitical assertions of sovereignty?

- What is it that we might learn from the relationally co-creative and intersubjective processes of conversive communications (combining senses of both the conversative and the conversional) that, evidenced in oral storytelling, enable persons to become part of diverse worlds through the media of language and story—thereby coming to empathic understandings of place and ancestry?

- How is the oral storytelling event (and its written literary forms) relevant to our understandings of the mechanisms by which persons' perceptions and lives engage and encompass (or not) diverse worlds, cultures, times, and places?

- And finally, what light can be shed by looking at the temporal point of Spain's 1492 as a critical axis around which pivot the intertwined and knotted histories of diasporization, colonization, and Manifest Destiny?

In bringing these questions together, Simon J. Ortiz's poetry and vision serve as lenses by which each of these questions can be posed and considered, for we cannot begin to approach attempts, in the aftermath of 1492, to erase knowledge, beliefs, practices, traditions, language, and stories without seeking recourse to the expressed articulations of that story from the vantage point of those peoples at the receiving end of that attempted erasure. Roger

Dunsmore points out that Ortiz understands "the pain of five centuries of colonialism. He knows the loss because he has lived it—he also knows the life, the renewal, the fertile power in everything, including us. And he just tells it, sings it, moves it in language" (2004, 27). This is what is key in Ortiz's writing: he understands the expressed power of language and story as a means for that renewal, and he demonstrates that power in his poetry. As Ortiz states, "A story is not only told but it is also listened to; it becomes whole in its expression and perception" (1984, 57). In the telling and in the listening, even in relation to the difficult stories of loss, death, and absence, there is the co-creative power of conversive orality that invites engagement, connection, and healing.

■ 1492's Centrifugal Turn

Any work of Native American literature is, by definition, in one form or another the story of the colonization of the Americas, for which the year 1492 is a fulcrum. Spain, as a Muslim country for eight centuries, had been renowned as an inclusive center of knowledge, diversity, and beauty where scholars and artists throughout Europe journeyed to further their learning. The arrival of the Inquisition in Spain and the concomitant expulsion of Muslims and Jews initiated a powerful centrifugal impetus that extended outward as the West (western Europe) focused heavily on faraway lands with a materialist and capitalist vision that sought material resources that, in turn, fueled further expansionism. As the colonizing nations of Europe looked outward, colossal diasporas began—both volitionally and violently. Following upon the heels of Spain's Jewish and Muslim diasporas, three cataclysmic movements occurred that irrevocably altered the landscape of the western hemisphere: Europeans poured out of Europe seeking colonial wealth, land, and power; west Africans were horrifically diasporized into objectified forms of slavery that the world had not previously seen[2]; and the Indigenous peoples of the western hemisphere were suppressed through genocide, dispossessed of their lands, relocated into slavery, and otherwise displaced, marginalized, and impoverished. Elizabeth Cook-Lynn notes that the horrors of that time endure for Native peoples: "The arrival of Columbus in the New World in 1492 was the beginning of a massive reign of terror and genocide that has not abated" (2000, 92). The perceptual shift that crystallized in 1492 magnified and globalized the objectification of lands, cultures, and persons—all of which came to be viewed by the colonial elites in terms of a distanced alienation and disconnectedness. While there were exceptions to this rule, the larger consequences of the ideology of Manifest Destiny resulted in the almost total takeover of what is now the United States by non-Native peoples who, like temporary renters, see little need to live as empathic caretakers for lands to which they may have only a tenuous connection—most recently evident in the American government's prior intransigence on issues of global climate change.

Specifically in relation to the United States, the melting pot mythology and state ideology of the twentieth century presumed that the harmony of diverse peoples could come from the eradication of difference, with the diversity of cultures, traditions, religions, and languages eliminated through standardized and, in the case of Indian boarding schools, forced assimilationist education. By the end of the twentieth century, the vacuity and error of such policies became patently clear in light of the global imperatives that demanded strengths in multicultural communications, familiarity and, ideally, fluency with diverse languages, and a respect for the religions of the world: all areas in which the United States had become functionally, and unconscionably, illiterate. The illusions of essentialist isolation and purity, manifested in implicitly imperial state policies, were then translated to horrifically ignorant ends, as racist and nationalist ideologies of the state were transmitted to the largely uneducated masses by means of right-wing talk radio. The academic and real-world essentialisms of twentieth-century America are starkly evident in the earliest studies of Native America by ethnographers who produced Native studies that sought to distinguish, define, and categorize the very tribal groups and nations who were being further separated by the governmental system of reservations.[3]

Notwithstanding such powerful forces of division, Native peoples and, in fact, all peoples of the world, prior to the age of colonization and empire building of the past five hundred years, maintained extensive trade routes and routes of seasonal or relocational migrations. To varying extents, peoples and cultures have been in contact and mutual influence with other peoples and cultures throughout time (Clifford 1994, 325). Regional and tribal common-alities in music, language, history, and story provided what Sophia Lehmann describes as a language "bridge within a particular culture or community, between various members of the community; and then as a bridge between communities and cultures"—thereby helping individuals to feel at home even when geographically distant from their own homelands (1998, 116). The cata-clysmic effects of global empire building disrupted the regular and occasional regional and, even more far-reaching, global interactions among people. Instead of direct intercultural engagements among diverse peoples, the pri-macy and centrality of European and Euroamerican empires demanded that communications, interactions, and trade be negotiated through the mediacy of the imperial powers.

This process severely ruptured and deformed the more equitable and di-rect intercommunications among tribes and larger groups of peoples, thereby obscuring their historical interconnections, interdependencies, and mutual transformations—and relegating whatever and whoever was not empire to the subaltern peripheries. Ines Hernandez-Avila and Stefano Varese point out the enduring consequences of this politics of separation: "Historically, the colonially engendered fragmentation of indigenous peoples created a corollary fragmentation of indigenous knowledge systems and a rupturing of hemispheric information networks that were in place before contact" (1999, 85). It is ironic that the consequences of colonialist diasporas are now being mediated in new ways such that now the entire planet is implicated in what Barbara Kirshenblatt-Gimblett refers to as "a convergence of diasporas" where the prior fragmentations are beginning to yield to the intersections made possible by far-reaching human migrations and "by communication technologies" (1994, 342–43). The growing interest in hemispheric and global indigeneity is helping to restore previously disrupted communications links; the writing and study of Native American literatures has provided a powerful connective sharing of stories, histories, and cultures across tribes, national borders, and throughout the western hemisphere.

■ The Intersections of Indigeneity and Diaspora

Interrogations need to be made of the intertwined conditions of indigeneity and diaspora to elucidate the constitutive elements that determine a person's and a people's perceptions, interpretations, and evaluations of the lands where they live—regardless of where and what those lands might be. As Ortiz articulates, when people maintain a close, integral, and interpersonal relationship with a geography and its community (which need not be their ancestral, indigenous homelands), an empathic commitment to those lands and its peoples gives the individual a coherent sense of connection and *home* even when one lives in diaspora, far from home (e.g., the Native American girl Indigo who survives and thrives in Europe better than her Euro-American guardians in Silko's *Gardens in the Dunes* [1999]). While it is true that many of the Native peoples of the Americas still live on or near their ancestral homelands, indigeneity, throughout the Americas and elsewhere, needs to be understood in conjunction with the realities and discourses of diaspora, not only in relation to those many Native American peoples living away from their tribal lands, but also in interpretive analysis of the conditions of diasporic distance that can take psychological form even when one's geography is in relative proximity to those homelands (as in the case of the Laguna veterans in Silko's *Ceremony* [1977] who even when home from World War II perceive and live in psychic distance from their perceived "dead and dying" lands and tribe). Conversely, individuals who live far from the homelands of their people (identified in terms of familial, tribal, village, or regional affiliations) may still maintain a strong sense of their respective geographies of place and community-belonging by bridging diasporic distance, if not making it disappear.

Discussions of geographic indigeneity and diaspora need to investigate the conversive complexities of communal relationality that both create and reflect the conditions of spatial belonging that transcend the physical boundaries of geography. When James Clifford asks, "How do diaspora discourses represent experiences of displacement, of constructing homes away from home?" he presumes that such moves are definitionally removes, that diasporic dispersals are invariably "experiences of displacement," and that homes in a new place are "*away* from home" (1994, 302). As he explains, "These, then, are the main features of diaspora: a history of dispersal, myths/memo-ries of the homeland, alienation in the host (bad host?) country, desire for eventual return, ongoing support of the homeland, and a collective identity importantly defined by this relationship" (305). For Clifford, diaspora signifies alienation in one's present geography and a nostalgized connection to one's past home, noting that "diaspora exists in . . . tension with nativist identity formations . . . [T]ribal cultures are not diasporas; their sense of rootedness in the land is precisely what diasporic peoples have lost" (308, 310). Samir Dayal concurs, asserting that such "double consciousness" reflects a psychic duplicity that prevents a full participation in either cultural geography: "Di-aspora studies thematizes the diasporic as astride at least two cultural identity positions without being tied unproblematically to either" (1996, 52).

Even though the "hypermobility" of today's populations "not only di-vides and disperses people and activities," as Kirshenblatt-Gimblett clarifies, it "also collapses spaces of dispersal [which are increasingly] defined and mediated by communication technologies" (1994, 342–43). In fact, Daniel and Jonathan Boyarin note that "diasporic cultural identity teaches us that cultures . . . , as well as identities, are constantly being remade . . . as a prod-uct of such mixing" (1993, 721). As Jack Forbes affirms specifically regarding the recent migrations northward of the indigenous peoples of Latin America, "Millions of Mexicans of indigenous origin have joined us, along with hun-dreds of thousands" of Native peoples from other Latin American countries; "Thus, our American Indian population has become much more diverse and has taken on many new characteristics, such as increased urbanization and dispersal" (1998, 17). Therefore, if we are to understand the indigene-ity of the Americas as expressed in Native American literatures, we need to do so in considered juxtaposition with worldwide indigeneity and diaspora, questioning notions and realities of the colonized and the colonizer, the disenfranchised and the empowered, the impoverished and the imperialist, all as a means of interrogating, interpreting, and understanding the underly-ing conditions that determine a person's actual and perceived relationship to community and place.

The situation of Europe in which those in power are predominantly indig-enous Europeans while those who have come from elsewhere are reduced to the margins of European society is the inverse of the situation in the Americas, where the diasporic peoples of Europe colonized Native peoples throughout the western hemisphere. It is the rare nation in the western hemisphere that even today has an indigenous head of state (e.g., Chavez in Venezuela and Morales in Bolivia). There is a profound irony in the global shifting demographics of an increasingly and horrifically inequitable capitalistic expansionism that today is transforming colonized indigeneity into a colonial diaspora worldwide. The historic rioting and rebellion depicted in Gillo Pontecorvo's 1965 film *Battle of Algiers* is now manifested in the diasporic disillusionment, anger, and violence depicted in Udayan Prasad's 1998 film *My Son the Fanatic*, which shows the transformation of a modern Muslim young man in Europe into a fundamentalist Islamist convert. We see the colonialist mentality of Manifest Destiny being repeated iteration upon iteration in the continuing clash of cultures and peoples, and yet as Edmund T. Gordon and Mark Anderson point out regarding the diasporized peoples of Africa, "Like any sense of peoplehood, Black identities are formed and transformed in relation to other identity constructions. . . . [P]rocesses of travel, communications, and cultural exchange create forms of community and consciousness that subvert norms of race, nation, and capitalism" (1999, 289).

To understand how a conversively creative language of engagement facilitates deep personal connections to place and community, Acoma Pueblo poet, scholar and storyteller Simon J. Ortiz's writing provides a primer, demonstrating how a late twentieth and early twenty-first-century Indigenous poetry can provide the means for intercultural communications that can transcend both personal affiliations (tribally Indigenous or diversely diasporized) and the broader public geopolitics of place and nationhood without the erasure of either. Ortiz shows us that through story, a person can enter worlds and histories that are otherwise alien to her or his experience. In *from Sand Creek,* Ortiz invites his readers to listen to interwoven stories from and about American veterans in VA hospitals, the gritty and gnarled legacies of Manifest Destiny affecting Indians and non-Indians alike, individuals' struggles to survive in the increasing alienation of twentieth-century America, and all of this framed within the consequences of the infamous 1864 Sand Creek massacre of Arapaho and Cheyenne elders, women, and children. In *Fight Back: For the*

Sake of the People, For the Sake of the Land Ortiz shares a story about "Coso Hot Springs, a sacred and healing place for the Shoshonean peoples, enclosed within the China Lake Naval Station" (1980, 31–35). A Paiute man related the story of that place to Ortiz, an Acoma man, who, in turn, relates the story to his readers in his poem "That's the Place Indians Talk About," inviting us all to get a sense of the importance and sacredness of a place closed off and desecrated by the United States government. In these and others of Ortiz's poems and stories, he demonstrates how a deep sense of place, belonging, and community can be communicated and realized (becoming real) across times, worlds, and geographies through the power of conversive storytelling. Distances are affirmed, yet traversed within storied moments. What might otherwise appear to be impermeable divisions of tribe, geography, or race prove to be far more traversable and proximate as poetry and story invite listener-readers to conversively co-create a "sense of commonality between people who [thereby] share history and experience" (Lehmann 1998, 103).

Gertrude Stein wrote that "a rose is a rose is a rose," but the objectification inherent in this assertion ignores the co-creative and intersubjective meaningfulness that conversive relations constitute with whatever it is that one comes into relationship with. The realities of indigeneity and diaspora are far more complex than the geographies of place that determine one's proximity to or distance from ancestral homelands. This is patently evident in the current geopolitical realities of the United States' borderlands with Mexico. The ostensibly controlled border, in fact, provides the main route of illegal human crossings and one of the main routes of narcotrafficking into and arms trafficking out of the United States. Are the mass northward migrations of Latinos an indigenization as Forbes affirms or a diasporization, as Hernandez-Avila and Varese describe those movements? As they point out, "Diaspora and life in foreign countries, for those from Mexico in the south, or away from the reservations, for those from the north, is becoming the way of existence of ever larger sectors of indigenous people of the Americas" (1999, 79). They affirm that these indigenes "return to their communities and/or landbases to renew and replenish, maintaining their geocentric contacts and connections" (79).

Yes, in many cases, there are physical returns to the south that do "renew and replenish," but as Ortiz shows us, that which constitutes belonging and relationship can extend far beyond the geographical limits of ancestry and tribe to embrace other places and persons. Persons do not need to physically return to ancestral geographies to be renewed, for such renewal can be effected through storied remembrances and participation. Our understandings of the importance of geocentric connections need to be broadened in light of the actual experiences of persons' lives both within the bounds of their ancestral homelands and beyond in conditions of diaspora. The philosopher Ludwig Wittgenstein explains that the appearances of things and events are often obscured because of diverse causes and circumstances, and that what might appear to be similar or the same, in fact, may be very different (and what might appear to be different might be more similar than the appearances lead us to presume). While this point may seem obvious, discussions regarding the geocentrism inherent in indigenous and diasporic analysis have insufficiently interrogated the extent to which both indigeneity and diaspora are experienced divergently in diverse cases.

The geographical distance inherent to conditions of diaspora may indeed contribute to a person's sense of alienation and *anomie,* but in other cases, geographical distance might be a means of expanding the boundaries of home and community. The example of national borders is elucidative. Wittgenstein writes that borders may serve to keep people apart, but they may also be a means of engagement:

> If I surround an area with a fence or a line or otherwise, the purpose may be to prevent someone from getting in or out; but it may also be part of a game and the players be supposed, say, to jump over the boundary; or it may shew where the property of one man ends and that of another begins; and so on. So if I draw a boundary line that is not yet to say what I am drawing it for. (I.499)

We can see this in the case of the peoples who have traditionally lived along the lower Rio Grande valley that currently separates the United States and Mexico. For centuries and, arguably, millennia, these peoples were part of the larger regionalism of the area, establishing and maintaining extensive trade routes and intertribal relations. The Rio Grande helped to define a river valley region, but it was not a means of dividing peoples whose ancestral lands straddled both sides of the river. Now as the result of the Euro-American colonization that defines the borders of the United States and Mexico, the very same river has become the symbol and reality of the national and tribal partitioning that has transformed what had been a naturally permeable region for the trading, hunting, and nomadic migrations of an earlier time. Movements that in the past were within familiar lands have been geopolitically transformed into movements of diaspora, but as Simon Ortiz has profoundly expressed, "A river is more than just a river," and geography is far more than just latitudes and longitudes. If we are to live meaningfully in ways that make our ancestral lands or any other place our home, a deep interaction with that place and its history is necessary—what Ortiz himself states is integral to his "own writing [which] comes from a similar dynamic of reciprocity shared by the land, water, and human culture" (1997, xv).

■ Conquest, Land, and the Regenerative Power of Story

Even though the interwoven stories of indigeneity and diasporization elucidate and demonstrate the problematic legacies of Manifest Destiny's crossing of peoples, Ortiz shows us that they also bespeak new possibilities that have arisen from those convergences. To overlook one or the other is to erase the global histories and global present that define us all. Ortiz understands these interwoven realities intimately in ways that the vast majority of Americans can only imagine. His Indigenous roots run deep; as an Acoma man, Ortiz's Indigenous ancestry stretches back well over a thousand years in what is now the American Southwest. In fact, the ancient pueblo village of Sky City is the oldest continuously inhabited community in the United States. The Acoma people's connections to their lands and the lands of the regions of the Southwest are indeed ancient and enduring, as evidenced in the repeated refrain of his volume, *Fight Back:* "For the sake of the people, for the sake of the land" (1980, title page, 1, 2, 35–36, 41). He explains this commitment in a prose section that precedes the poem "It Was That Indian" in which he tells the story of the uranium boom in Grants, New Mexico, a mining and railroad town that, for a number of decades in the mid-twentieth century, was a booming border town to Laguna, Acoma, and Navajo lands.

The poem emphasizes the environmental racism and injustice that underlay that boom, which ironically was reputed to have been started by one Navajo man's discovery of the nearby uranium. Ortiz writes that "some folks began to complain / about chemical poisons flowing into the streams / . . . / and uranium radiation causing cancer" (1980, 3). I remember that back in the early 1980s when I lived in Gallup, New Mexico (to the west of Acoma), it seemed that just about everyone knew someone in the area with cancer, and anecdotally, nearby towns and communities seemed to have high numbers of cancer cases. For example, the town of Thoreau (between Gallup and Grants) eventually had its public water wells tested, and they evidenced levels of radiation substantially above what was allowable by law. All of the wells were shut down, and potable water had to be trucked in for months to the Anglo and Diné (Navajo) ranching community until safe wells could be dug. The radiation and other contamination was largely due to the coal and uranium mining in the region, including the Black Jack coal mine and the infamous Jackpile open pit uranium mine, subsequently listed as an EPA Superfund site (Office of Surface Mining; Shuey). Just to the other side of Grants is the ranching community of Prewitt, where cancer cases were well known to many of us even forty miles away in Gallup (United States Environmental Protection Agency 1990; Department of Health and Human Services 2005). Beginning twenty-five years ago, high levels of benzene and other contaminants were found in the wells of Prewitt because of an abandoned refinery (another EPA Superfund site—those sites whose toxicity and danger is so severe that they warrant federal oversight by the Environmental Protection Agency).

Whether it is in defense of the environmental integrity of the land or Indigenous people's rights to their ancestral lands, Ortiz articulates the enduring links between people and a landscape. His poem "It Was That Indian," speaks about the sacredness and desecration of the lands of his home, for the lands of his people, and also more broadly for the lands of all the peoples of the American Southwest. There is a tribal specificity in the poem, evident in his statement that concludes the prose introduction: "The following story and poem narratives speak for the sake of the People and for the sake of the land. Hanoh eh haaze kuutseniah—the People's fightback is critical" (1980, 2). Throughout time, Ortiz's people have been taught the importance of their culture and that their survival has always been integrally connected to the land upon which their primarily agrarian history has been based. That survival became more tenuous after the arrival of Europeans in the Americas. The collection *Fight Back* explicitly honors the past struggles of Ortiz's Acoma and fellow Pueblo brethren who suffered the horrific early effects of their Spanish and Mexican colonizations. The volume is offered "in commemoration of the Pueblo Revolt of 1680 and our warrior Grandmothers and Grandfathers." In that year the Pueblo tribes of the Rio Grande valley, including the Acoma, Laguna, Zuni, and Hopi people to the west, attacked and defeated the Spaniards in their colonial base in Santa Fe, forcing the Spaniards and Mexicans to withdraw back to the south (1980, ii). In this one historical honoring, the tangled and interwoven legacies of diaspora and indigeneity assert themselves in defining ways that inform the entire collection and, for that matter, virtually all of Ortiz's work. The Spanish and Mexican diasporas that led to the colonization of the Pueblo peoples and their centuries of struggle and survival yielded new ways of being Pueblo that demanded the integrations of diverse cultures, worlds, and peoples that, paradoxically, served as the means of insuring tribal integrity and sovereignty.

Ortiz's commitment to the primacy of his Indigenous and tribal orientation is evident in his poem "Mama's and Daddy's Words," which begins in his own tribal language: "Duwah hahtse dzah. / This is the land. / It is our life, your life, / my life, life. / Hahtse. Nya. Kutra tsahtee. / Land. Mother. Your breath, living" (1980, 40). The very reality and essence of the Acoma people is integrally interwoven with their ancestral lands, the land that is "Hahtse. Nya," their breath and lifeblood from that "Mother." As this poem and others of Ortiz's remind him and us, as his parents reminded him, "You have to fight / by working for the land and the People, / . . . / to work for the land and the People" (41). As a contemporary poet who has lived most of his adult life away from Acoma Pueblo, Ortiz translates his people's commitment to tribe and tribal lands, broadening them for a changing global demographic. In his own language, he writes, "Emii i Hahnoh. / Amoo o Hahnoh," which he translates into English in this way: "Compassion for all the People. / Love for all the People" (41). As this poem evolves, tribal specificity is enlarged with teachings about the importance of Acoma land and its people being extended to embrace the earth and all its peoples. Here, Ortiz stories the centrality of the Acoma people and their lands as a means of telling the larger story of the global ecological imperatives that remind us of the crucial responsibilities that humans have in relation to the health and ecosystemic balances of the planet.

The very next poem in *Fight Back*, "Returning It Back, You Will Go On" speaks directly to the readers, with the second-person voice shift that is one of the more common conversive tools used by oral storytellers to bring listeners into the unfolding stories. This pronoun shift to "you" overtly opens up the world of the "fight" to include any reader of the poem. Ortiz begins the poem starkly, addressing the capitalist objectification and commodification of the earth's natural resources that led to dire consequences for the people and lands of the American Southwest: "Corporate power companies / from the East and from the West / are now buying the processed uranium / from the corporate oil and mining companies / who mine the land. / That's Indian land. / . . . / Power companies and corporations, / railroads, agribusiness, electronics, / states, cities, towns, / the men and women who work for them" (1980, 41). All of us who read this poem, in one form or another, are implicated in the colonization and appropriation of these lands, whether we work for those companies or merely use the electricity that we would not have were it not for the global plundering of uranium, coal, timber, waterways, and so on. And yet Ortiz crafts this poem with the storytelling conversivity and inclusivity that seeks not to alienate or distance any of his readers, but rather to welcome them into the storytelling fold of the poem so that we can all hear this difficult and painful story and others as a means of learning, as a means of growth and change, as a means of healing—for ourselves and for the land. In this way, regardless of our respective ancestries and homelands, we can all enter the storytelling world of a poem that invites us to come together with each other and with the land, even those lands that are geographically distant from where we live but with which, through the creative power of language and story, we make meaningful connections in our own co-creative ways.

Affirming this co-creative power of language and story, Ortiz reminds us all that we must "give back . . . plant something . . . harvest it . . . speak about it . . . / With great care and planning, / with compassion and love, / you will grow, you will go on" (1980, 42). Like the change of seasons that invariably brings the renewal of spring after winter, in what ecocritic Joni Adamson describes as Ortiz's "garden ethic," Ortiz suggests that regardless of the catastrophic experiences of imperial and corporate colonialism, the people will survive, and Ortiz knows well the crucial role of language in that process (Adamson 2001, 61). As David L. Moore points out, "If what makes a poet is openness to that power in language, one of the particularly magnetic qualities in his writing is the fearless way that Ortiz maintains such openness in the midst of a devastating history" (2004, 35). Adamson notes how the Acoma people's stories helped them to articulate and make sense of a world that was out of their control:

> But after the Spanish and later the Mericano entered their homelands, depleting the natural resources on which they had depended for centuries, the people became dependent on the wage economy and experienced change, alienation, and loss on a scale unprecedented in their cultural memory. However, just as they always had before, the people went out into the changing world and incorporated into their oral traditions the understanding they were gaining of both social and environmental changes. They linked stories of the tall grass, abundant harvests, and clear, fast-running water with stories of oppression and loss—not out of a sense of nostalgia, but because they were making connections. (2001, 60–61)

"Returning it back, returning / it back, you will go on, life will go on. / That's what the People say. / That's what the land says" (1980, 42). Ortiz affirms connections with the land, with the People, with his Acoma homelands and his own Acoma people, and with all the land and all the people. As I wrote in the introduction to the special issue of *Studies in American Indian Literatures* devoted to Ortiz's work, "Ortiz speaks the realities of one Acoma man's, of Native people's, of indigenous people's, and possibly all people's lives and struggles in the face of colonizing oppression and genocide that is horrifically relevant on a global scale today" (2004, 6). Whatever Ortiz writes is rooted in his Acoma ancestry; nevertheless his own life and experiences complicate the tribal specificity of this commitment to "the People" (the Acoma people) and the land (Acoma homelands), for he crafts and offers his poetry and words with a clear sense of their conversively cocreative possibilities that make the tribally specific accessible, relevant, and poignantly meaningful to his listener-readers.

■ The Transforming Power of Conversive Language and Story

In the vast majority of cases around the world, colonizing empire builders constructed superficial relations with peoples, cultures, and lands that blocked their acquisition of natural resources. Accordingly, these Indigenous peoples and their surrounding environments, including indigenous lives, cultural traditions, and tribal knowledge, came to be viewed as little more than objects to be appropriated and consumed. This appropriative model has been perpetuated as subsequent generations of the diasporized and Indigenous have, in turn, struggled to establish and maintain meaningful relations with the places, peoples, and cultures in whose midst they now live. Wielding the divisive and disempowering tool of discursive silence, colonial oppressors erased Indigenous languages, substituting Euro-colonial languages as the media for linguistic communications. The effect of this diminishment and, in all too many cases, total erasure of oral tongues cannot be overstated. Hernandez-Avila and Varese explain, "In the best of circumstances, indigenous peoples have nurtured, sustained, and reproduced a core identity that encompasses traditional wisdom, a spiritual rootedness to the land (as cultural geocenter and as hemisphere), and the complex of expressions that comprise the oral tradition" (1999, 86). Colonization created fissures in that core identity that were big enough for individuals' lives to fall through.

Ortiz knows well the personal alienation and dislocation that lie in the crevices of the world's interstitial nowheres: "As an Acoma Indian in the Americas, the dreaded reality of despair, death, and loss because of oppressive colonialism has been too often present, and I cannot deny that. No one can, certainly no one who understands and has undergone debilitating colonization. My personal experience and history have been burdened with too much of that" (1994, xv). Keeping a poetic journal through a brutal South Dakota winter yielded invaluable stories of survivance that helped him in his own struggles towards interconnectedness: "On a daily basis and in a moment-to-moment way, I found this poetry reconnecting my life to all Existence with a sense of wonder and awe" (1994, xiii–xiv). Blaeser emphasizes the extent to which the transforming power of language is part of "Native belief systems and literary accounts [in which] the creative power of words and thought is not confined to mythic time. Past and present, words and thought are believed to have a certain power, and this power is enlisted to order all manner of things in American Indian life" (1996, 20).

Since language and interpersonal communications have been crucial tools in the process of human integration within communities and geographies, the work of Native writers like Simon J. Ortiz who consciously inform their writing with the influence and training of their respective tribal oral traditions elucidates contemporary conditions of diaspora and *anomie*. Noting the importance of language for diasporized people's senses of self and place, Lehmann points out that "disparate diasporic communities are now faced with the shared struggle of articulating a cultural identity in which history and home reside in language, rather than nation, and in which language itself must be recreated so as to bespeak the specificity of cultural experience" (1998, 101). Indeed, throughout time, persons and cultures have used language as a powerful connective means to distant times and places. Analogously, language has also served as a vehicle facilitating immigrants' connections to a new place. Drawing on Ortiz's collection *Out There Somewhere* that foregrounds the struggles to survive colonization and its various geographic and psychological dislocations, Sophia Cantave notes the linguistic desperation of her African and black Caribbean peoples who used prayer and song and story to help them survive slave horrors and disorientation "to redefine an alien landscape into a geography of belonging" through "that spirit of Indigenous agency (as Africans became part of the American landscape) and personal resistance to cultural and physical erasure" (2009, 246–47, 248). As

Harold Scheub, African language and literature specialist, affirms in relation to stories, "Story is at the heart of the way humans see themselves, experience themselves within the context of their worlds. . . . Story is a means whereby people come to terms with their lives, their past; it is a way of understanding their relationship within the context of their traditions" (1998, 21). The conversive nature of storytelling brings persons together in potentially deep and transforming verbal intercourse where the words and story serve the larger relational ends of interpersonal growth and community building.

The transformative implications of conversive language use are beginning to find documentation beyond the disciplinary bounds of the literary anecdotal. Psychologists and other mental health workers are actively exploring the transformative power of storytelling to assist individuals in perceiving themselves and their situations anew. Psychiatrist Amit Bhattacharyya explains that "in the main, the patient has to make some meaning out of what he discovers about himself and his environment. That is what gives him insight and power to survive or modify his life so that he enjoys better mental health. . . . That invariably means the reconstruction of a life story" (1997, 12). Clinical psychologist Peter Harper and play therapist Mary Gray remind us that "the creation and telling of stories has been used universally by cultures, communities and individuals to provide hope, meaning, purpose and understanding in life. . . . They are a vehicle through which people are able to develop understanding and coherence in their worlds" (1997, 42). Lamenting the decline of active storytelling in Western cultures, they posit this lack as a central factor in the problematic egocentrism, alienation, and purposeless that has seemingly become endemic worldwide (42, 46).

Many Native American writers have found literary ways that reach beyond the limits of self and tribe to provide literary models of engagement that invite their readers into worlds that deliberately cross ethnic, national, and cultural boundaries—which they accomplish without erasing or diminishing cultural and tribal integrity. In fact, in most cases such expansions concomitantly affirm tribal presence and significance. Writers such as Ortiz, Silko, Blaeser, Gordon Henry, and Carter Revard, among others, craft poetry and stories that interweave diverse worlds, times, places, and peoples in ways that interrogate presumptive essentialisms while articulating the evolving complexities and diversities that have always been part and parcel of personal and cultural growth and self-definitions. Whether it's Blaeser finding "home" in an urban powwow in Chicago, many miles away from her White Earth Anishinaabe community in Minnesota (1994, 12–13); Silko crafting an Indigenous character who experiences deep storytelling connections with the ancient stories of the diverse cultures of Europe (1999); medievalist Revard who interweaves his Osage and Ponca worlds with the stories and bards of medieval England (Brill de Ramírez and Beidler 2007); or Henry, who brings together different persons, histories, and cultures all within the scope of one poem (1993); these writers show us the power of language and story to effect perceived and actual changes in one's surrounding geographies in the mutually transforming process of conversive relations that enable individuals to become integral parts of new worlds, places, and communities. These stories provide much-needed healing articulations for a planet with increasing numbers of imploding and failed nation states and their forgotten peoples. In contrast, too many other contemporary literatures reflect the current global, national, and interpersonal discord, alienation, and division, as the movements and proximity of diverse cultures and peoples lead to what is presented as their inevitable corollaries: hostility and violence.

In the preface to his poetry collection *After and Before the Lightning*, Ortiz reminds us that human survival requires far more than the mere physiological needs of shelter, food, and clothing; there is a psychic need to live connectedly, relationally, without despair and *anomie*. Living far away from home, Ortiz learned, in just one year on the Rosebud Indian Reservation, that place and its people could become a deep part of him as he, too, became part of that world, and in so doing, he found/made a new home. "When the poems came about and I wrote them, I felt like I was putting together a map of where I was in the cosmos. . . . As an Acoma Indian in the Americas, the dreaded reality of despair, death, and loss because of oppressive colonialism has been too often present, and I cannot deny that. . . . I am most conscious of my life as a journey, and what I write is a map that comes about every moment for me" (1994, xiv, xv, xvi). Ortiz's poetic maps show him (and his listener-readers) vital directions for surviving our brutal winters (literally in the Lakota homelands and, more generally, metaphorically). Here and elsewhere, Ortiz demonstrates the power and efficacy of poetry and story to reorient, expand, and enrich the worlds of one's experience—both lived and imagined, which, in fact, become intertwined and understood in their conjunctions. In such wise, we see the possibilities for varyingly diasporized people to co-create a sense of home in places other than their ancient home-lands without any diminution in the primacy of those ancestral lands.

In the poetry and stories that he crafted from his time on the Rosebud reservation, Ortiz weaves himself even more integrally into that world, and, even more remarkably, he invites his readers as conversive listener-readers to join him in those storied worlds. Neither we nor Ortiz experience those lands in the same way as would the Lakota people for whom those lands are their ancestral lands, but we can become part of that place in our own ways. Ortiz dedicates the volume using the traditional Lakota greeting "For all my relations" (xvii). In this way, Ortiz affirms the relational connections that developed deeply during that year, without in any form or fashion attenuat-ing the far deeper connections that the Lakota have for their own homelands; as he affirms regarding his "Lakota friends who are the grandmothers and grandfathers, mothers and fathers, daughters and sons, sisters and brothers of their people. They are the true caretakers of their beautiful prairie land. Always among each other and with the land, they are relations" (xvii). They are relations to and with each other, relations to and with their lands, rela-tions to and with Ortiz. Here Ortiz affirms his sense of place and belonging within a geography that is far from his own Acoma homeland while, at the same time, affirming the ancestral sovereignty and sacredness of those lands to the Lakota.

Avoiding the tendency for a reductive hemispheric essentializing of In-digeneity while, nevertheless, recognizing the commonalities across tribes, Ortiz articulates stories of placefulness that transcend and affirm tribe, race, and ancestry. In the example of "Charley, an American white man married to a Lakota woman," Ortiz reminds us that "it is possible to pay attention to land and have a belief, art, and ingenuity. And be a white man married to an Indian woman" (86). Ortiz, several Lakota men, and Charley work hard together to build Charley's new home, and Ortiz *stories* that work in his poetry as beams, joints, and walls come together: "There. It fits now, the people, land, / the sacredness, sky, and walls joined" (87). Belonging. A place that is a home for the Lakota people, for a white man, and for an Acoma man as they all "sit in the kitchen at their trailer, tell stories, jokes, drink coffee" (86). On Rosebud, far away from the ancestral lands of the Acoma Ortiz, the Euro-American Charley, and Ortiz's non-Lakota readers, through poetry and story, Ortiz familiarly welcomes us all into that world as we conversively read (listen) ourselves into their kitchen as the informal storytelling, laughter, and hard work bring us all together.

Navajo poet Luci Tapahonso describes the healing energy that comes from such conversive storytelling as centered in caring and love: "Being a part of telling stories is very much a way in which affection is shown if a person is included within the circle. . . . And so it's a way to show affection and to be included within either listening to or sharing of stories" (1996). The geometric image of the storytelling circle offers a restorative model for persons and peoples to come into more direct and balanced relationships as fellow points/members of the circle. Ortiz depicts such a coming together in community and story with Lakota, Acoma, and Euro-American people (interacting in person and, for Ortiz's listener-readers, through the vehicle of language and poetry). The relational center within storytelling and orally informed literatures leads Karl Kroeber to warn that this "social interchange [in storytelling] . . . is misunderstood if the actively contributory force of *any* participant is ignored" (1992, 19). Just as all the points on a circle are equal to each other and necessary to the wholeness of the circle, in *After and Before the Lightning* Ortiz shows us the ability of diverse humans from diverse places to interact in a conversively intersubjective manner that affirms the distinctive importance of each while also subsuming each as parts within the larger focus of the unfolding stories. The absence of such interpersonal and intercultural interweavings is patently obvious on a global scale. For example, the rioting in France in 2005 of the diasporized peoples from various Caribbean and North African nations showed the world the consequences of the colonialist divides that alienate and impoverish those relegated to conditions of subalter-ity—in this case, the Indigenous people's aggrandizement at the expense of the disenfranchised diasporic minorities in their midst. The consequences of a residual imperial separatism of peoples and cultures are dire, and yet, as Ortiz shows us, diasporic distancing and alienation (as in the case of an Acoma man far from his own homelands) can provide the opportunity for bringing peoples and places together under the conversive rubric of life and story.

■ Indigenous Directions Home for Diaspora Studies

In the preface to *from Sand Creek,* Ortiz articulates the complexities of "home" for the colonized and diasporized. For American Indians, home in America requires integration into a nation whose very existence has been predicated upon their absence. "Indians had been conquered. . . . We had been made to disappear. We were invisible. We had vanished. Therefore we had no history. And it was almost like we deserved to have no history. That was the feeling" (1981, 6). The official histories of the United States and America put the Indigenous peoples of those lands under the scarred trace of erasure—what Ortiz describes as the "insulation of amnesia" (6). The restorative history of Ortiz's volume centers around the horrific atrocity that took place on 29 November 1864, when troops under the command of Colonel John W. Chivington ignobly attacked six hundred peaceful Southern Cheyenne and Arapaho people (the vast majority of whom were women, children, and old people) who were camped at Sand Creek. When Ortiz was in a Veteran's Administration Hospital not far from the site of the massacre, he was able to hear the story of Sand Creek from descendants of survivors of the massacre; he was also able to walk the lands of that place as he, himself, struggled with finding his own place in a country and world that continued to deny his presence and subjectivity as a contemporary American Indian. As Ortiz begins the first poem of the volume, "This America / has been a burden / of steel and mad / death," and yet walking the place that is Sand Creek, Ortiz cannot deny the springtime renewal that he saw around him, evidenced in the "flowers / and new grass" (9).

The reality of Sand Creek, once storied into poetry by Ortiz, makes that place, its history, and the Indigenous peoples of those lands accessible and meaningful to those readers who engage the words and poems in the co-creative manner of conversive storytelling listeners. Ortiz uses spacing on the page to open up the poems and histories more fully to his readers. The extensive blank spacing is akin to the oral storytelling tools of emphasis and silence during which the listeners are given the reflective time necessary to ponder the story and its vignettes more deeply and in considered interconnection. The book's episodic and associative organization parallels the structural intricacies of oral storytelling, in which stories, vignettes, persons, times, and worlds are interwoven in the process of the larger unfolding story. Each blank space on the page offers the reader open time for his or her interpersonal, co-creative interweavings of the vignettes, poems, and stories, thereby making them deeply and personally meaningful. In her discussion of Afro-Caribbean women's relational storytelling, which creates a meaningful placefulness that interweaves their diasporized African pasts within the new world's geography, Lehmann notes how they "combine different voices, languages and media to create one text [that, in turn,] is readapted and reworked with each telling as part of a collaboration between speaker and audience which takes its form from the interplay between them" (1998, 108, 109). Silence and its concomitant space for reflection and listening may well be the most crucial strategies in such conversive communications. Native writer and educator Anna Lee Walters (Pawnee/Otoe-Missouria) confirms this in noting that she was taught that there are two parts to language, the words and the silence and that it is during the silence that knowing occurs (1992, 13).

It is quite remarkable that through the medium of language and one man's conversive efforts to know a place, his listener-readers (without even physically traveling to Colorado) can join him in learning from the history of Manifest Destiny as it was played out at Sand Creek. Evelina Zuni Lucero (Isleta Pueblo) places Ortiz's distinctive lens within the rubric of Pueblo Indian "philosophy of life that permeates his thinking," noting that his poetry "is layered and dense with meaning and moves in multiple directions" (2009, 3). Ortiz wields a range of poetic tools to powerfully rhythmic, emphatic and empathic ends as the Cheyenne and Arapaho, the Colorado soldiers, Puritan witch burnings, urban skid rows, U.S. veterans and V.A. hospitals, Andrew Jackson and Kit Carson, and European immigrants come together in the larger story of Sand Creek.[4] As Ortiz asks: "Who stole the hearts and minds of the humble hard-working folk until they too became moralistic and self-righteous: senators, bishops, presidents, missionaries, corporation presidents?" (1981, 50).

> They were simple enough.
> Swedes, Germans,
> Mennonites, Dutch
> Irish, escaping
> Europe.
> Running.
>
> They shouldn't have stopped
> and listened to Puritans.
> And learned
> that mountains were chains
> to be crossed like breaking
> something. (1981, 51)

Whereas the first stanza welcomes the waves of European refugees into the Americas, Ortiz begins the second stanza ominously pointing to their catastrophic colonization: "They shouldn't have stopped." This unpunctuated line break underscores the stopping, the conquest that shouldn't have happened; qualifying that categorical critique, the next line quickly clarifies that it is not diaspora per se that is the problem, that it is not the presence of Europeans in the Americas that is the problem, but that it is the conquest, the violence, the horror that was and is the problem.

Later in the collection, Ortiz writes: "If they could have / dreamed untroubled / and gentle dreams, / dreams would have been roads. / Instead, self-righteousness / became a necessary style . . ." (1981, 75). The ambiguity at the end of this poem's first line "If they could have" opens up the poem within the historical frame of Manifest Destiny's possession and conquest. The further ambiguity of the third person pronoun includes the conquerors ("If *they* could have") and conquered ("If *they* could have") in alternative possible readings, both who were left bereft of "untroubled / and gentle dreams." Additionally, the rhythmic ambiguity in the line offers a beginning iamb that is followed by a metrical foot that could be read as either another iamb (emphasizing "have" and "their" ownership) or as a trochee (emphasizing "could" and the speaker's desires for a different past, an alternative story). Repetition ("dreamed," "dreams"), para-rhyme ("could have" and "would have"), and assonance ("self-righteousness" and "necessary") emphasize the poignancy of a story that could have been different but wasn't, a story whose history can never be fully told without the profound awareness of its enduring legacy in a people (Indigenous and diasporic) who are the "mutant generations" of America (1981, 87). It is this story of America that Ortiz desperately wants his readers to listen to deeply, in order to understand the history that defines contemporary America and to begin to dream a different dream: "That dream / . . . will not be vengeful / but wealthy with love / and compassion / and knowledge." (1981, 95).

In coming to a deeper understanding of the United States through the specificity of the Sand Creek massacre, it is important to clarify that the understandings that readers can glean will in no form or fashion be the same as those of the Arapaho or Cheyenne people for whom the tragedy of Sand Creek is their ancestral legacy, but this is not to say that others' understandings are any less meaningful, albeit different. Even though he is American Indian, Ortiz is neither Arapaho nor Cheyenne, but any person's deeply experienced personal story, once interwoven with other stories, makes those other stories part of the larger developing tapestry of the person's life. In this way, interconnective meanings and understandings become possible, and people's lives are accordingly enriched as those meanings help to make their lives that much more meaningful and purposeful. As the First Nations elder from the Yukon Territory Mrs. Angela Sidney described this process, "Well, I've tried to live my life right, just like a story," continually learning from her people's historical and traditional stories that, throughout time, have given persons restorative meaning, wisdom and balance (Cruikshank 1990, 20).

In his telling of Sand Creek, Ortiz demonstrates the capacity of stories to be reworked and molded to fit meaningfully within different languages, times, and geographies as a means of making those stories accessible to virtually any reader. The volume begins with a connective grasp, at a distance, of "*This* America," then shifts in the final poem to embrace "this heart / which is *our* America," inviting us all to come together without vengeance but with "compassion / and knowledge" (95, my emphases). Over ten years ago, Robert Warrior asked, "To what extent do the various conceptual and analytical categories currently available in American Indian scholarship provide an adequate framework for the emergence of a mature Native cultural and literary criticism?" (1995, xiii). One response to this question is for scholars to step beyond the limiting parameters of contemporary critical debate and, instead, to turn to the literatures themselves to see what critical pathways they elicit. Matthew E. Duquès asserts that Ortiz's writing helps us to rise beyond those "dichotomies that desecrate difference, learning not only from our own past genocides and massacres, but also recognizing the arduous yet fruitful process, circumscribed to a site, geographic or otherwise, that is regeneration" (2004, 98). The engagement of diaspora studies offers important new directions for Native American literary studies, pointing to global relevancies even beyond the scope of indigeneity while, at the same time, affirming the centrality and relevance of tribal domain.

Far from being less relevant in a post-9/11 world, a critical nexus of literary analysis that engages Native American literatures in new and meaningful ways is imperative in a world in desperate need of models for cross-cultural communications and stories. As Womack makes very clear in his call for literatures and scholarship that explicitly respond to the real-world needs of Native peoples, "The attempt . . . will be to break down oppositions between the world of literature and the very real struggles of American Indian communities, arguing for both an intrinsic and extrinsic relationship between the two" (11). This is why it is crucial that we make efforts to understand why, as Kroeber reminds us, "wherever real storytelling takes place, an essential human freedom exists" (1992, 4). Whether it is in the hemispheric indigeneity of Leslie Marmon Silko's *Almanac of the Dead,* her global ecologies of place in *Gardens in the Dunes,* or Sherman Alexie's post-9/11 assertion that "the end of essentialism is flying airplanes into buildings," the exigencies of the global imperatives of terrorism, abject poverty, climate change, and the trafficking of arms, drugs, and humans require analyses that extend beyond the past groundbreaking discourses of indigeneity in order to engage, in important ways, the contemporary, past and future realities of diasporization.

As Ortiz reminds us, perhaps the most powerfully integrative means available to assist persons anywhere on the globe in centering themselves within their respective geographies has been and continues to be a relationally based, conversive storytelling.

NOTES

1. The larger hemispheric and global sophistication of twenty-first century Indigenous literary scholarship is evident in the many new collections and monographs, including the pioneering work in *Going Native: Indians in the American Cultural Imagination*, by Shari M Huhndorf (2001); *American Indian Literary Nationalism*, by Jace Weaver, Craig Womack, and Robert Warrior (2005); and *Reasoning Together: The Native Critics Collective*, edited by Craig Womack, Daniel Heath Justice, and Christopher B. Teuton (2008).

2. See Kevin Bales's *Disposable People: New Slavery in the Global Economy* (Berkeley: University of California Press, 1999).

3. See my recent *Native American Life-History Narratives: Colonial and Postcolonial Navajo Ethnography* (Albuquerque: University of New Mexico Press, 2007) regarding the problematic ethnologization of tribal cultures and the subsequent misreading of those texts.

4. For a more developed analysis of Ortiz's poetics, see my introductory essay "A Geography of Belonging: Ortiz's Poetic, Lived, and Storied Indigenous Ecology" in *Simon J. Ortiz: A Poetic Legacy of Indigenous Continuance*, eds. Brill de Ramírez and Lucero (25–52).

WORKS CITED

Adamson, Joni. 2001. *American Indian Literature, Environmental Justice, and Ecocriticism: The Middle Place*. Tucson: University of Arizona Press.

Bales, Kevin. 1999. *Disposable People: New Slavery in the Global Economy*. Berkeley: University of California Press.

Bhattacharyya, Amit. 1997. "Historical Backdrop." In *The Therapeutic Use of Stories*, edited by Kedar Nath Dwivedi, 1–18. London: Routledge.

Blaeser, Kimberly M. 1994. *Trailing You: Poems.* Greenfield Center, N.Y.: Greenfield Review Press.

———. 1996. *Gerald Vizenor: Writing in the Oral Tradition.* Norman: University of Oklahoma Press.

Boyarin, Daniel, and Jonathan Boyarin. 1993. "Diaspora: Generational Ground of Jewish Identity." *Critical Inquiry* 19.4: 693–725.

Brill de Ramírez, Susan Berry. 1999. *Contemporary American Indian Literatures and the Oral Tradition.* Tucson: University of Arizona Press.

———. 2004. "Introduction: 'A Spring Wind Rising . . . Listen. You Can Hear It.'" *Studies in American Indian Literatures* 16.4 (Winter): 3–8.

———. 2005. "'Flying Airplanes into Buildings': An Interview with Sherman Alexie and Alex Kuo." Unpublished interview. Teleconference. October.

Brill de Ramírez, Susan Berry, and Peter Beidler. 2007. "Scholarship and Stories, Oxford and Oklahoma, Academe and American Indians: The Relational Words and Worlds of a Native American Bard and Storytelling Medievalist." In *The Salt Companion to Carter Revard,* edited by Ellen L. Arnold, 202–18. Cambridge: Salt Publishing.

Brill de Ramírez, Susan Berry, and Evelina Zuni Lucero, eds. 2009. *Simon J. Ortiz: A Poetic Legacy of Indigenous Continuance.* Albuquerque: University of New Mexico Press.

Cantave, Sophia. 2009. "Reading Simon Ortiz and Black Diasporic Literature of the Americas." In *Simon J. Ortiz: A Poetic Legacy of Indigenous Continuance.* Edited by Susan Brill de Ramírez and Evelina Zuni Lucero. 246–63. Albuquerque: University of New Mexico Press.

Clifford, James. 1994. "Diasporas." *Cultural Anthropology* 9.3 (August): 302–38.

Cook-Lynn, Elizabeth. 2000. "How Scholarship Defames the Native Voice . . . and Why." *Wicazo Sa Review* 15.2 (Autumn): 79–92.

Cruikshank, Julie, in collaboration with Angela Sidney, Kitty Smith, and Annie Ned. 1990. *Life Lived Like a Story: Life Stories of Three Yukon Native Elders.* Lincoln: University of Nebraska Press.

Dayal, Samir. 1996. "Diaspora and Double Consciousness." *Journal of the Midwest Modern Language Association* 29.1 (Spring): 46–62.

Department of Health and Human Services. 2005. Agency for Toxic Substances and Disease Registry. "Preliminary Public Health Assessment: Prewitt Abandoned Refinery."

Http://www.atsdr.cdc.gov/HAC/PHA/prewitt/par_p1.html. Accessed 5 December.

Dunsmore, Roger. 2004. "Simon Ortiz and the Lyricism of Continuance: 'For the Sake of the People, for the Sake of the Land.'" *Studies in American Indian Literatures* 16.4 (Winter): 20–28.

Duquès, Matthew E. 2004. "Revisiting the Regenerative Possibilities of Ortiz." *Studies in American Indian Literatures* 16.4 (Winter): 96–98.

Forbes, Jack D. 1998. "Intellectual Self-Determination and Sovereignty: Implications for Native Studies and for Native Intellectuals." *Wicazo Sa Review* 13.1 (Spring): 11–23.

Gordon, Edmund T., and Mark Anderson. 1999. "The African Diaspora: Toward an Ethnography of Diasporic Identification." *Journal of American Folklore* 112.445 (Summer): 282–96.

Harper, Peter, and Mary Gray. 1997. "Maps and Meaning in Life and Healing." In *The Therapeutic Use of Stories,* edited by Kedar Nath Dwivedi, 42–63. London: Routledge.

Henry, Gordon. 1993. "Sleeping in the Rain." In *Earth Power Coming: Short Fiction in Native American Literature,* edited by Simon J. Ortiz, 93–96. Tsaile, Ariz.: Navajo Community College Press.

Hernandez-Avila, Ines, and Stefano Varese. 1999. "Indigenous Intellectual Sovereignties: A Hemispheric Convocation. An Overview and Reflections on a United States/ Mexico Binational Two-Part Conference." *Wicazo Sa Review* 14.2 (Autumn): 77–91.

Huhndorf, Shari M. 2001. *Going Native: Indians in the American Cultural Imagination.* Ithaca: N.Y.: Cornell University Press.

Kirshenblatt-Gimblett, Barbara. 1994. "Spaces of Dispersal." *Cultural Anthropology* 9.3 (August): 339–44.

Kroeber, Karl. 1992. *Retelling/Rereading: The Fate of Storytelling in Modern Times.* New Brunswick, N.J.: Rutgers University Press.

Lehmann, Sophia. 1998. "In Search of a Mother Tongue: Locating Home in Diaspora." *MELUS* 23.4 (Winter): 101–18.

Lucero, Evelina Zuni. 2009. "Voice of Experience, Vision of Continuance." In *Simon J. Ortiz: A Poetic Legacy of Indigenous Continuance.* Edited by Susan Brill de Ramírez and Evelina Zuni Lucero, 2–25. Albuquerque: University of New Mexico Press.

Moore, David L. 2004. "'The story goes its own way': Ortiz, Nationalism, and the Oral Poetics of Power." *Studies in American Indian Literatures* 16.4 (Winter): 34–46.

Office of Surface Mining.2001. *Annual Evaluation Report for the New Mexico Abandoned*

Mine Land Reclamation Program: Evaluation Year 2001. http://www.osmre.gov/
Reports/EvalInfo/2001/newmexicoAML01.pdf. Accessed 18 May 2009.

Ortiz, Simon J. 1980. *Fight Back: For the Sake of the People / For the Sake of the Land. INAD
Literary Journal* (Albuquerque: Institute for Native American Development: Native
American Studies—University of New Mexico) 1.1. 1–75.

——. 1981. *from Sand Creek: Rising in This Heart Which Is Our America.* Tucson: University of Arizona Press.

——. 1984. "Always the Stories: A Brief History and Thoughts on My Writing." In
*Coyote Was Here: Essays on Contemporary Native American Literary and Political
Mobilization,* edited by Bo Schöler, 57–69. Aarhus, Denmark: SEKLOS/University
of Aarhus.

——. 1994. *After and Before the Lightning.* Tucson: University of Arizona Press.

——. 1997. "Introduction: *Wah nuhtyuh-yuu dyu neetah tyahstih* (Now It Is My Turn to
Stand)." In *Speaking for the Generations: Native Writers on Writing,* edited by Simon
J. Ortiz, xi–xix. Tucson: University of Arizona Press.

Scheub, Harold. 1998. *Story.* Madison: University of Wisconsin Press.

Shuey, Chris. 2007. "Uranium Exposure and Public Health in New Mexico and the Navajo
Nation: A Literature Summary." Southwest Research and Information Center. http://
www.emnrd.state.nm.us/MMD/MARP/Documents/MK023ER_20081212_Mar-
quez_NNELC-Acoma-Comments-AttachmentE-UExposureSummary.pdf. Accessed
18 May 2009.

Silko, Leslie Marmon. 1977. *Ceremony.* New York: Viking Penguin.

——. 1999. *Gardens in the Dunes.* New York: Simon and Schuster.

Tapahonso, Luci. 1996. "Interview with Luci Tapahonso." Interview by Jim Meadows.
WCBU-FM, Peoria, Ill. 24 April.

United States Environmental Protection Agency. 1990. National Priorities List. "NPL Site
Narrative for Prewitt Abandoned Refinery." Http://www.epa.gov/superfund/sites/
npl/nar768.htm. Accessed 5 December 2005.

Walters, Anna Lee. 1992. *Talking Indian: Reflections on Survival and Writing.* Ithaca,
N.Y.: Firebrand.

Warrior, Robert. 1995. *Tribal Secrets: Recovering American Indian Intellectual Traditions.*
Minneapolis: University of Minnesota Press.

Weaver, Jace, Craig S. Womack, and Robert Warrior. 2005. *American Indian Literary
Nationalism.* Albuquerque: University of New Mexico Press.

Wittgenstein, Ludwig. 1984. *Philosophical Investigations.* Translated by G. E. M. Anscombe. Oxford: Basil Blackwell.

Womack, Craig. 1999. *Red on Red: Native American Literary Separatism.* Minneapolis: University of Minnesota Press.

Womack, Craig, Daniel Heath Justice, and Christopher B. Teuton, eds. 2008. *Reasoning Together: The Native Critics Collective.* Norman: University of Oklahoma Press.

The(st)ories of Ceremonial Relation: Native Narratives and the Ethics of Reading

SILVIA MARTÍNEZ-FALQUINA

■ Theoretical Motivations: Native Writing/Reading as Ceremony

This essay starts from the premise that, in our interpretation of Native texts,[1] we can and should establish creative dialogues between storytelling and criticism, assuming that theories incorporate narrative patterns and show traces of stories in their articulation, and that stories imply and show a familiarity with theory, or can be theory, functioning as critique, especially in terms of their redefinition of the relations between writer, text, reader and critic. I am therefore dealing with the various readings of the(st)ories, including the story in theory and the theory in story, story as theory and theory as story, story theories and theory stories.

Ethnic creative writing often incorporates a critical response to Western authority, reminding us that so-called minorities have not usually had the same access to a theoretical voice as those in power do. Furthermore, we also need to take into account the specific origin of Native authors, in whose ancient traditions it was common for performances to include a commentary on themselves, thus practicing metafiction and self-reflexivity long before (post)modernism. On the other hand, Native writing has a primary ceremonial motivation, broadly understood as an opening of the possibility of transformation for the participants in the process. It is from these assumptions that my paper intends to engage in a creative dialogue with Ojibwe poet and fiction writer Gordon Henry's fictional and autobiographical narratives, in order to show the theory of reading offered in them that may lead to our transformation, and to prove how one author presents the issue of Native identity in a way which is complex enough to unsettle simple positionings and question any kind of preconceptions we may be tempted to embrace when meeting with the text.

■ The(st)ories of Positioning: Four Bears' Leg

As bell hooks accurately puts it, "When we write about the experiences of a group to which we do not belong, we should think about the ethics of our actions, considering whether or not our work will be used to reinforce and perpetuate domination" (1989, 43). Indeed, when writing about so-called minority cultures we may inadvertently be contributing to the unethical project of appropriation and oppression of the other started and continued by the western center of power and definition. It is therefore absolutely necessary to approach these texts in awareness of our positioning, while we try our best not to impose our own presuppositions and make the text fit into them, but, inasmuch as this is possible, carefully listening to the texts instead, letting them speak to us and exert their transforming power over us.

In order to explore the way a text by Gordon Henry guides us towards an ethical understanding or series of choices of interpretation, I will examine those sections of Henry's short story web *The Light People* (1994)[2] that deal with a lost human leg found in a museum and the court case leading to its return to its deceased Native owner.[3] As for the ethical aspects of my own reading, I will start from James Phelan's assumption that the communicative situation of narrative—somebody telling somebody else that something happened—is itself an ethical situation. The teller's treatment of the events will inevitably convey certain attitudes toward the audience, attitudes that indicate his or her sense of responsibility to and regard for the audience. Similarly, the audience's response to the narrative will indicate their commitments to the teller, the narrative situation, and to the values expressed in the narrative. (1998, 319)

As Phelan also outlines, an ethical reading of any text implies a concern for position, "a concept that combines *acting from* and *being placed* in an ethical location" (319), and it is also important to note that

the default ethical relation between implied author and authorial audience in narrative is one of reciprocity. Each party both gives and receives. Authors give, among other things, guidance through ethical complexity and expect to receive in return their audiences' interest and attention. Audiences give that interest and attention and expect to receive in return authorial guidance. (321)

Henry's text deals with issues of positioning and interpretation, the apprehension of truth, and a concept of justice and ethical responsibility towards the other that necessarily has to include ethnic difference. When Moses Four Bears has his leg amputated, his family dresses it in Ojibwe ceremonial legging and moccasin and asks young Oshawanung to bury it beside the river. However, a blizzard prevents him from fulfilling his promise to bury the leg, which mysteriously disappears until one of his own descendants finds it in the Minneapolis Natural History Museum several decades later. The Four Bears family then takes the museum to court in order to have the leg returned, and this motif is used to reflect about relevant themes for Native American peoples such as appropriation, objectification and the questionability of western ways of knowledge.

The short story web starts with a Native point of view, that of Oshawa, the young man who comes across the leg in the museum, and it incorporates

Oshawanung and the descendants of Four Bears. This Native community will soon be opposed to "[t]hose people" (1994, 123), the western museum who speaks the language of ownership, as well as to any Indian politician who "would view the leg as an issue not of family but of all Indian people across the whole uninvolved country" (124). Its others are therefore not only colonizing westerners but also opportunist Natives which might overgeneralize and misuse their request. The hearing begins with the opening arguments, where two opposing visions of truth are contrasted. The Four Bears family's attorney Catullus Cage starts:

> It is a hot day in August. We are witnessing a trial for the return of a human leg. But we are not all sitting at the same place in the same construct. Some of us are sitting up toward the front of the courtroom, where most of the dialogue and most of the action deciding this trial will take place. Some of us are sitting in the audience, outside the dialogue, outside the action. This difference in perspective may possibly affect our perception, reception, apprehension of the evidence presented to us in the course of the trial, but I believe the truth will become clear to each and every person who visits this courtroom during the tenure of this case, because that is what this case is about, the apprehension of truth. (127–28)

Indeed, although all participants are sitting in the same physical space, because of variations in location within that construct, not all of them will interpret reality in the same way, which can be extended to each reader's perception of the other. However, the text also proposes a way to achieve truth which is directly related to the Ojibwe worldview:

> In this case the apprehension of truth rests on understanding how something cut off from human existence comes to represent a mere object of limited human possibility. And in this case we will learn how perhaps possibilities for human existence are greater than the perceptions of the museum, the keepers of limited objects. We apprehend the truth as we become part of the story, and the story always brings the truth back to

us in some form. In this case, the form is the leg of Moses Four Bears, deceased tribal elder. In this case, the form has come to this courtroom to reassert a misunderstanding, a misconception, a mishandling of some part of the story that is our past. (128)

According to this Native voice, truth lies in stories and their capacity to integrate, for human reality has to be conceived of as related, and not in isolation like the limiting point of view of the museum argues through its representative Tony Nugush:

How ironic to speak of truth at a trial that involves a physical part of a human being that exists in the absence of thought on the part of that human being. Old man Four Bears is gone, and his mind is gone with him. Who, then, does this leg belong to, assuming that this leg once was attached to Four Bears? My clients and I are of the contention that there is no direct proof that the leg in question is the leg Moses Four Bears walked around with for sixty years. As for stories and truth, we all, every one of us, can imagine that a story is true, but the thought generating a story doesn't always convey the same relationships of images and symbols from the teller to the receiver. In this courtroom we should be beyond the once-upon-a-time stage. (128–29)

The western, colonizing language thus articulated discards the value of stories as it separates mind from body, subordinating the latter and thus conceiving of Four Bears' leg as an object. Since, to Nugush, "[t]his leg has no name, no face to go with it" (129), it merely exists as the museum's possession, and he will reject any given proof—no matter how obvious—that it actually belonged to Four Bears, showing the shortsightedness and partiality of his monologic western code.

As he illustrates the process of border construction between the two positions—where each is a narrative with an inherent logic which claims to possess the truth—Henry guides us through the choice between memory and ownership as two ways to apprehend the truth. On the Native side, he resorts to personal closeness and specific contextualization. Willow Four

Bears testifies what she remembers about the day her father lost his leg: not only was she there listening to his instructions about what to do with the leg, but she had also made the moccasin in which it would be dressed. In things like moccasins, she says, "the signature is in the mistakes of the maker, in imperfect work" (135), and this is contrasted to Nugush's theoretical, ridiculed claims that somebody might have copied the design in order to appropriate the leg for themselves. The next witness is Oshawanung, who should have buried the leg but could not because a storm made him search for refuge and leave it behind. He claims to have a clear memory and haunting dreams about the lost leg, and his speech is thoroughly personal too, for it is for the sake of his own peace of mind that he will see to its proper return and reburial. Both accounts of what happened at the time are interconnected and consistent, and each narrators' presence in the events is emphasized by means of personalization and specific referents, as well as oral features, direct speech and visual images that call for the implication of the listeners.

On the museum side, the witnesses' speeches to justify ownership of the leg are abstract, theoretical and disconnected from reality. The curator of the museum resorts to impersonal, official language and circular definitions to demonstrate that the educational institution "is everything a natural history museum should be" (145). He considers the leg an authentic and representative artifact whose extraordinary scientific value is given by its being real, meaning its having existed at a certain point in time, while simultaneously rejecting its continuing connection to any real being. Similarly, the Doctor in Anthropology who found the leg and sold it to the museum offers a parody of the reasoning of western science representatives, who foolishly speculate about the meaning of the leg—trying to interpret it as the result of torture, a ritual to test the manhood of warrior initiates, or a prayer for good fishing, all obvious echoes of the savage *indian* stereotype—and who finally admit that "the leg and the reason it was in the box could not be explained by any expert in our small circle. Still, we understood the value of the leg" (155). This academic discards the possibility of resorting to the people in the nearby Ojibwe village for information, for, he says, "my most immediate analysis told me the leg was older, of a time prior to the times of the people in the community. . . . So what could they possibly tell me, or what would they tell me?" (156–57). Both witnesses' conception of knowledge is so limited that it makes them blind and deaf to anything outside their own code, which totally invalidates any conclusion they may reach about the other.

This text ultimately represents a court case where the law needs to be more or less neutral and objective, and assign the truth to one side. The judge resolves in favor of the Four Bears family and so do we, for the right ethical choice becomes very clear. Henry guides us towards this choice in a particularly effective way: he avoids direct confrontation or categorical affirmations on the narrowness and inadequacy of the museum vision. Instead, using humor as a trickster weapon, he lets his characters define themselves in contrast with one another. As a result, we choose and understand the value of personal stories over official history, context over its absence, which is why we read Catullus Cage's closing arguments as the winning conclusions:

> Their use of Moses Four Bears' leg shows arbitrary judgement, pious self-righteousness framed in the interest of research, an understanding of natural history and language that affords certain seers the option of not seeing how their views affect the seen. . . . The deeper, more cumbersome story rests in five hundred years of human history on this continent, in the arbitrary manner in which Eurocentric intellectual culture mongers and mythmakers have judged the first inhabitants of this land. They've killed them, set plagues upon them, and then after they are dead, these same people, or at least their descendants, want to remove the remains of the dead and study them, catalogue them, and display them. Returning Moses Four Bears' leg to his homeland, according to the wishes and the judgement of his family, may seem like a small part of that larger story, but such a return would be only proper and just, given the evidence at hand. (158–59)

By centering our interest and attention on listening to the voices speaking in the text, we not only hear their own definitions of themselves and the other—westerners believing they know the Natives, the Natives ironically questioning that they do—but we can also creatively redefine an ethical relation of responsibility towards the Native text as other. On the one hand, we

actively choose one vision of truth over another, thus showing our commitments and attitudes towards the privileged values expressed in the narrative.
The holistic, relational approach is shown as more valid than separation and
ownership, and although this truth may be working as a necessary fiction or
a strategic essentialism, it is solidly supported by people's memory, which is
shown as superior to any abstract hypothesis or theory. On the other hand,
readers are called to assume a responsibility whereby we admit dialogue to
be the only possible way to interpret the world around us. If we bring limiting, self-centered and self-authorized presuppositions to the reading, we are
teased and proven shortsighted and hard of hearing. As a result, we inevitably
become uneasy with our ways of knowing, examining our own prejudices in
the process. As readers, we have no choice but to ask ourselves a series of
ethical questions: if the leg is the form that the truth acquires in this case,
how do we read the leg, and why? Do we see it as a separated or an integrated
object, within or without reality? Are we, in the end, literary critics who think
about Native texts and people as separate, to-be-appropriated parts or as full,
autonomous, voiced beings with a story to tell?

■ The(st)ories of Re/Visioning: Entries into the I

Once our position as readers and critics has been unsettled, and our means
to apprehend the truth have been put to the test of responsible perception
and relation to the world, our epistemological constructs are given a further
turn by Henry's lesson on seeing and reading in his autobiographical short
piece "Entries into the Autobiographical I" (2000). "Entries" is structured
as a sweat lodge ceremony that plays with static definitions of genre and any
clear-cut borders between written and oral. The ritual, thus articulated as
written orality, consists of four doors framed by an initial evocation and a
final invocation.

Henry's "Evocation" refers to land and ancestors "farther back beyond
the current conventions of names and numbers, beyond the skins and
skeins of dark heavy liquid" (2000, 165), and he prays that he may "live in a
good way with the gifts of creation" (165). The First Door of the ceremony

following this evocation is entitled "I as Not I," and it consists of a list of more than two hundred labels that he rejects. "I am not," he mentions, for example, "postmodern or modern; a sign, or a signifier, between signifieds; surreal or existential; neo-traditional or beat; transcendental or metaphysical; confessional, shaman, warrior, or sun priest; trickster, nationalist, exile, or anthropocentric" (165). Henry includes both positive and negative stereotypes in an exhaustive list of expectations generally associated with the *Indian*, a constructed, stereotypical, and prevailing invention of the West. But his definition of the self in opposition is not a simple one, for the author is also well aware of the need to admit his relation to these images: "No, I am none of these," he claims; "Still, they are my relations and for them I am thankful" (167). What started as an escape from essentialism in the definition of identity, then, has to combine difference *and* relation, becoming an affirmation of the self that cannot and will not escape the acknowledgment of the other, and this dialogic vision is one of Henry's most outstanding and productive postindian achievements.

In the Second Door, Henry becomes "I as Traveler I," he starts playing with the first-person pronoun / organ of vision homophony—I is the eye that sees, the subject of vision who sees and interprets the world in his own terms, thus subverting the Western colonizing impulse to see, categorize, and dominate—and he resorts to poetic form to represent biographical facts in chronological order: he mentions White Earth, his reservation of origin, his Bear clan, his childhood sickness and constant travels as the son of a father in the military, his Catholic education and school games and friends, and the significant elders in his life. Often using the first-person plural to place himself in community, he mentions his search for identity as a young man, troubled, looking for answers and putting great events and particular anecdotes at the same level of significance in his learning process. He marries, has three daughters, keeps on traveling, and he rediscovers Native spirituality in sweat lodge ceremonies, naming ceremonies and ultimately, the thirsty dance ceremony, "when the idea of self / becomes too much / for others / to carry, when we know / we are truly home" (2000, 173–74).

The Third Door, "I as Alter I—An Autobiographical Meta-Tale on Writing" mixes prose, poetry, and fiction to recount the development of Henry's relationship to writing. It all starts as the need for words to make up for the lack of images due to his limited vision and a lost camera, and it evolves from a writing workshop, where he is expected to write about stolen land, to the inspiration of his ancestors through dream:

> There was a past I couldn't live in, a past of languages and words I never learned, a past of words my father couldn't share. So as a child I was never a speaker and the comfort I received grew not out of words, but out of the resilience of a Native presence of my father's grandparents and their ways. . . . When I stopped thinking of myself I knew who I was and where I came from and I believed in this dream the way I believe that the spirits of the ones who raised my fathers raised me up. (2000, 176)

After a personal crisis when he has "no desire to live or write" (178), Henry is healed thanks to traditional elder Francis Cree, from Turtle Mountain, who teaches him strength and acceptance and opens his ceremonies to him. His recovery is manifested in his giving in to giving up writing (178), for this learning helps him recognize "the gifts of creation." He writes,

> I began to understand the deep and profound ways of seeing that being in ceremony involved. These ways of seeing and understanding helped me to recognize the stories in all things; these ways of seeing helped me to try and see the cumulative past in the being present. My life opened and kept opening. (179)

The Fourth Door, "I as Still Open I—From Spain, 1994" is set in a metro station in Madrid and has the ceremonial element of fire as its link: the light that a street vendor gives him for his cigarette takes him to the sweat fires and stories back at home. The door is still open, his eyes are still open, and place is a ceremonial space of relation. The final "Invocation" closes the ceremonial circle and links the ancestors to the children in the future, thanking those who inspire the spirit of creation with good words and good works.

Throughout the text, Henry resorts to the I/eye homophony in order to subvert and revise narrative form and content. The first-person I is a traveling, open eye who exerts the power to see and interpret the world around him in his own terms. Traditionally, it was the Western subject who was able to see and thus categorize and dominate the Natives, but now it is the Native who looks back and writes back too. This is also related to a subversion of the ear and eye dichotomies, whereby the Natives of North America—as other indigenous peoples elsewhere—were supposed to privilege the sense of hearing by means of an oral tradition, whereas the West mastered seeing, reading, and writing. Contemporary Native American authors bring the oral tradition to writing in order to find a legitimate voice with a right to belong in American literature as they assert Native differences, a means to survive through transformation. This entails a negotiation between an oral tradition (Native) and a written tradition (Western), which necessarily subverts the oral versus written cultures approach that has supported dichotomies such as preliterate/literate, oral/visual, primitive/civilized. Since these pairs sustain a hierarchical system of cultural organization and prevailing power inequality, it becomes compelling to deconstruct them as absolute opposites, outlining their interdependence instead: the dialogue between the oral and the written thus becomes a means of ideological re/vision of the utmost importance for cultural relations.

All these meanings are directly related to the ceremonial structure of the text. The purpose of Native ceremony is to transform an individual's relation to his or her people, environment, ancestors, spirits, past, and place in the world. It is directly aimed at healing, where health, according to Karla Sanders, is understood as a state of "wellbeing and wholeness; it is the condition of emotional, spiritual, and physical balance within an individual as well as between that subject and his/her family and community" (154). Henry's textual ceremony creates a meaningful identity for him in dialogue with the other in its broadest possible sense, where dialogue always includes both difference and relation. In his definition of the postindian self, Henry resorts to Native American literature as a ceremony that is aimed at changing preconceptions about the other in the reader, underlining the power of language to transform the self and reality. Through ceremony, in Henry's words, one can see the stories in all things, and these stories offer a lesson on how to see/read the Native American self that can become theory.

My dialogue with this specific text starts from or has resulted in two basic assumptions:[4] firstly, that the reading of a Native autobiographical story entails an unstable moment of representativity, or a creative play between the one and the many, the particular and the general; and secondly, that the key to understanding a Native autobiographical text can be found both within itself and in all its relations, literary and extraliterary. Its interpretation necessarily engages the reader in a dialogue with other accounts of Native autobiography—theoretical and literary, past and to-be-published—and thus becomes part of an open conversation of significant stories and theories about Native selves.

Many Native writers will openly admit that they cannot speak for or claim to know about all the Natives in the United States. Besides being an act of honesty and responsibility, hesitating to assume the spokesperson role they are so often expected to fulfill entails an affirmation of the individual speaking voice and self. Nevertheless, and irrespective of the writer's intentions, the moment a Western reader knows about the ethnicity of the author, a series of expectations will unavoidably be activated. The story of an academic reading of a Native text—and all ethnic texts for that matter—often becomes a search for theory, a quest for connection, a transition from here to there, from the particular text to the general relevance. On the other hand, it is by no means uncommon for critics to establish a relationship to Native texts by reading them as examples that prove certain expectations, preconceptions, or theories. The best possible answer to these questions in ethical terms may be a recognition of individual positioning in the process of writing, reading, and interpreting. And of course, we need to be ready to listen to the story in the text, for it may speak differently than we expected. This is the case with Gordon Henry's "Entries," which shows us the process of ceremony learning and related open-eyedness, calling us to put our ways of reading and interpreting the Native American self under serious re/vision.

Most old stereotypes of the noble or cruel savage can be more or less easily recognized and discarded by many people today. But there are other more subtle—although similarly damaging—accounts of the same limitations, like the seemingly generalized admission that there is no such thing as the *Native American individual self*, which would likewise limit the participation of

Native Americans as individuals in the contemporary world. This idea is part of the generally accepted definition of the Native American as tribal and communal *instead of,* for example, urban and individual. My emphasis falls not on the positive characterization of these or other Native features, but on the ethnic either/or rhetoric, and in the negation implied in the affirmation of such differences. In *Ethnocriticism,* an illuminating study of Native American autobiography, Arnold Krupat assumes the existence of significant differences between the Native and the Western sense of self as shown in autobiographical texts (1992, 205). According to his view, the Native American self

> would seem to be less attracted to introspection, expansion, or fulfillment than the Western self appears to be. It would seem relatively uninterested in such things as the "I-am-me" experience, and a sense of uniqueness or individuality. More positively, one might perhaps instantiate an "I-am-we" experience as descriptive of the Native sense of self, where such a phrase indicates that I understand myself as a self only in relation to the coherent and bounded whole of which I am a part. (209–10)

In his subsequent articulation of the Western self as metonymic and the Native self as synecdochic, Krupat consistently underlines *difference and separation from* other individuals for the former, and *relation to* the group for the latter. Furthermore, he recalls Jane Fajans's distinction between "the *person* as a bounded entity invested with specific patterns of social behavior, normative powers, and restraints, and the *individual* as an entity with interiorized conscience, feelings, goals, motivations, and aspirations." Within this opposition, according to Krupat, "Native Americans (along with most of the world's people, it would seem) tend to construct themselves *not* as individuals *but* as persons" (1992, 210, emphasis added).[5]

The basic candidate for re/vision of this and related theories of the self is the insistent emphasis on negation and the focus on fixed, past images of the Native American. In fact, such generalization—which as strategic essentialisms can sometimes be useful and even necessary, especially for teaching purposes—cannot account for a Native individual personality that may be interested in introspection, expansion, or fulfillment even while she or he belongs in a group of people. That is, these generalizations do not recognize, as Gordon Henry's story does, that one does not have to be *either* an individual *or* a person, but can be an individual person who makes certain choices under specific conditions, and who can be both independent and social, without one denying the other. Far from meaning to silence the importance of community for Native Americans, who still have a fight to win over colonial fragmentation and separation, it is basically the ethnic and gender association in either/or terms that I feel openly uncomfortable with. I am also assuming that a theory will only be truthful when it keeps a reasonable relation to story. If a theory about a group of people does not correspond to the individuals in that group, then it should be revised; otherwise, it will lead to awkward questions of authenticity out of which little good can come. Being able to perceive the other as a full, complex human being capable of changing is by no means a trivial matter, and in the Native American case, there is an obvious risk in the more or less accepted assumption of a nonautonomous Native self in a world where the self is necessary in order to exist socially, politically, economically, or educationally. As I see it, the nature of the self is one more element of difference that, not too surprisingly perhaps, is often emphasized to the Natives' disadvantage in the modern world. And I wonder, couldn't we take the self, whatever its allegiances, Native or Western, as being placed in social, political, economic, historical, and educational contexts, and capable of transformation in cultural contact, so that differences are really a matter of emphasis rather than a matter of opposition? Would this not make mutual understandings possible in the present? Wouldn't that be our first and foremost aim, the main story in our theories, beyond repeated simplifications that do not exactly work when applied to living human beings? Would anybody like to be perceived as anything but a being capable of instability, even ambiguity, as human complexity and capacity for change, which are given us by the choices we make?

Gordon Henry explores, and calls readers to explore, this possibility in his text, which ceremonially constructs a dialogic identity for his individual self with different levels of relation as he makes a theoretical statement beyond the oppositions in other visions of the Native self. He teases association to "synecdoche, collective or unconscious, anima or inanimate" (2000, 167) in his list of "I-am-nots," which he denies but then recognizes as his relations, and this kind of dynamic relation requires a disposition towards change, as being in ceremony helps us see: Henry is a traveler and he will be a traveler, his life is articulated as a narrative of progression, he shows clear introspection, and the things that happen to him are things that happen to *him* as an individual, the most fundamental of which may be his particular recovery of the sense of community. It is in his individual road and set of experiences that this link with parents and grandparents is recovered, or newly acquired. That is, the communal is for him part of his life journey, and it should be viewed not as a marker of Native authenticity or essential nature but as a story of human choice placed in context.

As he teases out the content of autobiographical expectations about Native Americans in his story of human possibility, Henry's ceremonial form opens a re/vision of theory and an engagement in critical dialogues. By opening us to ceremony, he is directly asking us to read his life story not through stereotypes of any kind, old or new, but with open eyes that can see a human being in the process of changing, just as ambiguous and complex as a person can be perceived in person, with a central reference to the fire that takes him home in a circle but also a linear progress like any other living individual would be expected to experience. He is asking us not to classify him or his life in simple terms and to read him as we would listen to him in person, see him as we would in ceremony, open-eyed. The ethical aspect of the text is broadened as the responsibility of the reader becomes more obvious. This lesson makes it a good ceremony.

■ Creative Circles: Ethical Conclusions, Story Openings

As we start reading a story, previous knowledge is activated: we have heard and read more stories, we are aware of more theories, and our familiar stories and theories placed in the context of our experience are the lenses through which we see reality, the patterns into which we try to make the new material fit. In order to see the world fully and the sample of it that is offered to us in the text, and to believe what we see instead of seeing just what we believe in, it is important that our lenses allow for some unfocusing, that the frame is not cemented but loosely arranged, so that we can let the new story exert its transforming power over us. It is from this widely open-eyed standpoint that a story takes us back to a theory, revising and rebuilding it, and that the modified theory will take us back to the story once more, expanding the possibilities of perception in an unending circle of relations.

Henry's narratives of the Native body and self let us theoretically reconsider the apprehension of Native history and autobiography in such a way that both story and theory illuminate one another. His work becomes a good example of how a (Native) text can unfocus and disarrange, only to revise and rearrange creatively a reader's ways of reading, and thus fulfill the basic transforming function of ceremony. It is only fair that an individual person guide us to the way she or he should be perceived in her or his literature, and nothing but due attention to the instructions that Henry proposes—which will in turn illuminate the way we think about other people, Native or not—will respond to what is actually written there, for the text leaves us no alternative except to become active participants in this reading ceremony. Any provisional conclusion, which is nothing more than an opening, would have to admit that knowledge is possible, but it is also constructed, positioned, and questionable, and all we can do is look at ourselves and at the position we are occupying in the courtroom, in the sweat lodge, in the room where we are reading.

That said, this essay, like any essay, can be nothing more, and it will be nothing less, than a story interpretation, an interpretation story.

NOTES

The research carried out for the writing of this article was financed by the Spanish Ministry of Education and the European Regional Development Fund (MCYT DGI/FEDER, HUM2004-00344), in collaboration with the Aragonese Regional Government (DGA, ref.: H05).

1. Just as part of my assumption is my own positioning as a Western academic reader, part of my conclusion goes beyond such limiting ethnic associations, which is why my

reflections on how *I* or *we* are addressed by Native texts directly refer to lessons aimed at the Western reader, but are by no means restricted to such ethnic categories.

2. The short story web is a hybrid form between the novel and the short story by means of which authors like Henry articulate a dialogical or postindian conception of language and identity as an instrument of re/vision of both Western and Native formal and cultural assumptions. For a more detailed analysis of the form and its cultural implications in *The Light People,* see Martínez-Falquina, forthcoming.

3. This includes "Requiem for a Leg," "Oshawanung's Story: Waking in the Library," "Systems and Witnesses for the Museum," and "The Anthro's Tale."

4. I have no alternative but to make time circular here, for lack of the means to prove unambiguous linearity. I may have had those expectations—or some measure of them, or a predisposition towards them—before I actually read the text for the first time. I certainly reached or confirmed these ideas after reading the whole text and carefully thinking about it. I am not claiming to have adopted, inherited, or even learned a Native notion of time, which has been generally described as circular in opposition to Western linearity. It is the latter concept of teleological continuity, and the overall opposed simplification that I am consistently trying to question.

5. Krupat admits that "Indian sense of self" and "Western sense of self" are not monolithic (1992, 207), that not all autobiographies by Native people must take synecdoche as their defining figure or reject an account of individualism, just as not all Western autobiography is metonymic: he excludes Western women, briefly acknowledging in a note that, whereas men tend toward metonymic presentations of self, "women—in this like Indians and tribal peoples generally—tend toward synecdochic presentations of self" (217); certain forms of Christian autobiography; and writing devoted to political egalitarianism, all of which seems like a large exception to keep confirming the rule. He also applies his images to contemporary texts by Native Americans like Silko's *Storyteller* (1981) or Vizenor's *The Trickster of Liberty* (1987) (230–31). However, the fixed sense of difference and his emphasis on past, masculine definitions prevail in the development of his idea as presented above, an insistence by no means exceptional to Krupat's work but persistent in much of contemporary criticism and thought.

WORKS CITED

Henry, Gordon D., Jr. 1994. *The Light People*. Norman: University of Oklahoma Press.

———. 2000. "Entries into the Autobiographical I." In *Here First: Autobiographical Essays by Native American Writers,* edited by Arnold Krupat and Brian Swann, 165–81. New York: Random House.

hooks, bell. 1989. *Talking Back: Thinking Feminist, Thinking Black*. Boston: South End Press.

Krupat, Arnold. 1992. *Ethnocriticism: Ethnography, History, Literature*. Berkeley and Los Angeles: University of California Press.

Martínez-Falquina, Silvia. Forthcoming. "Gordon Henry's *The Light People:* The Native American Short Story Web and Postindian Identity." In *Cultural Representations in the Short Story Sequence,* edited by Jeff Birkenstein and Robert Luscher.

Phelan, James. 1998. "Sethe's Choice: *Beloved* and the Ethics of Reading." *Style* 32.2 (Summer): 318–33.

Sanders, Karla J. 1998. "A Healthy Balance: Religion, Identity, and Community in Louise Erdrich's *Love Medicine*." *Melus* 23.2: 129–55.

Bearheart: Gerald Vizenor's Compassionate Novel

MICHAEL WILSON

ike Mourning Dove's *Cogewea,* Gerald Vizenor's *Bearheart: The Heir-ship Chronicles* (1990)[1] combines two disparate narrative forms: an indigenous four-worlds narrative and a linear reversal of the narrative of westward American expansion. Unlike *Cogewea,* however, these two narratives are not contentious—in fact, they become intertwined in the first chapters and ultimately combine to form the unified narrative for the novel. *Bearheart,* then, sets aside binary, scientific desire for the purity or authenticity of indigenous forms, along with the subsequent belief that any mixing of traditions is a debasement. *Bearheart* instead revels in the intersection or crossroads between these forms; indeed, as a combination of these narrative forms, the novel itself becomes an embodiment of a vital, hybrid- or mixed blood space. To illustrate this hybrid space, Vizenor frequently turns to trickster stories from Anishinabe oral traditions, the crossroads character who allegorically enacts a dynamic tension between conventional and un-conventional behaviors, beliefs, and forms, who ultimately offers fluid yet stable, self-conscious yet powerful narratives of culture, identity, and political resistance.[2]

In the novel, the character who most clearly occupies this borderland is Proude Cedarfair, the leader of a group of thirteen mostly mixed blood pilgrims traveling from the headwaters of the Mississippi in Minnesota to the pueblos of the Southwest. Proude and his wife Rosina have managed to save their homeland, a stand of sacred cedar trees, from the engines of progress and from tribal avarice by leaving the trees in hopes they will be forgotten. As they travel to the Southwest, Proude and Rosina welcome other pilgrims to their party, most of whom lack their altruism and compassion, and who allegorically fall into two distinct types. On the one hand, certain characters are extremely dedicated to their cherished beliefs about "race," culture, and identity—even assigning a morality to these beliefs or "terminal creeds," as Vizenor frequently refers to them. On the other hand, other characters have little or no concern for social questions, much like the amoral tricksters from oral traditions who care only for their immediate desires. Mediating between these two alternatives is what Vizenor terms "the compassionate trickster" in the form of Proude, his protégé Inawa Binwide, and to some extent Rosina.

In the introduction to his early collection *anishinabe adisokan: Tales of the People* (1970), Vizenor first refers to this trickster as "compassionate" because of the trickster's qualities as a helper and sometimes a healer. These stories initially appeared in the late 1800s in *The Progress*, a newspaper on the White Earth Reservation, and were originally edited and published by Theodore Hudon Beaulieu, a relation to Vizenor. Revised further and annotated by Vizenor, *anishinabe adisokan* contains stories about cultural and history, including trickster stories that demonstrate how the trickster helps human beings understand and live in the world. For instance, in one of the stories the infant trickster tells his grandmother: "My name is manabozho and I shall do many things for the comfort of you and your people" (Vizenor 1970, 95). Manabozho's notable feats include obtaining fire for his grandmother, exacting revenge for the perceived murder of his mother, and defeating an evil gambler. Sometimes gaining inspiration from his dreams, the trickster provides instructions on how to build a birch bark canoe, how to use herbs for healing, and how to make beaver pelts into blankets. The trickster, in fact, saves the Anishinabe people from destruction, for, the stories tell us, his defeat of the evil gambler determined "the destiny of *manabozho* and the salvation of the *anishinabe* people" (149).

While his compassionate qualities are predominating in these seven trickster stories, the stories in *anishinabe adisokan* also show that the trickster can be vengeful and at times even cruel. Manabozho, for instance, threatens his grandmother's life when she withholds information about his parentage; he also (unjustly) kills a whale and later desires to kill the *manito,* "the spirit of the *anishinabe*" (Vizenor 1990, glossary). Writing later of the trickster in *The People Named the Chippewa,* Vizenor comments: "More than a magnanimous teacher and transformer, the trickster is capable of violence, deceptions, and cruelties: the realities of human imperfections" (Vizenor 1984, 4). In part because of the trickster's unpredictable qualities, Paul Radin claims that the trickster is essentially amoral: "He possesses no values, moral or social, is at the mercy of his appetites, and yet through his actions all values come into being" (1972, xxiii).

Similarly, Carl Jung, whose essay "On the Psychology of the Trickster Figure" is included in Radin's volume, argues that the trickster does not correspond to human laws and reason: "In his clearest manifestation, he is a faithful copy of an absolutely undifferentiated human consciousness, corresponding to a psyche that has hardly left the animal level" (1972, 200). As an expression of the unconscious, Jung argues, the trickster is a parallel to the shadow in the human psyche—that is, the often unacknowledged and sometimes irrational desires and emotions that manifest themselves in dreams and or in unexpected words or actions. As a communal phenomenon, Jung further argues that this collective unconscious takes form (becomes "personified and incarnated") as a trickster in societies where the "people get together in masses and submerge the individual" (206). As part of Jung's overall vision of the human psyche, then, the trickster corresponds to the infantile, even "evil" aspect of the psyche that exists in dualistic tension with "higher consciousness," both of which comprise an "energic system" that is "dependent upon the tension of opposites" (209).

Like Jung, Vizenor proposes a dualistic, energic system to explain tricksters and their function in societies; but unlike Jung, Vizenor does not place the trickster on one side of the equation as the antithesis to civilization. Nor does he agree with Radin's conception of the trickster as essentially amoral, writing in *Earthdivers* that his own version of the trickster is "not the trickster in the word constructions of anthropologist Paul Radin" (1981, xii). Instead, Vizenor writes, the trickster mediates between two differing forces, "balanc[ing] the world between terminal creeds and humor with unusual manners and ecstatic strategies" (xii). Thus, Vizenor argues that the trickster, rather than being a figure of amorality, actively creates a balance between stasis and change, the conventional and the unconventional, the Apollonian and Dionysian. Indeed, negotiating the space between the moral certainty of "terminal creeds" and the abrogation of responsibility in pure chance, the trickster is in fact a moralizing force in certain societies and in literature. Theoretically, Vizenor's trickster is more closely associated with the African trickster figure Esu-Elegbara, described by Henry Louis Gates Jr. Gates argues that Esu-Elegbara is an ultimate mediator, providing a medium of exchange between the gods and man—both the "guardian of the crossroads" and also the "master of that elusive, mystical barrier that separates the divine world from the profane" (1988, 6). Jung himself suggests similar properties for the trickster, likening the trickster to Mercurius, who possesses a "dual nature, half animal, half divine" (1972, 195), although Jung focuses in his essay primarily on the "primitive" aspects of the trickster figure in indigenous oral traditions. Both Vizenor and Gates, however, foreground the trickster's power to negotiate between differing sides in putative opposition, demonstrating the trickster's conceptual usefulness as an interpreter and therefore as a source for theories and practice of literature.

In both his fiction and his cultural criticism, Vizenor asserts the continuing value and even necessity of trickster traditions for their teaching not only about indigenous philosophies but also about current theoretical discussions of language and literature. Consequently, he objects to Jung's position that the trickster "gradually breaks up under the impact of civilization" (Jung 1972, 202) arguing instead that the trickster is "a revenant holotrope in new and recurrent narratives" (Vizenor 1989, 205). Vizenor's most sensitive critic, Kimberly M. Blaeser, likewise emphasizes that Jung undermines the trickster figure's application to contemporary indigenous people:

> Jung, too, succinctly museumizes the trickster stories of the Winnebago and denies both their satiric sophistication and any claim to contemporary applicability by characterizing the myths as a "remnant" and distinguishing between the contemporary tribal people for whom the mythic "still 'functions' provided they have not been spoiled by civilization" and the "thoughtful observer" who can presumably theorize more knowledgeably and disinterestedly about this "remnant" of culture. (1996, 141)

Jung certainly argues that the trickster evolved from a lower level of consciousness, and thus his dualistic (energic) system between civilization (the animus) and the trickster (the shadow) is necessarily hierarchical. In the early stages of their development, "before the birth of the myth," Jung reasons, American Indians were "groping . . . in mental darkness" (1972, 202). Only when they had attained a "higher level of consciousness" could they picture or objectify the "lower and inferior state" in the form of the trickster figure (202). Ultimately, for Jung, the history of human consciousness is a narrative of evolution in which healing and liberation occur when the higher plane of consciousness brings light to the mental darkness in *agnoia* or the unconsciousness.

Vizenor's concept of the compassionate trickster resists theories that create hierarchies between the conscious and the unconscious, encouraging positive manifestations of the unconscious in creativity, play, and self-criticism. Vizenor further demonstrates that such categorizations frequently result in binary exclusions, where the conscious mind—and its attendant signs, reason and intelligence—become defined as the absence of indeterminacy, contradiction, and creativity. As a result, reason becomes relegated to the simple repetition of existing ideas and language, the hardening of convention, and the valorization of the comforting but static visions of common sense and uncomplicated clarity. Vizenor calls such comforting beliefs "terminal creeds," signifying how beliefs and belief systems becomes ends in themselves (terminal), lacking the vital capacity to change, adapt, and self-criticize. In contrast, compassionate tricksterism—in the form of the novel itself or the character Proude Cedarfair—deconstructs such oppositions, reminds us that the conscious and unconscious exist as necessarily part of each other, and foregrounds the power of the liminal space between such oppositions as common sense and creativity, genre and innovation, indigenous and nonindigenous. Indeed, *Bearheart,* like many of Vizenor's works, asserts that the liminal, trickster space of crossing over—often in the form of the "mixed blood"—is neither powerless nor tragic, but is potentially quite strong and liberating.

■ Two Metanarratives

Just as the novel reflects Vizenor's concept of compassionate tricksterism through its allegory of characters, so too does the novel reflect his dynamic through its use of two forms of narrative: an episodic travel narrative and a somewhat generic version of the four-worlds prophecy of certain Southwest tribes.[3] Although *Bearheart* is a more open-ended book than Leslie Marmon Silko's *Ceremony* (published one year before *Bearheart*), it is actually structurally similar because it combines a linear narrative with an indigenous story form, with both narratives merging at the end. Vizenor's conception of the linear narrative is different, however, because he offers it primarily as a critique of American colonialism. When asked whether the novel is a pilgrimage in the tradition of Dante, Chaucer, and Bunyan, Vizenor replies, "My first consideration was a conversion of the themes of discovery, western expansion, and manifest destiny" (2000, 96). By pointing specifically to Manifest Destiny, Vizenor thus challenges one of the most willfully blind terminal creeds in the history of the Americas, a concept that not only justified the greed for Mexican and Indian land and California gold, but actually regarded such inhumanity as being natural, inevitable, and even ordained by God. John L. O'Sullivan, the originator of the term, writes in 1845 that it is the nation's "manifest destiny to overspread and to possess the whole of the continent which Providence has given us for the development of the great experiment of liberty and federated self-government entrusted to us" (1845). A concept that even now continues to be taught uncritically in American schools, Manifest Destiny is an attempt to provide an quasi-religious alibi for the basest of human instincts, and, like so many stories about American history, it masks, wittingly and not, an underlying horror that Americans wish to ignore or forget. *Bearheart,* then, takes this concept and reverses its teleological movement, rejecting outright the presumed moral valence of providential progress and its attendant devastating effects.

As the pilgrims journey southward, they continue to witness the results of providential progress, as they themselves move backward in time toward the precolonial, indigenous city of Mesa Verde ("walking backward," as the Hopi clowns tell them). The movement of the pilgrims enacts a reversal of the phylogeny of America, which has taken the ethos of greed to its logical end: namely, the loss of natural resources and the devaluation of humanity in the pursuit of personal gain. The narrator tells us: "Economic power had become the religion of the nation; when it failed, people turned to their own violence and bizarre terminal creeds for comfort and meaning" (Vizenor 1990, 23). When, for example, the pilgrims enter the town of Big Walker in an automobile (a rarity because few cars have fuel), the people in the town fight each other for no other reason than to have a chance to ride. Eventually the excessive weight from the passengers causes sparks to fly underneath the car, igniting the gas in the tank and killing many of them. This irrational desire to ride a car illustrates, in macabre microcosm, how an entire society continues to embrace consumption as an ethos even while it takes them to their death. At other times, the novel foregrounds the coincidences of their reversal of the narrative of westward expansion, even to the point of absurdity. For example, when traveling down the Mississippi River, the pilgrims encounter hungry and angry "whitestudents" from a nearby college who are anxious to sink their boat and eat their dogs. To ward off enemies as did his great-great-grandfather, the explorer Giacomo Constantino Beltrami, "Bigfoot" Saint Plumero takes the form of a compassionate trickster, distracting the students from their ill humor by opening a red umbrella and dancing around the boat in precisely the same way that Beltrami did many years before to avoid confrontation with indigenous people (72). In fact, Bigfoot not only uses the same method as Beltrami, he also uses the very same umbrella, purchased at an estate sale in the cities, at exactly the same spot to distract the hostiles in the area.

Along with this linear reversal of westward expansion, the novel also employs the indigenous narrative of the emergence of human beings through four worlds, thus combining, in the manner of a compassionate trickster, narratives from both Native and non-Native traditions. In the opening chapter "Heirship Chronicles," the narrator describes the first two of these worlds as filled with creation and magic, when the earth turtle emerged from the waters and the animals spoke to humans. The third world, however, loses its life-affirming qualities, and reflects the deathly conditions the pilgrims find during their journey: "The third world turns evil with contempt for living and fear of death. Solemn figures are slashed open on the faces of tribal dream drums" (Vizenor 1990, 5). Only the philosophy of the compassionate trickster can overcome the end result of terminal creeds that have ravaged the continent: "In the fourth world evil spirits are outwitted in the secret language of animals and birds. Bears and crows choose the new singers" (5).

The narrative of the emergence through four worlds occurs in several ways in the novel. For example, in the prefatory section entitled "The Letter to the Reader," *Bearheart* playfully suggests that the fourth world is the retirement of an old bureaucrat working at the Bureau of Indian Affairs as a keeper of records. He writes: "We are finished with the third world now, and we wait here in the darkness, less than one month from federal retirement" (Vizenor 1990, vii). In fact, the personal history of this bureaucratic author of the *Heirship Chronicles* foreshadows both the narrative structure and thematic concerns in his work. For example, although the youthful American Indian Movement (AIM) activist Songidee Migwan treats him with contempt, the old bureaucrat has undergone considerable hardship in his life (his own version of the third world), having been taken as a child to boarding school and punished in progressively worse ways as he tries to escape. As a youth, he attempted to escape four times, suggesting the fourth world emergence that his life is about to perform, in the form of retirement. This sequence also adumbrates the four generations of Proude Cedarfairs, as well as the journey of the Proude and Inawa through the third world to transcendence in the fourth at the close of the novel. Furthermore, it is after his fourth escape that the old bureaucrat learns the vital role of the compassionate trickster dealing with the evil of the third world. He tells us that he and his animal helpers "learned to outwit the government in darkness" (viii) as a means of remaining "untamed" and surviving without "assimilation" and "tribal death."

As the author of the novel proper (*The Heirship Chronicles*), the old BIA official uses similar imagery to begin and end the narrative: in the Minnesota cedars, the Fourth Proude "dreams in sudden moods and soars through stone windows on the solstice sunrise" (Vizenor 1990, 5), adumbrating the stone windows and soaring transcendence both Proude and his protégé Inawa Biwide find at Chaco Canyon. Furthermore, the BIA author parallels the four-worlds narrative with four incarnations of Proude Cedarfairs. The first Proude is a compassionate trickster who outwits evil "in the secret language of animals and birds," frightening encroaching loggers by growling like a bear and laughing at them as they leave. But the methods of the compassionate trickster are lost on his son, the second Proude, who learns, through his service in World War I, the ways of warfare. The second Proude becomes an activist and uses tactics he learned while in the American military rather than humor to defend the cedars against corrupt tribal officials. Eventually, the second Proude is shot to death by tribal policemen while he is on his way to fight with the members of the American Indian Movement at Wounded Knee. With the third Proude, the pendulum swings back toward compassion and humor: he was raised by women who "taught him to seek peace and avoid conflict" so that he "abhorred violence more than evil and corruption" (14–15). He dies prematurely from a lightning strike while bathing in the river, but his legacy continues with the fourth Proude, who sacrifices his own peaceful existence in the sacred cedar so that they might be saved.

The four Proude Cedarfairs are able to halt the narrative of Manifest Destiny by denying the minions of progress ownership of the cedar forest: the loggers, corrupt tribal officials, the two bicycle-riding federal employees, and finally Jordan Coward. Each, in turn, loses out to the ecstatic strategies of the Proude Cedarfairs, even though they begin their quest completely resolute in the terminal belief that they have claim to the woods. In the case of the loggers and Jordan Coward, an elected tribal president, the Proude Cedarfairs employ humor, fear, and trickery to ensure the survival of the trees. With the two federal employees, the fourth Proude first learns about their "insecurities" before later becoming a "clown"—"a compassionate trickster for the afternoon, a bear from the cedar" (Vizenor 1990, 20). Then, as a compassionate trickster, the fourth Proude uses bluntness and humor to create a union between these two very different federal employees. The federal man is physically weak but has an intuitive connection with the cedar forests, perhaps through his father, who, ironically, lost his reservation summer cabin when the tribal government took it back. The federal woman, in contrast, is physically strong but refuses to acknowledge anything except the letter of the executive order to cut down the trees. She disdains human contact and becomes angry with Proude for emphasizing "sexual differences" (29). By mere suggestion, the fourth Proude prods the federal man and woman into a sexual liaison that connects the hard-edged federal woman to the fecund, life-giving properties of the cedar forests; she then neglects to mention in her report that the trees even exist.

■ *Bearheart* as a Moral Novel

Introduced early in the novel, the federal man and federal woman foreshadow two general types of characters whom Rosina and Proude meet throughout their travels: those who adhere to terminal creeds, and those who challenge the bounds of convention, often through their sexual desires and practices. In the tradition of indigenous oral stories, especially those in Vizenor's *anishinabe adisokan,* the characters often suggest, almost allegorically, an affiliation with general ideas of the conventional and the unconventional (although not allegorical to the extent of those characters in, for instance, *Pilgrim's Progress*).[4] Perhaps because the novel follows in this indigenous oral tradition, the characters in *Bearheart* lack developed psychologies in the tradition of modern realist fiction; it is unclear, for instance, why most of the pilgrims choose to follow Proude southward except that they seem to recognize his shamanistic power. Kimberly Blaeser suggests that "while most of the American Indian novels in print are still clearly plot-centered, Vizenor's writing is more idea-centered" (1996, 202). Where desires are explained (Lilith Mae Farmer's love of her dogs, Bigfoot Plumero's love of his statue and later his desire for Rosina) or when desires are shown (Little Big Mouse's desire to possess the victims of pollution), such desires are highly unconventional and always result in violence. On the other side, those who adhere too closely to terminal creeds or conventions either perish in violence (Belladonna Darwin Winter Catcher) or do not complete the trip to the Southwest (Justice Pardone Cozener and Doctor Wilde Coxwain). In the final pages of the novel, the only survivors are those who manage to negotiate between these two extremes: Proude and his wife Rosina, and two other pilgrims, Inawa Binwidi and Pio Wissakodewinini, who arrive damaged, both becoming blinded for their efforts, unable to realize the final vision of transcendence that ends the journey.

In fact, for all its violence and its stylistic innovation, *Bearheart* is finally a moral novel, holding up the ethos of compassionate tricksterism as the only viable response to the dual forces of terminal beliefs and chaos, both of which create and later predominate in this futuristic vision of a world that is no longer in balance. In an early essay about Bearheart, Mareen Keady writes: "As strange as events of *Bearheart* may be, Vizenor's novel is really a teaching tale about truth and choice, about those who are willing to sacrifice their 'Terminal Creeds' for real meaning, and those who will not" (1985, 62).⁵ More recently, Vizenor says in an interview, "The pilgrims who died on the journey lost the games because of their own greed, intensities, cultural reductions, traditional simulations, terminal creeds, absolutist views, and because of their temptations to court authority" (1999, 109). In episode after episode, Proude and his fellow pilgrims encounter a third world filled with violence and death, and it is essential that they be highly adept at negotiating with evil through humor, avoidance, and, in the case of Proude, shamanistic power from the spirit of the bear. Despite Proude's presence, however, they are not always successful, for Proude and Rosina lose almost as many pilgrims as they pick up along the way. Consequently, the novel becomes a kind of moral crucible, in effect burning away those characters that are unable or unwilling to maintain the difficult balancing act of the compassionate trickster.

Belladonna Darwin Winter Catcher is perhaps the clearest example of a character that cannot complete the pilgrimage because of her terminal beliefs. As Maureen Keady writes: "The cookie that kills her is, in effect, the poison of her own false-pride and superiority" (1984, 64). At the walled community of Orion, the "famous hunters" and "horse breeders" perform a kind of social purification by killing visitors who adhere too closely to their dogmatic beliefs. Their motivation for such drastic acts, the novel suggests, is that hunters in Orion are exposing the spiritual death of passing pilgrims. A woman from Orion tells Bishop Parasimo, "People are the living dead with the unquestioned church in them" (Vizenor 1990, 192). Like the trophies the hunters and horse breeders kept in former days, the Orion community maintains a large, leather-bound book containing the signatures and "one line thoughts" of all those who have failed to pass their test. During a banquet, Belladonna speaks for the pilgrims and chooses to discuss tribal values, but she relies upon clichéd, binary distinctions between her indigenous values and those of the hunters and breeders. Because Belladonna uses blood as a signal marker of her identity as an indigenous person, her task is theoretically hampered from the outset because, as we learn from the previous chapter (and as her name suggests)[6] she herself is a mixed blood. The inhabitants of Orion have little difficulty dismantling her claims, suggesting, for instance, that she relies on an "invented" concept of Indians, that she presumes to speak for all Native people, and that does not speak from "real experience and critical substance" (196). Although frustrated and angry, Belladonna is quickly brought back to good humor with false praise and admiration, indicating, one breeder says, that Belladonna's (or anyone's) terminal beliefs are closely associated with narcissism.[7]

Yet, because the community of Orion has little compassion for those who hold terminal creeds, it too has its own peculiar kind of narcissism. Indeed, Orion is cut off from the rest of the world by its imposing red walls, metaphorically emphasizing the genetic (blood) makeup of the community. The writing on the wall to the entrance reads (in part): "Within the red walls live several families who were descendents of famous hunters and western bucking horse breeders. Like good horses, we are proud people who keep to ourselves and our own breed" (Vizenor 1990, 189). As Bishop Omax Parasimo observes, Orion appears to contain elements of the creed it rejects: "Your wall is more terminal than the church" (193). Although the community of Orion, like Proude, abjures terminal creeds, it lacks Proude's tolerance, compassion, and thus at least the possibility of any positive engagement with the world. Through their incessant questioning, the people of Orion keep themselves in a constant state of uncertainty to avoid any possibility of possessing terminal creeds. Their approach, however, places them within the well-known postmodernist dilemma of having, on the one hand, the salutary function of exposing the presumed "naturalness" of terminal creeds, but on the other hand, the difficulty of having any positive ground upon which to engage the world in meaningful ways. As Linda Hutcheon writes regarding a similar dilemma for postmodernism and feminism, "There has been an understandable suspicion of the deconstructing and undermining impulse of postmodernism at a historic moment when construction and support seem more important agendas for women" (1989, 20). In its depiction of Orion, *Bearheart* critiques certain forms of postmodernism, suggesting that its narcissism extends to both those holding terminal creeds and those who have nothing more to offer than the never-ending deconstruction of the world.

While exposing the dangers of terminal creeds, the novel equally critiques the amorality of narcissistic tricksters as well—in particular, the trickster figures Bigfoot Plumero and especially Matchi Makwa. Having little regard for others in the novel, Matchi Makwa most resembles Paul Radin's formulation of the trickster who possesses "no values, moral or social" and who is "at the mercy of his appetites." Indeed, as with many tricksters from indigenous oral traditions, his appetite for sex results in his death. When he and other pilgrims attempt to free witches hanging from a ceiling in a restaurant in Oklahoma, Matchi Makwa and the witch are so overcome with their sexual desires that they immediately copulate on a restaurant table, where the restaurant owner finds and kills them. Matchi Makwa appears particularly disdainful of his structural opposite Belladonna Darwin Winter Catcher, the purveyor of terminal creeds. When Belladonna lovingly quotes the translated words of Ten Bears, the Comanche chief, Matchi Makwa responds, "Superserious crap" (Vizenor 1990, 113). And later, when Belladonna bemoans the fate of the cancerous cripples, Matchi Makwa calls her musings "squaw rubbish." The reason Matchi Makwa makes such outlandish statements, the narrator tells us, is that he "seeks most opportunities for public attention, flourishing on the disadvantage of others" (145). Proude also makes clear that, although Matchi Makwa's mother married a mountain bear, Matchi Makwa himself "never speaks with bears." Indeed, because Matchi Makwa uses language that separates rather than heals ("Our women were poisoned part white"), Proude refers to Matchi Makwa's use of language as "terminal" (59). Only on the occasion of meeting the cancer victims does Matchi Makwa express sympathy for others, and even here the novel suggests that he does so involuntarily: "Their incomplete bodies lived whole through phantoms and *tchibai* dreams. Matchi Makwa twitched and limped from the silent suggestion of phantoms claiming his sympathetic limbs" (145).

Unlike Matchi Makwa, Bigfoot Plumero often expresses compassion for others, but his compassion takes on unusual forms, even grotesque forms, making him capable of loving a statue and of exacting brutal revenge when it is taken from him. For example, before he encounters Proude, Bigfoot cares for Belladonna after she is raped by three men, having carried her home from the courthouse in Big Walker and possibly saving her life. In his travels with the pilgrims, Bigfoot drives through Big Walker so that Belladonna can accompany them southward. At the same time, like certain trickster figures from indigenous traditions, Bigfoot is both a creator and destroyer, capable of great good and great harm. For instance, because of his deep love for a large-footed bronze statue, Bigfoot viciously kills the anthropologist Orrel Hanson, who stole the statue from Bigfoot and planned to sell it to a dealer— a murder that is as carefully planned as it is cruel. Bigfoot also kills Sir Cecil Staples, the evil gambler, whom Proude Cedarfair defeats and incapacitates through preternatural means in an ancient game of chance. Because Sir Cecil is no longer able to mesmerize others with his chromium eyes, Bigfoot's act of righteousness is gratuitous and simply repeats the cruelty Sir Cecil wrought upon weaker people in the world. Finally, although Bigfoot is one of the few characters who negotiates the third world and completes the journey to the Southwest with Proude and Rosina, ultimately he—like Matchi Makwa—dies because of his uncontrolled sexual passion, forcing himself upon Rosina while Proude and Inawa transcend to the fourth world.

While Matchi Makwa and Bigfoot Plumero constantly demand attention from others, Proude Cedarfair is almost always reserved, even distant, rarely offering more than a few (sometimes enigmatic) words of wisdom about their circumstances. Yet without question Proude is the center of the group, attracting and uniting this incredible diversity of characters, just as he brings together the federal woman and federal man in the opening chapters of the novel. Similar to Professor Gates's description of Esu Elegbara, Proude is a copula among diverse characters in the novel—a complex and "classic figure of mediation and of the unity of opposed forces" (Vizenor 1990, 6). As a compassionate trickster, Proude looks beyond his own personal desires, taking "care to balance the world between terminal creeds and humor," exerting his considerable powers at significant moments in the novel. In the episode with Sir Cecil, for instance, Lilith Mae Farrier attempts to win precious gasoline for the pilgrims but loses because, according to Sir Cecil, she "was possessed for one toss of the dish but then lost her good power through her own selfish need for praise and credit" (129). Because Proude lacks Lilith Mae's narcissism and also because he possesses preternatural powers, he easily defeats the evil gambler, ridding the world of a severe imbalance of good and evil. (Lilith Mae is so consumed with narcissistic fears about her body after death that she immolates herself and her dogs with gasoline.) Later in the novel, Proude likewise exhibits the qualities of a compassion trickster when, following the deaths of Belladonna Darwin Winter Catcher, Matchi Makwa, and Bishop Parasimo, he ceremonially takes care of their remains, acting as a kind of bridge between this world and the next. With Belladonna, Proude must also see that her unborn children receive sacred names so that they may too enter the next world.

Rosina likewise acts on behalf of her other characters with a compassion that recognizes their deepest and spiritual needs. For instance, Rosina lovingly embraces Sister Willabelle, whose scars from a childhood trauma initially repulse her. Toward the close of the novel, Rosina comforts Pio Wissakodewinini, who became blind at the close of the journey because she/he opened Proude's medicine bag and gazed upon the powerful cedar figures. It is also telling that, during the word contest to determine Sir Cecil's gambling opponent, the pilgrims mostly choose words that reflect themselves and their own narcissistic desires. Matchi Makwa, for instance, lists obscenities; Bigfoot Plumero lists the names of presidents (a comment on his sexual organ), Belladonna the names of historical indigenous leaders, and so on. In contrast, Rosina and Proude choose the names of people they met along the journey, indicating that their thoughts are generally on the welfare of others. Furthermore, their altruistic compassion is distinct from other examples of compassion based once again upon narcissism, which appears from the hunters and breeders at Orion, who feign concern for the pilgrims, especially Belladonna, and also with Little Big Mouse, whose compassion for the mutilated cancer victims is actually an expression of her desire to possess them. In this episode, Little Big Mouse admires the wings of the scolioma moths because they remind her of her childhood with her mother and her dreams of flying. The moths recognize Little Big Mouse's narcissism, telling her, "You are perfect and now you want our imagination and visions for your own" (Vizenor 1990, 149).

Proude's compassion for his traveling companions, however, does not prevent him from finally leaving them to ascend to the fourth world, suggesting that he either accedes to his own version of narcissism (his transcendence ultimately helps no one but himself and Inawa) or that he understands that his powers are insufficient to affect the social conditions of the third world. The novel indicates that Proude's goal of transcendence works against his connection with others, particularly Rosina, who maintains a strong connection to her family and the pilgrims around her. It is Rosina, for instance, not Proude, who expresses concern for their daughters living in the cities, and it is Rosina who sends Proude back to the lighting hills in hopes that Bishop Parasimo might still be alive. The narrator tells us that Rosina's "life was personal. She did not see herself in the abstract as a series of changing ideologies" (Vizenor 1990, 39). As a consequence of Proude's preoccupation with transcendence, the novel implies, particularly with Hopi clown's sharp reference to Proude's "rude prize," Rosina acquiesces to Bigfoot's sexual overtures, indicating the severity of the break between Proude and Rosina, and ultimately resulting in Bigfoot's death. While Proude is able to influence nature, speak to animals, and see into the future, his powers are limited within the overarching and pervasive sense of evil in the third world. Despite his compassion for other pilgrims, for instance, seven of the thirteen pilgrims die, mostly through extreme violence. In their most desperate circumstances, when imprisoned at Santa Fe, New Mexico, Proude appears as helpless as the rest, when the group saves itself only by working for its own preternatural vision with the help of Bigfoot's "precious vision vine leaves" (232).

■ The Postmodern Politics of *Bearheart*

Whether Proude's transcendence is an act of narcissism, or whether it is recognition of immovable social circumstances (or some combination of both), the transcendent conclusion of *Bearheart* is likely predetermined by the narrative structure of four worlds' emergence set up early in the novel. Nonetheless, the conclusion to this four-worlds trajectory offers little or no hope for the people Proude and Inawa leave behind: Unlike the cedar forests that Proude leaves earlier in the novel, the rest of the world does not benefit from Proude's departure. But just as the novel has two narrative trajectories, so too does it have two quite different endings. The first is the transcendence of Proude and Inawa; the other is the possibility of resistance to the destruction and violence of the third world residing in the fireside voices of Diné singers near White Horse (New Mexico), whom the remaining four pilgrims encounter after a brief stay at Walatowa (Jemez). The narrator tells us: "Evil had been turned under with the sunrise and their sacred voices. The good power of the dawn was attracted toward their rituals. . . . The men laughed and laughed knowing the power of their voices had restored good humor to the suffering tribes" (243). The novel offers the power of indigenous ceremonialism as a kind of cure to the tremendous ills of the third world, referring to N. Scott Momadays's *House Made of Dawn,* a novel that makes similar assertions about the power of the oral tradition to keep evil at arm's length. In the second half of Momaday's novel, the protagonist Abel cannot resist his desire to exact revenge upon a corrupt (evil) policeman in Los Angeles for accosting him and his friend Ben Benally. As a consequence, the policeman almost kills Abel, beating him severely and leaving him for dead. In this terrible condition, Abel remembers the teachings of his pueblo and finally seems to understand the proper way of dealing with evil, namely, through the ceremonial dawn running at Walatowa that begins and ends the novel. These runners are charged with dividing the world at dawn between good and evil—"They were whole and indispensable in what they did; everything in creation referred to them. Because of them, perspective, proportion, design in the universe. Meaning because of them" (Momaday 1968, 104). Abel ultimately returns home and joins the dawn runners, helping the pueblo and himself by properly dealing with evil, even if he stumbles and loses pace with the other runners because of his damaged body.

House Made of Dawn examines in extraordinarily sensitive ways indigenous philosophies of good and evil, and includes the Navajo, Kiowa, and Pueblo oral traditions as part of its narrative. But its narrative methods—for example, flashbacks and psychological fragmentation—reflect the conventions of the written modernist tradition rather than indigenous oral traditions. (It is for this reason that I have not included Momaday's works nor James Welch's in this study.) In contrast, like *Ceremony* and to a lesser degree *Cogewea*, *Bearheart* completes a narrative substantially based upon Native oral traditions, in this case a generalized version of the Hopi, Diné, and Pueblo creation narratives. As Vizenor says in an interview, such four-worlds narratives are specific to indigenous communities:

> But actually, the number four in the way of the words depends on the
> time, place, and native creation story. Bearheart, the old man, envisions
> the fourth world, a season of creation and transmutation, and a world of
> shamanistic journeys and visionary survivance. (1999, 98)

On one side, the movement toward this generalized tradition with the Diné singers provides in the practical ceremonial life of indigenous people; on the other side, the move to transcendence is, at least for those in the third world (as well as readers of the text), decidedly unknowable, almost completely outside the conventional, comprehensible universe. Therefore, just as the novel mediates between terminal creeds and chaos, so too does the ending mediate, as a kind of compassionate trickster, between both the physical and spiritual worlds as well as between textual (modernist) and oral traditions (four worlds).

In avoiding a conventional narrative of closure, *Bearheart* also avoids the philosophical problems of terminal creeds. The novel remains open-ended, with several strands of the narrative unresolved, providing both complicity and critique of closure and perhaps modernism in general. In other words, the novel foregrounds the fictional nature of closure, and instead asserts its own ontological status as a fictional text. That is, the novel shows that it is not an objective reflection of reality, nor the product of an omniscient narrator or even one that especially inspires much confidence. Rather, through form, technique, and narrative structure, *Bearheart* foregrounds the textualness of his fiction, and indeed any fiction, and thus critiques as a kind "terminal creed," the world-building omniscience that must resolve tensions in the novel.

Because Vizenor's fiction often moves deftly among a variety of discourses, writers such as Alan Velie and Craig Womack consider Vizenor's work to be an example of postmodernist fiction. In his essay "The Trickster Novel," for instance, Velie argues that *Bearheart* (and postmodernist novels in general) has the salutary effect of unsettling "mainstream culture and ideology," particularly realistic fiction, which has "the air of total authenticity" (1989, 130). Velie rightly suggests that realistic fiction often offers the illusion of authenticity, not because it reflects reality more accurately, but because it accurately reflects the conventional codes of novelistic discourse—language, genre, character development, and so on. That is, realistic fiction provides readers with what they expect, the novels *seem* or *feel* real, whereas fiction such as *Bearheart* disrupts the conventional flow of reading, reminding readers to question and critique the conventional worlds—and not just fictional worlds—they inhabit. As Blaeser writes, "By unmasking all rules, revealing their true nature as fragile social constructs, [Vizenor] encourages readers to relinquish their moral props and to reevaluate things on their own merits" (1996, 185).

While Craig Womack agrees that Vizenor's aesthetic has the effect of deconstructing fixed concepts in language and culture, he challenges the value of this approach on two fronts. First, he argues that this postmodernist approach leaves no stable ground upon which to claim an identity or to fix a political movement. Second, Womack asserts that the poststructuralist language of Vizenor's aesthetic limits his audience "to a handful of academics, effectively cutting himself off from Native people" (1997, 99). To ensure that literature has the ability, in Jane Tompkins words (1986), to do "cultural work," Womack argues that Vizenor should balance his postmodernist preoccupations with "free play" against the "fixed meanings" within the reality of indigenous social and political concerns. (1997, 98) Yet as Louis Owens points out, Vizenor's trickster figure anticipates this specific criticism by "containing" both sides of the apparent Hegelian dialectic: the stasis of "terminal creeds" and the "infinite proliferation of possibility . . . so common to postmodern literature and theory" (1992, 234). Focusing on the question of indigenous identity, Owens argues that Vizenor's works offer a provisional identity within the dynamic open-endedness of narratives. He writes, "Through language, stories that assert orders rather than order upon the chaos of experience, a coherent, adaptive, and syncretic human identity is possible without the 'terminal' state of stasis" (1992, 235). We can apply this concept of "syncretic human identity" to the compassionate tricksters in the novel, as well as the novel itself, for it provides two kinds of narrative that correspond to the two sides of the "dialectic."[8] In this way, *Bearheart* responds to Womack's call for Vizenor and his critics to "mediate theory with tribal worldviews" so that his work will have sufficient grounding to be applicable to tribal life (Womack 1997, 100).

Furthermore, *Bearheart* also portrays, often graphically, contemporary realities of human violence and depravity, as well as more general political concerns about fuel shortages, indigenous land rights, and materialist philosophies replacing the value of human relationships. Through its use of postmodern metafictional techniques and its genre (futuristic fiction), the novel distances readers from this violence; nevertheless, readers often have extremely strong reactions to the graphic events in the novel. Louis Owens, for instance, relates his experience with three female Native students who reported him to the dean of his college because they were upset with the novel's "wild humor" (1990, 248). In an interview, Vizenor likewise relates his interaction with a class of college students who were angry with the violence in the book, especially the violence toward indigenous women. Vizenor says: "My first response was to say, 'What, then, is not true in this novel?' The students could not think of anything untrue in *Bearheart*. So the descriptive scenes of violence were what troubled them, not that the scenes were not true" (1990, 110).⁹ Furthermore, because *Bearheart* includes graphic scenes of death, it seems to me that the novel insists that we respond emotionally to it, but with a measure of distance that also insists that we recognize that these circumstances—like fictions themselves—are potentially of our own making if we continue to subscribe to terminal creeds. Thus, by combining the techniques of realism and metafiction, *Bearheart* mediates between two distinct approaches to constructing fictional worlds and thus performs a function parallel to that of its protagonist, Proude Cedarfair.

Womack's second criticism focuses on Vizenor's frequent references to contemporary theorists such as Jacques Derrida and Roland Barthes when describing the attributes of the compassionate trickster. Contemporary theory provides Vizenor with convenient shorthand to describe the ways that indigenous trickster figures embody the conventional and the unconventional, the sacred and the profane, a constant dynamic that prevents indigenous traditions from hardening into dogma. In addition, Vizenor (like Derrida) frequently employs neologisms—for example, *postindian, socioacupuncture,* and *paraeconomics*—that have the effect of breaking down conceptual (sometimes unconscious) preconceptions of indigenous people. Indeed, these conceptions are frequently reinforced by the apparently clarity of such of terms such as *Indian, treaty rights,* or *sovereignty,* each of which contains complex and sometimes contradictory meanings, even within tribal communities.¹⁰ Consequently, what appears to be clarity in writing and other communication that employs these terms may actually be the illusion of clarity—a kind of mask of resignation to the unconquerable elusiveness of language. At the same time, however, neologisms (and literary theory in general) sometimes have the effect, as Womack points out, of limiting the readership of Vizenor's essays to persons in the field of indigenous studies, perhaps rendering Vizenor's work incapable of adding a political voice in support tribal "sovereignty." Although there is no way to tell how literature of any kind affects federal Indian policy, Womack is probably correct that Vizenor's theoretical works are not often read by public officials, indigenous or otherwise. Yet this statement is also probably true with regard to all literary studies, including indigenous essays and fiction, even works that do not especially challenge the readership with either its form or content.

Furthermore, *Beartheart* itself questions the value of self-referential language, especially in the chapter "Word Wars on the Word Wards," where government employees play endless word games upon old government documents and recorded conversations. With the help of linguistic machinery that analyzes language for attributes such as heat content, the government employees at the Word Hospital are primarily interested in rendering language clear (no contradictions) and present (synchronic). They tell the pilgrims that "what we want out of our lives is more clearness and meaning to our words" (Vizenor 1990, 164). Later, they say that "we are still working out models and paradigms and experiments on our language to learn where we are and where we will be, all at the same time that we consider the moment at which we meet and speak" (165). The Word Hospital, then, operates upon the belief or theory that language is a medium for the exchange of communication, attempting to set aside the irreducible complexity of language for the illusion of clarity. Moreover, because the government employees can only use language to determine the meanings of language, their task is an ever-receding horizon, an Escher print of two hands drawing one another. Nevertheless, the Word Hospital receives funding because the government believes that there is a political connection between clear language and conventional institutions. Their reasoning: a breakdown in the meaning of words means a breakdown in law and order, institutions, families, and communications.[11] Yet, as the novel shows, such dreams of a clear and comprehensive social order or of social narratives, such as Manifest Destiny, through conventional language can seem to exist only by ignoring or even erasing certain unpleasant complexities, such as the existence of indigenous peoples.

After hearing the terminal philosophy of the workers at the Word Hospital, the tricksters Bigfoot Plumero and Matchi Makwa (as one might expect) immediately respond with nonsensical but humorous language, the kind of language that exists to communicate an emotion, not the clear communication of thought. The employees at the Word Hospital have difficulty with this kind of language, just as they had difficulties with the pilgrims' unspoken communication with animals and Bishop Parasimo's communications with his hands. The Word Hospital employees must reduce communication to understand it on their terms, indicating the degree to which their theory of language is inflexible and inadequate (terminal), unable to comprehend the full range of human communication. They can only understand emotion, for instance, by using machines to color-code the varying degrees of language, rather than understanding it through the maze of human experience. The narrator tells us: "The machines were humanized while the humans were mechanized" (Vizenor 1990, 167). Despite this dismal vision of the future of language, the novel also offers the possibility of a much different kind of language that is emerging in this posttechnological third world. The chapter begins with an almost nostalgic tone about a new or resurgent ethos of human communication and interaction that occurs among the many disenfranchised travelers along the interstate. "Oral traditions were honored," the narrator tells us. "Myths became the center of meaning again" (162). In the absence of an industrial society, the pilgrims now gather around a fire in an idyllic setting, where "Proude told stories about his father and grandfather and the sovereign nation." In the ruins of the third world, the novel offers the nostalgic but hopeful return to a communal, changing indigenous oral tradition.

Finally, throughout his writing career, Vizenor has certainly written highly theoretical works, most notably his *Fugitive Poses: Native American Indian Scenes of Absence and Presence.* But Vizenor has also written a number of quite conventional works, such as his autobiography *Interior Landscapes* and his articles for the *Minneapolis Tribune* collected in *Crossbloods: Bone Courts, Bingo, and Other Reports.* Although Vizenor may be "cutting himself off from Native people" by employing the language of theory, he also addresses in straightforward language issues such as education, treaty rights, water rights, and the American Indian Movement. Both forms of writing—the theoretical and the practical—offer audiences variations of the same melody: that fear of uncertainty and the desire for clarity drive people to embrace terminal creeds, often disregarding the human cost, whether in personal questions such as indigenous identity or social concerns such as progress and Manifest Destiny. It is within his novel *Bearheart,* however, that Vizenor creates worlds where tricksters travel with terminal believers, where narratives of conquest merge with narratives of transcendence, and where theoretical and practical considerations merge into compassionate narratives of caution and possibility.

NOTES

1. The novel first appeared as *Darkness in Saint Louis Bearheart* (1978) and was revised and reissued as *Bearheart: The Heirship Chronicles* (1990). Vizenor said the reason for the name change was that the book is already known to most people as *Bearheart* (1999, 95). For a discussion of the differences between the two versions and the reappearance of characters in *Bearheart* in Vizenor's subsequent works, see Blair 1995.

2. As Roland Barthes, whom Vizenor frequently cites, tells us in *The Pleasure of the Text:* "Neither culture nor its destruction is erotic; it is the seam between them, the fault, the flaw, which becomes so" (1975, 7).

3. Wolfgang Hochbruck points out that some Native traditions consider the present world to be the fourth. He speculates that Vizenor might have had in mind the conditions of the contemporary reservations: "Within the context of *Bearheart,* however, the pilgrims' progress (of course, this is one of the intertexts) into the fourth world makes the one they leave the third, which is what tribal politicians have claimed on several occasions: that their reservations are actually part of the Third World" (1992, 275). A. Lavonne Brown Ruoff writes: "Vizenor's descriptions of the four worlds of Indian people combine the emergence and migration myths of Southwestern tribes with the flood myths of the Algonkin-speaking tribes" (1985, 71).

4. For a discussion of the possible relationship between *Bearheart* and Bunyan's allegorical *The Pilgrim's Progress,* see Rigel-Cellard 1997. See also Ruoff (1985), who writes: "Accompanying Cedarfair on his journey is a bizarre collection of followers that represent various figures from Indian mythology as well as human vices and virtues" (71).

5. Keady (1985) discusses those characters who fall victim to their narcissistic terminal creeds, especially Belladonna Darwin Winter Catcher.

6. Her name is likewise a combination of two views of the world, Winter Catcher offering an indigenous vision of the world, Darwin suggesting the totalizing narrative of natural selection.

7. Paul Pasquaretta suggests that gambling stories in *Bearheart* demonstrate how the novel rejects cultural narcissism: "In Vizenor's *Bearheart,* gambling stories are also employed to advance particular attitudes, values and, most importantly, modes of expression. These may be regarded in terms of the things they oppose—terminal creeds and cultural narcissism" (1996, 30).

8. I hesitate to use Hegelian terminology with its connotations of upward progress, a

concept the book itself critiques.

9. The novel similarly questions the idea of distance with our relations with oral traditions, providing an old indigenous story about a woman having sexual relations with dogs who later became hunters. Couched in the protective, distancing epistemology of anthropology, sexual relations with animals are not especially troubling for many readers. Yet, when the idea is placed in contemporary circumstances, many of us readers are taken aback. Thus the novel implicitly questions our relation to older oral traditions.

10. In a section of his book entitled "Sovereignty: An Inappropriate Concept," Taiaiake Alfred (1999) points out that the concept of sovereignty has come to mean a limited amount of power for indigenous nations within the borders of the United States and Canada. For example, the word *sovereign* no longer means "freedom," but instead means a state of perpetual colonization.

11. Two writers who argue for such a connection between clear language and institutions are E. D. Hirsch (1988) and William Bennett (1992). Both are surprisingly confident, for example, in the ability of a single sentence to summarize the complexities of novels, and argue that such clarity is the substance of American culture. If all Americans had this level of "cultural literacy," they argue, the conversation about American policy would be much more informed. Such an approach, however, offers only the illusion of clarity, or if clarity, then a sort that exists only with the exclusion of such complications as American Indian history.

WORKS CITED

Alfred, Taiaiake. 1999. *Peace, Power, Righteousness: An Indigenous Manifesto.* New York: Oxford University Press.

Barthes, Roland. 1975. *The Pleasure of the Text.* Translated by Richard Miller. New York: Noonday Press.

Bennett, William John. 1992. *The Devaluing of America: The Fight for Our Culture and Our Children.* New York: Summit Books.

Blair, Elisabeth. 1995. "Text as Trickster: Postmodern Language Games in Gerald Vizenor's *Bearheart.*" *MELUS* 20.4 (Winter): 75–90.

Blaeser, Kimberly M. 1996. *Gerald Vizenor: Writing in the Oral Tradition.* Norman:

University of Oklahoma Press.

Gates, Henry Louis, Jr. 1988. *The Signifying Monkey: A Theory of Afro-American Literary Criticism.* New York: Oxford University Press.

Hirsch, E. D., Jr. 1988. *Cultural Literacy: What Every American Needs to Know.* New York: Vintage Books.

Hochbruck, Wolfgang. 1992. "Breaking Away: The Novels of Gerald Vizenor." *World Literature Today* 66 (Spring): 274–78.

Hutcheon, Linda. 1989. *The Politics of Postmodernism.* New York: Routledge.

Jung, C. G. 1972. "On the Psychology of the Trickster Figure." Translated by R. F. C. Hull. In *The Trickster: A Study in American Indian Mythology,* by Paul Radin, 195–211. 1956; New York: Schocken Books.

Keady, Maureen. 1985. "Walking Backwards into the Fourth World: Survival of the Fittest in *Bearheart.*" *American Indian Quarterly* 9:61–75.

Momaday, N. Scott. 1968. *House Made of Dawn.* New York: Harper and Row.

Owens, Louis. 1992. *Other Destinies: Understanding the American Indian Novel.* Norman: University of Oklahoma Press.

O'Sullivan, John. 1845. "Annexation." *United States Magazine and Democratic Review* 17 (July): 5–10.

Pasquaretta, Paul. 1996. "Sacred Chance: Gambling and the Contemporary Native American Novel." *MELUS* 21.2 (Summer): 21–33.

Radin, Paul. 1972. *The Trickster: A Study in American Indian Mythology.* Commentaries by Karl Kerényi and C. G. Jung. 1956; New York: Schocken Books.

Rigel-Cellard, Bernadette. 1997. "Doubling in Gerald Vizenor's *Bearheart*: The Pilgrimage Strategy or Bunyan Revisited." *Studies in American Literatures* 9.1 (Spring): 93–114.

Ruoff, A. Lavonne Brown. 1985. "Gerald Vizenor: Compassionate Trickster." *American Indian Quarterly* 73:67–73.

Velie, Alan. 1989. "The Trickster Novel." In *Narrative Chance: Postmodern Discourse on Native American Literatures,* edited by Gerald Vizenor, 121–39. Albuquerque: University of New Mexico Press.

Vizenor, Gerald, ed. 1970. *anishinabe adisokan: Tales of the People.* Minneapolis: Nodin Press.

———. 1981. *Earthdivers: Tribal Narratives on Mixed Descent.* Minneapolis: University of Minnesota Press.

———. 1984. *The People Named the Chippewa: Narrative Histories.* Minneapolis: University of Minnesota Press.

———. 1989. "Trickster Discourse: Comic Holotropes and Language Games." In *Narrative Chance: Postmodern Discourse on Native American Indian Literatures,* edited by Gerald Vizenor, 187–211. Albuquerque: University of New Mexico Press.

———. 1990. *Bearheart: The Heirship Chronicles.* Minneapolis: University of Minnesota Press. Orig. pub. as *Darkness in Saint Louis Bearheart* (St. Paul: Truck Press, 1978).

Vizenor, Gerald Robert, and A. Robert Lee. 1999. *Postindian Conversations.* Lincoln: University of Nebraska Press.

Womack, Craig. 1997. Review of *Gerald Vizenor: Writing in the Oral Tradition,* by Kimberly M. Blaeser. *Studies in American Literatures,* ser. 2, 9.4 (Winter): 97–100.

Story, Braid, Basket: The Woven Aesthetics of Jeannette Armstrong's *Whispering in Shadows*

JANE HALADAY

What Aboriginal authors bring to world literature is our ability to braid
our oral traditions with the written word and tell stories about ourselves
and our nations and our communities in a way that no one else can.

—Richard Van Camp, "Miracles"

The literature of Native North American writers is replete with images of indigenous cultural forms including quilting, basketweaving,
braiding, and beading, as descriptors of the storytelling process and
as structuring devices for stories themselves. Poet Elizabeth Woody,
an enrolled member of the Confederated Tribes of Warm Springs,
describes the act of reading cultural texts in a variety of forms as an ancient
indigenous activity:

I was taught through the act of writing that words could mean and create many things. Apart from other "Tellers" or "Teachers," these words
existed in the physical realm by being in books. Books are not new to
us, or limited in form. The petroglyphs on rock in the Columbia River
Gorge are part of my literary heritage. The mnemonic device of beadwork, necklaces, and the personal imagery of dress items were books in
themselves. The songs and prayers that I hear from others are markers
in a lineage of great tradition, both personal and spiritually inherited.
(1994, xi–xii)

For many Aboriginal and Native women writers, the sense of patterning language into stories readily derives from the visual and aural designs experienced
through related art forms and natural phenomena, providing an integrated
theoretical framework for conceptions of writing and storytelling acts. Mixed-
blood Tsalagi and Huron author Allison A. Hedge Coke observes that

the memories I have imprinted in my mind from making bark and pine-
needle baskets and from weaving fabric are significant for my writing
today. These weaving skills may produce layered imagery, a tangle of raw
material shaped into something tangible through gentle strokes of the
fingers and the mind's eye. (1998, 115)

Similarly, Anishinaabe poet and writer Kimberley M. Blaeser, in describing Cherokee author Marilou Awiakta's text *Selu*, notes Awiakta's skill in
"weav[ing] together the activity and the analysis of storytelling," which "invites her readers to become involved in the process of connecting her stories
and ideas about stories to her life" (1998, 268). Recognizing these woven
aesthetics is fundamental, notes Blaeser, "to develop an interpretive theory
about Native literature," and "the patterns, physical images, and dynamics
we identify must be allowed to arise from within the texts themselves, and
the theoretical approaches must be flexible enough to take into account the
motion of ongoing life and ongoing story" (268).

Like Hedge Coke and Blaeser, Okanagan writer and activist Jeannette
C. Armstrong demonstrates a theory of woven motion as a central force

informing her writing. Motion for Armstrong is generated by the relationship between Okanagan ancestral lands and the people's language that arises from those sacred earth places, the interplay between the animate entities of earth, rock, water, wind, animal, and plant life that is fluid and constant in Armstrong's life and writing. "I am claimed and owned by this land, this Okanagan," Armstrong declares in her essay, "Land Speaking." "Voices that move within as my experience of existence do not awaken as words. Instead they move within as the colors, patterns, and movements of a beautiful, kind Okanagan landscape" (1998, 176). Armstrong's literature, particularly her poetry and her second novel, *Whispering in Shadows*, enacts her theory of fluid boundaries and active flow between human beings, homelands, language, and other artistic expressions of the sacred including painting, music, and writing. In *Whispering in Shadows*, Armstrong incorporates poetry, letters, third- and first-person narratives, and Coyote stories that span time and location by weaving them together through telling the life story of protagonist Penny Jackson.

This essay articulates a theory of storytelling arising in both the structure and content of *Whispering in Shadows* through the metaphor of indigenous weaving as cultural practice and creative process. For indigenous North American basket weavers, the process of weaving is as significant in the production of the basket as are the preparation and gathering of materials and the finished basket itself. In like manner, Native and Aboriginal writers carefully select and cultivate their words to create meaning through their stories' emergence within and beyond the printed page. Indigenous attitudes toward baskets, as toward stories, are that they are living beings to be treated with care and respect; like stories, the baskets most valued are those that continue to be used. As baskets must be fed in order to nourish their spirits, stories must be read and told to nourish theirs, to fortify readers and listeners, and to consolidate community. Blackfeet scholar Leroy Little Bear, Jr. emphasizes that Native storytelling

> is not just the words and the listening but the actual living of the story.
> . . . The Native American paradigm comes to life as the author weaves
> through ecology, relational networks of plants, animals, the land, and

the cosmos. It is a renewal ceremony of Native American knowledge, a storytelling of the discoveries of regular patterns manifesting themselves in the flux. (Qtd. in Cajete 2000, xii)

Although Little Bear, Jr. is here specifically discussing ideas of Native science, his words apply equally to the process of Armstrong's construction of *Whispering in Shadows* and to the basketweaving process. Basket makers must be of good mind as they weave, and while many weavers understand the appearance of the finished basket from the start, perhaps having envisioned it in dreams, others follow the basket's guidance as it takes shape within their hands to become what it was meant to be. At the heart of the theory of indigenous basketweaving, then, is the ongoing transaction between weaver and woven materials, the organic relatives the weaver honors and cares for not only as she weaves, but throughout the seasons to ensure their continuance and to participate in what Little Bear, Jr. calls "a renewal ceremony of Native American knowledge."

In like manner, the story Armstrong crafts in *Whispering in Shadows* manifests slowly through her conscious cultivation of significant themes and images over the course of the novel. Armstrong's text requires active interrelationship between Armstrong and her readers to weave together the lives, stories, settings, and themes involving protagonist Penny Jackson's human, plant, and animal relatives across time and throughout the Americas. The completed vessel of Armstrong's novel is one of multiple, interwoven centers spiraling upward and outward together,[1] a network of strands unified within a final pattern that continues the story's life beyond the final page of printed text.

The archive of Armstrong's nonfiction serves as guide for envisioning the shape of her novel. In her collaborative text *The Native Creative Process*—itself an interweaving of Armstrong's and Métis architect Douglas Cardinal's thinking and words on the title's theme—Armstrong explicates an indigenous approach to knowledge acquisition through a rhetoric of spiral motion:

The Native creative process places importance on the internal understanding of our individual selves as a process toward building relationships, moving outward to all other things. This becomes a means of

collective long term healthy continuance. This principle is expressed in
the open kind of societal structures which contain a cooperative symmetry concerned with continuance and yet facilitating the individual's
capacity to continuously change and be enhanced in a balanced way.
The spiral rather than the circle is used as a fundamental symbol for this.
(Cardinal and Armstrong 1991, 22)

In some form or another, Armstrong emphasizes the Okanagan value of "collective long term healthy continuance" in every interview she has given, every
essay she has written, and every activist project in which she engages. Thus
it is no surprise that a grounding in these values, and how to practice them
within, and despite, an ecologically destructive and humanly fragmenting
colonial mass culture, is one fundamental theme in *Whispering in Shadows*.
The strands Armstrong bundles together to form the novel's primary spiral
are land, language, and human relationships within these. These foundational coils are bound throughout the text by many interrelated symbols and
motifs, some of which are shadows, light, color, dreams, whispering, trees,
Coyote, and specific character relationships. Together, these images gradually
combine to reveal the larger shape of the story.

Over the course of the novel—which begins for Penny Jackson when
she is seventeen and ends with her death as an elder—Penny is an artist,
mother, and activist whose earliest memory is linked to her beloved great-
grandmother, Tupa, on the land of the Okanagan: "They sat together on
the still-cool and damp ground and carefully dug [yellowbells] down to their
bulbs. Her and Tupa, gathering" (2000, 11). Penny gathers together her
memories of Tupa as they spiral through the text to remind Penny that the
strength of her cultural upbringing, much of which was taught to her by
Tupa and underscores an Okanagan attitude toward living in harmonious
relationship with earth and our relatives of the natural world, will guide her
through difficult times. Armstrong writes in her online essay "Sharing One
Skin: Okanagan Community":

Our word for people, for humanity, for human beings, is difficult to say
without talking about connection to the land. When we say the Okanagan word for ourselves, we are actually saying "the ones who are dream

and land together." That is our original identity. Before anything else, we are living, dreaming Earth pieces. It's a second identification that means human; we identify ourselves as separate from other things on the land. (2001)

It is additionally significant that Armstrong links Penny's memories with Tupa to memories on Okanagan land because it is an ancestral grandmother spirit that most aptly describes in English the Okanagan relationship of people to the land: "The English term *grandmother* as a human experience is closest in meaning to the term *Tmixw* in Okanagan," Armstrong explains in "Land Speaking," "[m]eaning something like loving-ancestor-land-spirit" (1998, 176). Thus, while Tupa is an actual character who once lived physically and continues to live spiritually with Penny, Armstrong also weaves memories of Tupa throughout the novel at critical moments as symbolic reminders to Penny to honor her deep connection to Okanagan land, language, and practices. Consistently, Penny feels her most profound sense of spiritual connectedness when her physical body—as a "living, dreaming Earth [piece]"—is in direct contact with the body of earth. For example, at the first environmentalist rally Penny attends to save a stand of old growth redwoods:

She leans close to the tree, her cheek pressed sideways against the trunk and closes her eyes. Her words are barely audible in the still air. The sounds of her language mixing with the soft movement of ferns, the whispering of branches and the sound of birds overhead.

Ancient one. Thank you for your welcome. I offer copper and sweet tobacco. I seek your comfort and ask for my spirit to be filled with your beauty.

She can feel the tremble and vibration of the tree[']s movement under her cheek as she presses her ear closer to the damp bark.

It sounds like a long sigh. Like a breath drawn in and slowly let out.

She sits still, face against the tree, the tree's each sigh matching her own. A calm moves over her.

It feels the same as a relative holding me. Soothing me. (98–99)

Reflecting Penny's deepest beliefs, these themes of language and land relationship spiral upward from the novel's inception to inform every action and event in which Penny participates, from gathering roots with Tupa as a girl to the environmental protests and global human rights activities of her adulthood. The first pages of Armstrong's novel, like the start of a coiled basket, mark the center and direction that her story-building process will take. Sisters in indigenous rights activism are invoked in the novel's dedication,[2] and literary ancestor E. Pauline Johnson's poem "Moonset" introduces the motifs of whispering and shadows that Armstrong sustains in her own imagery throughout the text. The speaker in Johnson's poem blends her voice in conversation with the "soft responsive voices of the night," which include "The troubled night-bird, calling plaintively" and "The cedars, chanting vespers to the sea." The speaker does not fully understand the meaning of the cedars' chanting, yet she feels her soul converge with her fellow beings "in shadow-land."

As readers, we also "may not all [the] meaning understand" of Johnson's poem, or of Armstrong's placement of the poem (the only piece of writing in the novel that is not her own) as the first page of the text. Yet the earthy, restless, dreamlike tone invoked in "Moonset" works well as the "start" guiding the shape of the novel. Armstrong continues to weave dreams, the voices of trees, and multiple meanings of shadows throughout the story of Penny's life. "The Okanagan word for ourselves is sqilx{w}," Armstrong writes, "Which in literal translation means 'the dream in a spiral.' We recognize our individual lives as the continuance of human dreams. We know our lives to be the tools of the vast human mind which is continuing on into the future" (Cardinal and Armstrong 1991, 111). The dreams Armstrong weaves into Penny's story serve at various points to clarify, caution, or uplift when her waking thoughts seem unable to offer Penny the particular insights she may need.[3]

On the page following Johnson's poem, Armstrong places another poem, presumably written by Penny, that again references sisters, dreams, singing, and shape. Its direct relationship to Johnson's poem before it, and to the block of prose after it, again are not made explicit as Armstrong continues gathering the fibers of her story together to weave meaning into them through the process of telling Penny's life. The speaker in "frogs singing" tells us:

> my sister did not dream this
> she found this out when she walked
> outside and looked up and star
> rhythms sang to her pointing their spines of light
> down into her and filled her body with star song
> and all round her
> frogs joined
> the star singing
> they learned it
> long ago. (7)

Indirectly, "frogs singing" refers to Johnson's poem in that its central figure (the speaker's sister), as the speaker in "Moonset" also does, describes a moment of communion within natural life forces during which she hears their calls and their music, and, in "frogs singing," also feels her body literally penetrated with the rhythms of star song. "Frogs singing" adds the additional dimension of ancient time that is hinted at but not articulated in Johnson's poem, another significant strand that Armstrong will incorporate as she stitches together the more contemporary story of Penny and her family through the appearance of Coyote and Fox, and other references to Okanagan worldview and cultural practices. "Frogs singing" was also published two years earlier in Armstrong's essay "Land Speaking." There, Armstrong offers commentary on the poem's genesis that underscores the themes of Okanagan experience, earth relationship, and sister relationship that are woven throughout *Whispering in Shadows*. Armstrong writes:

"Frogs Singing"+ is the result of a long discussion on our language and worldview with my sister Delphine, who spoke only Okanagan until age twelve. She pointed out that the stars and the frogs in the Okanagan summer nights have the same rhythm and that in saying it to recall the sound and the night filled with stars, the rhythm filled her soul and became hers. (1998, 188–89)

This strand of meaning—that of corporeal human integration with other animate beings in the natural world—reemerges in a later scene in which Tupa encourages the child Penny's ability to speak to colors as grandmother and granddaughter conclude their day fishing by the lake with the "Turtles Landing Song" (46). Even more powerfully than "Moonset" and "frogs singing," this scene illustrates Penny's direct connections with and total absorption by a richly colored, musical, living universe replete with light, sound, and motion that resonates within and is not separate from the physical body. Little Bear, Jr., notes that "the Native American paradigm is comprised of and includes ideas of constant motion and flux, existence consisting of energy waves, interrelationships, all things being animate, space/place, renewal, and all things being imbued with spirit" (qtd. in Cajete 2000, x). Thus, as a young girl Penny absorbs the dancing colors of her Tupa's shawl as it arches over her like an awning; she sings to the colors' faces and Tupa sings with her: "Tupa's voice, talking in the language, sounded somehow like the ducks, the water, the bees buzzing and the song, all at the same time." This imagery is evidence of Okanagan holism and healthy experience, not a demonstration of Western literary techniques such as personification or synesthesia. Tupa encourages Penny to talk to the colors, reassuring her granddaughter that "they tell you things. Listen to them. They never lie." Tupa points out to the girl that the turtle in the lake is "swimming the song you were just singing" (45–46).

This is a primary scene in the novel enforcing the Okanagan attitude toward complete, healthy human interrelationship with all life-forms and natural occurrences. Significantly, Armstrong braids it between two scenes of tremendous anxiety for Penny. In the first, Penny at last works up the nerve to register for college after vowing she is "never going to stand in a work line again and have some fat fart fondle [her] ass just because he thinks [she] needs the job so bad" (41). In the second scene, following the scene at the lake, Penny anxiously attends her first college party and feels very much an outsider, thinking she "should've just stayed home" (46). In both of these culturally mixed colonial spaces, the confident Okanagan girl who speaks with colors and sings the song of swimming turtles in her Tupa's company feels completely out of her element, cut off and separated from the deep cultural knowledge and competence she possesses. By inserting Penny's positive memory of Tupa's Okanagan education at the lake between two painful scenes of engagement with institutional Euro-Canadian education, Armstrong emphasizes that Penny has not lost her core self, that she will remember her indigenous instruction, and that it this original education that will prove to be her strongest mooring.

• • •

The significance of the swimming turtles' song Penny and Tupa share has been visually woven into the text as early as page 7. The structure of the novel's first twenty pages, in fact, reveal the entire woven aesthetic of Armstrong's text in that they are mixed-genre story strands whose relationship only grows apparent as they are plaited into the larger narrative. As discussed above, the novel opens with a dedication to Armstrong's sisters on the same page as Johnson's poem, followed by a short poem on its own page, followed by the recurring visual motif Armstrong weaves into her novel, a graphic of four descending (or ascending, or horizontally drifting, depending on how one "reads" them) turtles above and to the left (to the west? toward the sunset direction?) of the novel's first prose paragraph, again on its own page (7):

This paragraph, describing an unnamed "she" whom we take to be Penny once we meet her on the following page, outlines a powerful mixed image of love as a consuming and destructive force that "owned" and "created a wreckage" of this unnamed female body. The "madness moved inside" to a hidden place: "It had found her; claimed her in the way it did to make her become what she must. This love. This is a map" (7). Here, Armstrong explicitly informs readers that her novel is a map whose path must be followed to make meaning; this is a story of becoming, for Penny and also for readers. What Penny will become, what each of us will become, Armstrong seems to suggest, will only be realized during the course of the journey. This map is not a generic mass production to be followed blindly; we are creating this particular map, this story, as we go, and only in looking back once our journey is finished will it become clear where we have been. Given that we are, in fact, reading a commercially produced text, Armstrong's suggestion of our individual mapmaking during the process of creating Penny's story through the transaction of reading becomes a subversive and decolonizing act. Armstrong overlays the colonial concept of "map" as a two-dimensional printed construct marking movements across and within geographic land spaces with the Okanagan concept of human bodies as "living, dreaming Earth pieces" to suggest that our own flesh is the living map of our life's journey within a continuum of earth ancestry and love. Earth is the mother's body that has birthed us and will re-embrace us in physical death, and both experiences are necessary and welcomed.

The prose narrative of Penny Jackson's life begins on page 8, where Armstrong introduces a second visual motif of italicized interior monologue to indicate Penny's unspoken thoughts throughout the story. There are no chapters in *Whispering in Shadows*, no abrupt breaks in the weaving of poetry, prose narrative, letters, the "Note Found in Her Dresser Drawer" (92), notes from Penny's sketchbook and diary, Coyote stories, and graphic arrangements such as font shifts, the swimming (or floating? or flying?) turtles, and a chart of Penny's growing consciousness, titled "Penny's Notes from Her Diary":

```
AWARENESS ------------------------------ CONSCIOUSNESS
        :                                    :
        :                                    :
   AS A PROCESS                         AS A PROCESS
        :                                    :
        :                                    :
   as a witness                         as a participant
```

Penny's awareness/consciousness "chart" (122) emphasizes the key theme of process that Armstrong stresses not only in *Whispering in Shadows*, but in her articulation of Okanagan worldview as a healthy way of life. As an engaged activist and Okanagan community member, Armstrong consistently underscores the necessary shape of active, deliberate community process as expressed in the Okanagan concept of *En'owkin*.[5] The *En'owkin* process is "a way of carrying out one of the main principles of our people—respect," Armstrong has stated. "This process does not presume an agenda, an outcome of direction." More significantly, the *En'owkin* model of community process emphasizes "that we care about how the other person feels. We are in community" (1995, 50). Like the processes of storytelling and basketweaving, the *En'owkin* process is consciously structured, although its shape may not be initially apparent and only gradually comes into being through interaction. Armstrong discusses the patience required for the success of the *En'owkin* process during the Okanagan community-building meetings she engaged in during the 1970s:

> I could see this structure starting to develop in my mind and under-standing that what seemed like the non-sacred and non-spiritual is really a spiritual act, if it is tied back to the understanding and to the process itself. If the structure is in synchronization with that process, so that it does not become something extraordinary or out of the ordinary, it becomes something very ordinary. In other words, it is so natural, that it is not even seen as a spiritual act. (1995, 50)

The structure of daily activities such as community meetings, basketweaving, and fiction writing—"so natural, that it is not even seen as a spiritual act," although it *is* deeply spiritual—arises from a consciousness inherent in Okanagan and other indigenous traditional worldviews. Through the fracturing of Aboriginal lifeways from the impact of multiple colonialisms, a holistic human consciousness—one that rejects the limitations of essentialist categorizations and binary thinking—must be recuperated, often painfully, by many indigenous and nonindigenous peoples alike. This is where the warp and weft of Armstrong's story structure in *Whispering in Shadows* offer a visual as well as an intellectual/artistic manifestation of an indigenous literary theory of resistance and reconstruction. As Penny travels between her home reserve and Euro-Canadian institutions of education and commercial art, she begins to fray, pulled apart by the destructive either-or forces of colonial capitalist demands. She accelerates toward psychological breakdown, which is ultimately triggered by her interaction with her gallery agent when she realizes the vast schism between her intentions in creating politically and socially conscious artwork and the desires of affluent mass cultural consumers for artwork that is comfortable and safe (2000, 202–6). Yet even during her descent into mental collapse—the ultimate psychic splitting apart—Armstrong's text steadfastly continues to stitch Penny's story around the growing spiral of the entire novel, a story that, for Penny as for Armstrong, begins in time immemorial and continues forward today.

In Okanagan worldview, as Armstrong expresses it in her various writings and as it informs *Whispering in Shadows,* people who are separated from their language and land—like the bundled central coil of a basket when pried apart—become weakened and vulnerable; their very survival is at stake. In describing the three parts of the Okanagan word for themselves as human beings, Armstrong explains that the word's first part relates to "a physical realm," while "the second part of the word refers to the dream or the dream state." She notes in "Sharing One Skin" that

> the third part of the word means that if you take a number of strands, hair, or twine, place them together, they become one strand. You use this thought symbolically when you make a rope and when you make twine, thread, and homemade baskets, and when you weave the threads to make the coiled basket. That third part of the word refers to us being tied into the part of everything else. It refers to the dream parts of

ourselves forming our community, and it implies what our relationships are. We say, "This is my clan," or, "This is my people. These are the families that I came from. These are my great-grandparents," and so on. In this way I know my position and my responsibility for that specific location and geographic area. That is how I introduce myself. That is how I like to remember who I am and what my role is. (2001)

As the weaver joins the plant relatives together into one integrated basket being, Armstrong weaves real and fictional relatives into the text, braiding their stories together at points of intersection, illustrating a pattern here and moving on again, spiraling events outward from a center point that continues beyond the novel's closing pages. Together, these separate parts gather meaning through their cohesive bond as one more powerful whole.

As it opens, *Whispering in Shadows* closes with another short poem, "earth love," which serves as the final stitch in Penny's story and draws the strands together by harking back to the two opening poems through another description of ultimate communion with nature, the death of the speaker's (presumably Penny's) human flesh and its reintegration with the beloved earth body: "I said that I would / give my flesh back / but instead my flesh / will offer me up / and feed the earth / and she will / love me" (296). This poem also spirals back to the first prose paragraph of the novel, the love map discussed previously that claimed the body of the speaker and made a wreckage of her. It may be that the wreckage of the body outlined in the beginning of the novel is Penny's eventual cancer, arising from Penny's deep love of the earth and her full engagement within it, down to the toxins now permeating earth's flesh and Penny's own.

Armstrong weaves her first allusion to Penny's cancer into the scene when Penny is working in the apple orchard with her partner, Francis. "Indian Summer in the Okanagan" is good for apples, but "in the hottest part of the summer, . . . the still air became hazy and heavy with the sharp smell of orchard spray" (23). As a young woman on her way to becoming a mother of three before splitting up with Francis, Penny's exposure to toxic chemicals foreshadows both her own later cancer and her more immediate involvement with issues of environmental and indigenous rights.

Immediately after she receives her cancer diagnosis later in the novel, Penny discusses with her friend Tannis how Okanagan worldview might frame her disease in terms of the return of the flesh-eating monsters that Coyote had vanquished long ago to make way for the coming of humans. "Those stories tell of how the world had to be rid of the flesh-eaters so we could survive," Penny tells Tannis. "How they conjured themselves and how they shape-shift and change their form continuously. They were banished but only if we kept the balance which was established. The balance is the natural order in this world. Now everything is out of balance. We are causing another transformation" (247).

In the closing pages, the spiral of Armstrong's novel returns to its most meaningful source, the land and the Okanagan women who pray to and within it in Okanagan language. That Okanagan culture will endure is announced through Armstrong's mirroring of Tupa in both Lena (Penny's older sister) and Penny, and of Penny's witnessing the prayers of Tupa and Lena that are, although separated by at least forty years, still woven together across time into a single, unbroken prayer. Internally, Penny takes up the prayer where Lena leaves off:

> *She sounded just like Tupa. I'm so thankful that she's here. Everything is right now with her finally home, and doing all the things in the old way like she's been doing . . . I am full inside with family on this good day. Give us your protection while we move in these mountains, with our wild relatives out here in our true home. Accept these small gifts that it be so.* (281)

With Lena home and her family together, Penny at last feels the shadow she had internalized at Tupa's death dissolve, replaced by the light of contented understanding. The collaborative process of *En'owkin* Armstrong writes into the text through Penny's relationships with Tupa and her other friends and relatives, especially the women, enacts the ideal of healthy Okanagan community, which provides a bulwark against Penny's fragmentation: "The [*En'owkin*] process empowers the community, creating unity and strength for the long term," Armstrong explains (1999, 9). The shape of the finished basket now visible, *Whispering in Shadows* reveals the complex interweaving of

Okanagan theories of holistic interconnectedness, through which the world might be radically transformed by people's mutual, conscious nurturance of the earth and of each other.

• • •

As Armstrong's novel demonstrates, an indigenous theory of weaving in literary aesthetics perpetuates ancient patterns and practices of production that are at once artistic, practical, and highly spiritual. Whereas baskets are "the oldest form of human manufacture" (Schlick 1994, 16) in material form, stories are the oldest verbal world-making forces in indigenous experience. In the tradition of oral storytelling events, the woven aesthetics in Native women's writings build community through storytelling processes and highlight forms reflecting a spiritual relationship to earth: the plant relations who are woven into baskets are another manifestation of the land language that sings itself into being through the human voice, in both indigenous and colonial languages. In constructing a literary theory of woven motion in their writings, Native North American women weave pieces of history, moments of humor, sacred worldviews, and individual authors' visions into unified, original creations. Expressing this theory in her poem "Threads of Old Memory," Armstrong writes:

> I am the dreamer
> the choice maker
> the word speaker
> I speak in a language of words formed of the actions of the past
> words that become the sharing
> the collective knowing
> the links that become a people
> the dreaming that becomes a history
> the calling forth of voices
> the sending forward of memory
> I am the weaver of memory thread
> twining past to future
> I am the artist

the storyteller
the singer
from the known and familiar
pushing out into darkness
dreaming splinters together
the coming to knowing. (1998, 185–86)

The decolonizing energy in Native North American women's woven storytelling aesthetics honors tribal traditions of dynamic relationships. The ease
with which Aboriginal and Native women writers gravitate toward a language
reflecting traditional cultural productions of tangible items that are created
for both sacred and secular use, that involve particular attitudes and relationships between living materials and human artists, that result in entities including beadwork, baskets, or books, and that simultaneously illustrate aesthetic
beauty, spiritual connection, and cultural self-determination, is powerful
evidence of the appropriateness of a Native literary theory rooted in motion
and shape. "It is possible to see the whorl on the baby's head as the visible
motion of the soul entering the new physical body," explains poet Elizabeth
Woody, a member of the Confederated Tribes of Warm Springs:

> The sound and vision in symbols store more information than I can
> comprehend. I like mystery. The life span is a string of patterns, as when
> I make beadwork, poetry, story or art—simplifications of complex life-
> patterns arranged into a comprehensible shape. Writing is a way to recall
> people's generously given motion and strength that can enter other lives
> and minds by its own momentum. (1994, xiii)

While reading *Whispering in Shadows* through a theory of woven aesthetics is
only one way to approach Armstrong's text, Armstrong's other written productions encourage theorizing her fiction through indigenous conceptions
of woven process and interconnected symmetry. Armstrong has discussed
the Okanagan concept of balance that arrives through conscious, nonde-
structive human activity, a process expressed in the Okanagan metaphor
yəyʕat stimʔ put, which translated, Armstrong explains, "says simply to make

certain that 'all things in the world are right'" (Cardinal and Armstrong 1991, 18). Yet enacting the "simplicity" of this metaphor requires conscious, constant vigilance. "In this simple phrase," Armstrong tells us, "lies the principle of deliberate non-destruction. A reminder to be aware of and to be protective of the sensitivity and the relationship between all beings and things, including us. The spider web is a physical construct which many native cultures draw on symbolically to imbed this principle in their storytelling as an expression of the creative process concerned with the connectedness of all things" (Cardinal and Armstrong 1991, 18).

In theorizing Armstrong's novel, which, like all her writing, stresses process and continuance and works constantly to be heard, seen, and felt in multiple dimensions, a rhetoric of woven shape and motion provides powerful critical possibilities for literary interpretation. Armstrong's story does not remain confined to the flatness of the printed page but, like an emerging basket, takes shapes from the first strand and arises from the page to weave its meaning within the heart and consciousness of each reader. Armstrong has stated that "any time people can pull together something, make something or build something, to pool together to make something happen, in other words to be able to work together and give of each other, that is a spiritual practice" (1995, 50). Armstrong's weaving of Penny's story in *Whispering in Shadows* is one more act in Armstrong's diverse project of Okanagan community building and indigenous knowledge transmission that strives to stitch delicate, individual fibers into a vital, more enduring whole.

NOTES

1. I thank Gordon D. Henry Jr. for sharing his theory of "sacred concentricities," an articulation of the concept of multiple centers in Native ceremonial symbolism and movement and their relationship to American Indian literatures.

2. Armstrong's dedication reads: "*This book is dedicated to the memory of my beautiful sisters:* / Ingrid Washinawatok El-Issa / *and* / Lahe'ena'e Gay." Both of these Native women were kidnapped and murdered in March of 1999, a year before the publication of *Whispering in Shadows,* while working with the U'wa indigenous people of

Columbia. Washinawatok El-Issa, Gay, and a third victim, Terry Freitas, were invited by the U'wa people to assist them in creating a cultural education and preservation program after the U'wa rejected the Columbian government's educational system for their children. While members of the Columbian "rebel" group Revolutionary Armed Forces of Columbia (FARC) claimed responsibility for the murders, there is specula-tion that U.S. government-backed Columbian militia helped destabilize negotiations for the release of Washinawatok El-Issa, Gay, and Freitas because of U.S. corporate in-terests in the oil resources on the U'wa people's homelands. See the American Indian Cultural Support website (http://www.aics.org/aics.html) and the Amazon Alliance articles on these events.

3. The first reference to Penny's dreams appears on page 35, when the unnamed speaker recalls that "they never leave that mountain. It is always there in her dreams. A quiet tree-filled valley filling her. A small green fir bough there in her dreams. Over and over it is slowly being turned around."

4. Armstrong capitalizes the title, "Frogs Singing," in her essay, but does not capitalize it in the novel.

5. Armstrong has variously spelled this Okanagan word in English as *En'owkin* and *en'owkin*, though she most often capitalizes it. Her essay "Let Us Begin with Cour-age" provides another powerful articulation of the *En'owkin* process.

WORKS CITED

Armstrong, Jeannette C. 1995. "The Spirit of the People Has Awakened and Is Enjoying Creation Through Us: An Interview with Jeannette Armstrong, Okanagan." Inter-view by Dagmar Thorpe. *Native Americas* 12.3: 50–53.

———. 1998. "Land Speaking." In *Speaking for the Generations,* edited by Simon Ortiz, 174–94. Tucson: University of Arizona Press.

———. 1999. "Let Us Begin with Courage." Center for Ecoliteracy, February. http://www.ecoliteracy.org/publications/index.html. Accessed 7 March 2009.

———. 2000. *Whispering in Shadows.* Penticton, B.C.: Theytus Books.

———. 2001. "Sharing One Skin: Okanagan Community." *Columbiana Magazine,* http://www.culturalsurvival.org/ourpublications/csq/article/sharing-one-skin. Ac-cessed 9 December 2006.

Blaeser, Kimberley M. 1998. "Like 'Reeds through the Ribs of a Basket': Native Women Weaving Stories." In *Other Sisterhoods: Literary Theory and U.S. Women of Color,* edited by Sandra Kumamoto Stanley, 265–76. Urbana: University of Illinois Press.

Cajete, Gregory. 2000. *Native Science.* Santa Fe: Clear Light Publishers.

Cardinal, Douglas, and Jeannette C. Armstrong. 1991. *The Native Creative Process: A Collaborative Discourse between Douglas Cardinal and Jeannette Armstrong.* Penticton, B.C: Theytus Books.

Hedge Coke, Allison A. 1998. "Seeds." In *Speaking for the Generations,* edited by Simon Ortiz, 92–116. Tucson: University of Arizona Press.

Schlick, Mary Doods. 1994. *Columbia River Basketry: Gift of the Ancestors, Gift of the Earth.* Seattle: University of Washington Press.

Van Camp, Richard. 2005. "Miracles," *Spirit Magazine,* Spring–Summer, 2–4.

Woody, Elizabeth. 1994. *Luminaries of the Humble.* Tucson: University of Arizona Press.

Of Good Listeners

Stories Are All We Are: Thomas King's Theory and Practice of Storytelling

TERESA GIBERT

> We wrote knowing that none of the stories we told would change the
> world. But we wrote in the hope that they would.
>
> —Thomas King, *The Truth about Stories*

hroughout his works, Thomas King deals with dichotomies such as
theory versus practice, myth versus history, stories versus histories,
private versus public, oral versus written, fact versus fiction, realism
versus fantasy, past versus present, and seriousness versus humor. Yet
instead of merely emphasizing contrast within each binary opposition, he prefers to blur the lines, resisting polarizations, questioning sim-
plistic differentiations, challenging clear-cut demarcations, and indicating
how complex both the relationships between the two elements of every pair
and the connections among the pairs themselves may become. For instance,
the multiple conjunctions of theory/practice with oral/written texts can be

■ 259

discerned when comparing King's essays and lectures (which devote a great deal of attention to elucidating how the oral and the written may be fruitfully linked in literature) with his novels and short stories (which provide excellent exponents of written orality).[1] Indeed, his most distinctive literary achievement is the "voice piece," a hybrid form that the author has glossed as a short story that "is meant to be read out loud," and that may fall flat "if you try to read it silently to yourself" because it "really exists in the sphere of the spoken word" (Davis 1996, 51).

King's self-defined position between two countries and his belonging to more than one ethnicity has provided him with a vantage point from which to deal with the paradoxes of hybridity. In several interviews, as well as in his creative writings, he has explicitly or implicitly revealed his personal attitude toward the United States, his birth country, and Canada, the country that he has called home for many years now. Furthermore, he has often addressed the sensitive issues of authenticity and legitimacy on the part of mixed-bloods whose degree of "Indianness" is questioned in spite of their firm determination to be seen as Natives. In 1990, when he edited *All My Relations: An Anthology of Contemporary Canadian Native Fiction*, he described himself as "a Native writer of Cherokee, Greek, and German descent" (217). In an interview held the same year, when he was asked his opinion about being labeled a "Canadian Native Author," he acknowledged that he was not born in Canada but in the United States, and that the Cherokee are not a Canadian tribe, adding:

> Now that becomes a problem only if you recognize the particular political line which runs between Canada and the US, and if you agree with the assumptions that that line makes.
>
> I think of myself as a Native writer and a Canadian writer. I doubt if I could call myself a Canadian Native writer, just because I'm not from one of the tribes from up here. (1991b, 107)

When interrogated by another interviewer, he insisted that he considered himself a Canadian writer (in part because of his citizenship, as well as the material and the landscape of his fiction), and restated the artificiality of the forty-ninth parallel, an imposed division that split tribal territories and still functions as a painful reminder of colonial history:[2]

> I guess I am supposed to say that I believe in the line that exists between the US and Canada, but for me it's an imaginary line. It's a line from somebody else's imagination; it's not my imagination. It divides people like the Mohawk into Canadian Mohawks and US Mohawks. They're the same people. It divides the Blackfoot who live in Browning from the Blackfoot who live at Standoff, for example. (1990a, 72)

In another interview—dated 1999, precisely the year that his third novel, *Truth and Bright Water*, was published—King commented on his mixed ancestry and his desire to reconnect with his Native heritage in a meaningful way: "Greek was the assumed, the given identity. Indian was the mystery, the unknown self" (1999b, J4). Considering roots a matter of choice to some extent, in 1994 he had already expressed his preference with the following words: "I'm Cherokee from Oklahoma, but I don't think of Oklahoma as home. If I think of any place as home it's the Alberta prairies, where I spent ten years with the Blackfoot people. I'm not Blackfoot, but that feels like the place I want to get back to" (1998, 95). More recently, in the Massey lectures he delivered in 2003 and later published as a book under the title of *The Truth about Stories: A Native Narrative*, he gave a fairly detailed autobiographical account of his troubled adolescence as a mixed-blood, coping with problems of racial identity and the traumatic experience caused by the disappearance of his Cherokee father before, as a child, he was old enough to know his parent (2005c, 2–8).

King's life experiences may explain why he distanced himself from the Cherokee, to whom he is genealogically linked, and felt more affinity with the Blackfoot, who constitute the major source of material that frames the realistic component of his novels and short stories. The ten years he spent teaching in the Native Studies Department at the University of Lethbridge, which is close to the largest reserve in Canada, gave him an opportunity to enjoy one of his favorite activities: listening to Blackfoot storytellers (1999a, 71–72). Probably for this reason, although the main technical inspiration for those of his "voice pieces" that are narrated by an imaginary traditional storyteller

comes from the Okanagan elder Harry Robinson, most of the characters who
people King's fiction are Blackfoot living in Alberta.

Thomas King displays a penchant for realism through his vivid portrayals
of contemporary Blackfoot who move to and fro from small border town to
reserve, while he deploys a fondness for fantasy as well. In his novels *Green
Grass, Running Water* (1993a) and *Truth and Bright Water* (1999c), for
instance, he develops intertwined realistic and fantastic plots. Likewise, he
combines elements derived from actual existence with those extracted from
the world of fantasy in the numerous playful scenes of magic realism that give
a distinctive flavor to the two collections of short fiction he has published
so far.[3] In many of these stories, supernatural events occur in the middle of
everyday life, while legendary figures of traditional Native storytelling (such
as the trickster Coyote) interact with realistically portrayed ordinary characters.[4] In an interview held in 1994, King himself noted the liberating effects
of fantasy, magic realism, and surrealism:

> What I learned from storytelling—from oral stories—was that those
> stories help to create a fantastic universe in which anything can happen.
> You're free to create that as you will. Which is freeing in the same way
> that I imagine magic realism and surrealism are freeing. (1998, 95)

Among the many cases in which King has felt free to mix realism and surrealism, special attention should be paid to one particular piece, the brief introductory narrative that became the title story of *A Short History of Indians
in Canada* (2005b), a volume that is not a condensed textbook in the area
of social studies, as its name would imply, but the author's latest collection of
short fiction. The story entitled "A Short History of Indians in Canada" first
appeared in the magazine *Toronto Life* in 1997, and was reprinted in 1999 to
represent King's literary art when the prestigious scholarly journal *Canadian
Literature* devoted an entire issue to the study of his oeuvre. The choice of
this specific piece seems to have been particularly appropriate, for it epitomizes the writer's work with regard to both form and content. Concerning
form, this narrative provides an excellent example of what King calls a "voice
piece," which begins abruptly with the following dialogue:

> Can't sleep, Bob Haynie tells the doorman at the King Edward.
>
> Can't sleep, can't sleep.
>
> First time in Toronto?
>
> Yes.
>
> Businessman?
>
> Yes.
>
> Looking for some excitement?
>
> Yes.
>
> Bay Street, sir, says the doorman. (2005b, 1)

Reducing report to a minimum, and without having recourse to a detailed description of the setting, this concise dialogue vividly sets up the scene: a sleepless businessman staying at a hotel in downtown Toronto is sent by the doorman to Bay Street in order to look for "some excitement," which readers may assume is the kind of entertainment supplied by any red-light district. But, typically playing with our expectations, the author startles us with one of his characteristic displays of magic realism. Instead of engaging in some sort of sexual activity, what Bob Haynie does in Bay Street is watch a flock of Indians crashing into the side of an office tower, as flying migratory birds sometimes do when they are attracted by the lights from the city skyscrapers. Two men jump out of a city truck in order to collect the bodies, and explain to the puzzled businessman how they deal with this "natural phenomenon": "The dead ones we bag, says Rudy. The live ones we tag, says Bill" (3). According to the two city employees, Bob has been lucky to witness a tourist attraction that is becoming rare nowadays, because the Indians are disappearing. Fascinated by the spectacle of the Indians, Bob returns to his hotel, where he thanks the doorman, who nostalgically remembers, "In the old days, when they came through, they would black out the entire sky" (4).

Out of the four main narrative modes, speech prevails in "A Short History of Indians in Canada."[5] And in spite of the absence of quotation marks, speech here is always direct speech, not reported speech. The dialogues between the businessman and the doorman begin and close this circular story, thus illustrating Thomas King's most common narrative structure, which makes us end right where we began. The oral quality of this story highlights King's exposition of his Native material, which focuses on the present while giving just a glimpse of the past, a time he consciously avoids.[6] The modern setting of the story—an urban center that smells of concrete and is full of skyscrapers—furnishes the lifelike elements that are later combined with the mythical ones in order to produce a piece of magic realism. Thus, King provocatively mixes everyday earthly events with supernatural, fantastic or surrealistic episodes so as to convey his political ideas in a persuasive manner. Additionally, his caustic sense of humor emphasizes the effect of this instance of social satire, which specifically addresses the notion of "the Vanishing Indian," one of the stereotypes that the author has often tried to counter in his writings.

All through his fiction, Thomas King places his serious concerns within a comic framework, turning to humor not merely for amusement, but to correct widespread misconceptions about Native peoples and their cultures. He resorts to jesting in order to more effectively deliver his earnest political messages about racism, stereotyping, appropriation, sovereignty, environmental degradation, land claims, cross-cultural adoption, and many other issues that have a bearing on the present lives of Natives. For instance, the stereotype of "the Vanishing Indian" together with the objectification of Native peoples and the commodification of "Indian culture" are the main themes of the second story included in *A Short History of Indians in Canada*. The protagonist of "Tidings of Comfort and Joy" is a white man who proudly collects specimens of nearly extinct First Nations peoples for his own pleasure and to entertain his house guests, just as one of his friends has taken up the hobby of gathering African ivories (2005b, 5–19). As is the case in most of his fictional writings, King ridicules or pokes fun at prejudice rather than employing a solemn tone to repudiate it. In an interview about the controversial children's book *A Coyote Columbus Story* (1992), he explained to reviewer Marke Andrews his main reason for adopting this kind of procedure: "Preaching doesn't work. I prefer to be laughing like crazy, then slip the knife in every so often" (1992, C15). Two years later, when interviewed by Jeffrey Canton, King addressed the same topic as follows: "You have to be funny enough to get them laughing so they really don't feel how hard you hit them. And the best kind of comedy is where you start off laughing and end up crying, because you realize just what is happening halfway through the emotion"

(1998, 97). In fact, King has never ceased to resort to the subversive humor that Margaret Atwood praised so enthusiastically at the very beginning of his literary career, when she observed about his early stories "One Good Story, That One" and "Joe the Painter and the Deer Island Massacre":

> They ambush the reader. They get the knife in, not by whacking you over the head with their own moral righteousness, but by being funny. Humour can be aggressive and oppressive, as in keep-'em-in-their-place sexist and racist jokes. But it can also be a subversive weapon, as it has often been for people who find themselves in a fairly tight spot without other, more physical, weapons. (1993b, 244)

Partly because King rejects the characterization of Natives as vanishing communities, he avoids the images that place them in the past. Instead, he often grounds his stories on contemporary popular culture, and focuses on the social realities of today's Canadian urban centers and reserves. However, he also ties the past to the present by introducing deliberate anachronisms, and by refashioning traditional tales in the midst of modern or even futuristic scenarios.[7] For instance, in the narrative entitled "The Garden Court Motor Motel," he parodies the creation story of the WOMAN WHO FELL FROM THE SKY. In King's hilarious new version, the woman fails to reenact her legendary performance in the swimming pool because the required elements are missing. The four water animals that are supposed to dive to the bottom of the water and bring up the dirt are nowhere to be seen. The turtle on whose back the dirt must expand in order to form the Earth is absent as well. The only person to whom the WOMAN WHO FELL FROM THE SKY can talk, without ever making herself understood, is the manager's son, an ignorant young man who is unable to recognize the mother of all peoples.

"The Garden Court Motor Motel" shares some features with the title story of King's first collection of short fiction *One Good Story, That One* (1993b), in which King had irreverently parodied the Genesis account of Adam and Eve, not just to make fun of the biblical story, but primarily in order to make his readers understand how one feels when strangers treat with disrespect what one holds as sacred. Furthermore, in *Green Grass, Running*

Water, once again the novelist evoked the Garden of Eden as an enclosed space where GOD exerted authority, claiming exclusive property, imposing selfish rules, and restraining Old Coyote's insatiable appetite for fried chicken, pizza, hot dogs, melon, and corn, that is, traditional and modern, as well as local and foreign types of food (1993a, 40–41 and 68–70). In this novel, the author not only imagined Jehovah interacting with Coyote, but also subversively envisaged how Changing Woman would land on Noah's ark when she fell out of the sky, rather than on the canoe that readers might expect.

Apart from comically dealing with these two creation stories in his fiction, in the first of his Massey lectures Thomas King has resorted to both of them seriously in order to compare and contrast a Native worldview with a Judeo-Christian one (2005c, 10–22). After recognizing the main stylistic differences between the account of the Woman Who Fell from the Sky and that of Adam and Eve in the Garden of Eden, King concentrates on the ideology propounded by each of them. He points out that the Native story of the woman called Charm starts with a formless world of water and mud, but thanks to the shared efforts of all the earth's inhabitants, the planet gradually develops into a setting where peace, equality, and balance are celebrated (23–24). Conversely, the biblical story begins in Paradise—devised by an omnipotent, omniscient, and omnipresent deity—but ends up in chaos, which is brought about by a single act of disobedience. Thus, King concludes his first Massey lecture by ironically suggesting what he says he does not mean: we should blame a civilization shaped by stories that are based on crime and punishment, that praise hierarchical relationships, that honor individuals who fight their way to the top, and that turn those who see themselves as God's Chosen People into arrogant Masters of the Universe with exploitative attitudes to natural resources.

All through the Massey lectures, collected in the book *The Truth about Stories,* King harmoniously blends theory and practice both by speculating on the enormous potential of storytelling and by narrating a considerable number of stories, which are woven into his analysis. Each of the five lectures begins with the story about how the earth floats in space on the back of a turtle. It is always the same story, but King remarks that there are changes every time that it is told in a different place to different people: changes in the voice of the storyteller, the details, the order of events, or the response of the audience. In the first three brief paragraphs of each lecture, using basically identical wording, King notes that the story of the earth and the turtle is told in five Canadian cities, located in five different provinces: Prince Rupert (British Columbia), Lethbridge (Alberta), Peterborough (Ontario), Trois-Rivières (Québec), and Moncton (New Brunswick). In all five lectures, the introductory creation story is followed by the same key sentence, "The truth about stories is that that's all we are," a dictum that refers to the title of the book and is repeated for the sixth time at the end of the volume, to open a final section entitled "Afterwords: Private Stories" (2005c, 153). In each lecture, King's key sentence is illustrated by a quotation drawn from a different Native author: the Okanagan artist Jeannette Armstrong (2), the Anishinabe writer and university professor Gerald Vizenor (32), the Metis singer Andrea Menard (62), the Laguna poet and novelist Leslie Marmon Silko (92), and the Cherokee storyteller and playwright Diane Glancy (122). Each of these five quotes calls attention to a particular aspect of storytelling: (1) Armstrong conceptualizes storytellers as listeners and speakers "of" and "for" their people, (2) Vizenor observes that storytelling helps us understand the world, (3) Menard celebrates the fact that the imagination revealed through storytelling may hold a nation's pride, (4) Silko remarks that storytelling is not only entertainment but may also be useful to fight off illness and death, and (5) Glancy concludes that some stories take seven days to tell whereas others take all our lives.

Each of the five quotations provides a starting point for King's theoretical discussions, which are mixed with stories, most of which are his own, while a few are extracted from the works of other writers. Personal recollections are grounded on collective memory in those of King's stories that deal with events and anecdotes from his own life and that, as a result, can be interpreted as pieces of individual and communal life-writing. To a great extent, all of his Massey lectures highlight the conceptual intersections between life-writing (as opposed to the traditional genre of autobiography) and history, both in practice and from a theoretical standpoint. For example, in the first lecture, his recollection of his mother evokes much more than a vivid portrait of a strong-willed and optimistic woman who raised her two sons by herself, facing all kinds of difficulties while making her way "from doing hair in a converted garage to designing tools for the aerospace industry" (2005c, 3). Apart from depicting a real person who seems to have inspired certain distinctive features of some of his fictional characters, the author's retrospective view of his mother renders a larger panorama, since her story epitomizes a whole social context marked by prejudice and discrimination against female workers trying to get job advancement in the mid-twentieth century.

The first of Thomas King's lectures contains fragmented memories of his childhood and adolescence, a time when he evaded the harsh realities of his earthly existence by imaginatively escaping to outer space.[8] Stories about other worlds and interplanetary travel allowed him to cope with his teenage angst, exacerbated by two intensifying factors: (1) "being poor in a rich country," and (2) "knowing that white was more than a colour" (2005c, 2). Although King claims that he vaguely remembers actual—or perhaps invented—scenes in which a man who might, or might not, have been his father took him to a small café, this parental absence is not a mere nonexistence that simply leaves a void. King's sense of loss used to trigger in him frequent dreams about an illusory future encounter with his father, who had left the family for good. The child was about three or four years old when this happened, and as he grew up, he would resort to imagining his father's death in order to avoid informing his friends of the actual situation. The intense suffering caused by such a mysterious disappearance elicits in the lecturer a chain of thoughts that helps readers understand why the theme of the missing father is so recurrent in King's fiction.

Will, the mixed-blood protagonist and first-person narrator of *Medicine River*, King's earliest novel, resents having "no vague recollections, no stories, no impressions, nothing" left by his father, except for a bunch of old letters that are addressed to his mother and that he surreptitiously manages to read (1991c, 7–8). The brief missives reveal a man who was full of good intentions, but always had an excuse for not even dropping by, or at least sending the money and the presents he had promised in his previous messages (2–9). In "The Dog I Wish I Had, I Would Call It Helen," four-year-old Jonathan is being brought up by his mother only, while his father does no more than make occasional long-distance telephone calls to keep on postponing the much awaited return home (2005b, 20–33). In "Noah's Ark," another short story included in the same collection, little Luke naively lets strangers know how his drunk father killed himself in an accident that not only made the young boy an orphan, but also took away the lives of two of his siblings (2005b, 112–26). In the story "Where the Borg Are," young Milton Friendlybear fails whenever he looks for a logical reason to account for his dad's strange desertion of his family; therefore, the ingenious schoolboy settles for a fantastic motivation, involving outer space creatures by whom he fears he might be kidnapped as well (2005b, 131–32). In King's novels and short stories, children are often impressed by mothers who always rise above adversity and by wise grandparents who furnish spiritual and material comfort. Compared with the satisfaction provided by such nurturing figures, the painful impact made upon youngsters by the unexplained absence of their irresponsible fathers is no less conspicuous.

In his first Massey lecture, however, Thomas King purposely refrains from dwelling on his personal trauma for too long, and even minimizes it by quickly switching to the various tragedies that affect humankind at large, such as starvation, land mines, suicide bombings, sectarian violence, and sexual abuse (2005c, 8). His argument about atrocities leads him to recall Leslie Silko's story of how evil came to the world and was set loose forever. Once upon a time, there was a contest for conjuring the scariest thing, and the witch who won it was the one who told a story "full of fear and slaughter, disease and blood" (9). It was indeed a terrible story that, once told, could not be called back. The story about the witch, drawn from *Ceremony*, simultaneously closes King's discussion on evil and serves as a prelude to his extensive disquisition on the power of stories not only to form our perceptions of the universe, but also to shape the world itself.

King's profound belief in the transformative power of stories, their outstanding ability to create and destroy, pervades both his critical and his fictional writings. It is perhaps the most recurring topic in his Massey lectures, where he ponders it extensively and in earnest, although on other occasions he mentions it in passing and jokingly. For instance, in the humorous observations he prefixes to his contribution to the collection *Our Story: Aboriginal Voices on Canada's Past*, he states that "I wrote it to change the world" is his third and favorite answer whenever he is asked why he wrote something (2005a, 157). Nevertheless, those seemingly light words about his creative process achieve an unexpected poignancy as soon as we perceive the author's irony by reading the piece of fiction that follows them, "Coyote and the Enemy Aliens," a tragicomic story in which he deals with the trauma endured by the people of Japanese heritage who lived in North America during the Second World War (2005a, 159–74).

In the Massey lectures, King seriously focuses on the transforming faculty of stories, often resorting to quotes from other writers, such as a paragraph by the Nigerian storyteller Ben Okri, who concluded: "If we change the stories we live by, quite possibly we change our lives" (2005c, 153). King's own assertion that "stories can control our lives" justifies his decision to offer readers such a detailed autobiographical account that, he insists, is not intended to play on our sympathies, but to make us aware of the impact of storytelling on the daily existence of any human being (9). Rather than expand his lectures with generalizations about abstract entities, the author resorts to specific people (including himself, his relatives, and friends) in order to express his main concerns about the articulation of personal identity through storytelling.

The paradoxes of hybrid identities and the difficulties in occupying what King calls "racial shadow zones" are examined throughout his fourth Massey lecture, which is haunted by memories of the Choctaw-Cherokee-Irish novelist, critic, and theorist Louis Owens. King expresses the deep sorrow that he felt when he learned about the suicide of his close friend, and comments on how much they had in common. In particular, they shared the same literary purpose, which King defines as follows: "We wrote knowing that none of the stories we told would change the world. But we wrote in the hope that they would" (92). The central story of this fourth lecture is one about Louis Owens, which Owens himself tells in his memoir *I Hear the Train*. It is a sad story about the unfulfilled hopes of hundreds of poor youngsters who were offered summer jobs but ended up being the innocent victims of a short-lived experiment in economic opportunity, ruined by governmental ineptness and commercial greed. The sorrowful story about Owens is juxtaposed with three cheerful anecdotes that King enjoys telling because, being a "hopeful pessimist" as much as Owens was (92), he needs stories that make him laugh and help him keep alive, stories he calls "saving stories" (119). All four stories are cleverly worked into a theoretical discussion on oral and written literature, a disquisition intended to refute the false assumptions that often lead people to privilege the latter over the former.

Native oral literature is a territory that Thomas King has often explored, first by undertaking research for his dissertation (1986), then by publicizing the assets of its chief practitioners (1990c), and, above all, by drawing inspiration from it in order to create his own contributions to what he once called "interfusional literature," that is, "a blending of oral literature and written literature" (1997, 244). What may strike readers of *The Truth about Stories* as new is that Thomas King conceptualizes oral stories as public stories, yet he conceives written stories as private ones (2005c, 154). Anticipating disagreement about his perception of these dichotomies, he contends that, notwithstanding public libraries and bookstores, the act of reading is essentially an individual's private experience, whereas in the case of oral storytelling the audience engages in a group dynamic. According to his particular distinction, there are stories he can tell out loud, while there are others he would never perform as oral pieces, but only dare to put forth in print.

Except for one "private" story that King chose never to perform in public as an oral piece but decided to place at the end of his book, confined to a series of "mute marks on a silent page" (2005c, 155), all the stories contained in *The Truth about Stories* are meant to be told out loud. They are, in his own terms, "public" stories for everyone to use freely, albeit always honestly, for listeners and readers are encouraged to share the moral responsibility of storytellers. This emphasis on ethics is the driving force behind the five Massey lectures, all of which end up inviting us to take the central story of the talk, and do with it whatever we wish—perhaps tell it to friends, cry over it, or forget it. However, there is an admonishment we should never forget, because it is repeated as the closing lines of every single lecture:

> But don't say in the years to come that you would have lived your life differently if only you had heard this story.
> You've heard it now.

NOTES

1. For a more detailed discussion, see Gibert 2006.

2. Sophie McCall rightly observes: "The Canada-US border has long been considered a soft border, more a state of mind than a physical presence. However, for Aboriginal peoples, the border is a constant reminder of colonial history. It is an enduring scar that not only obscures the violent appropriation of Aboriginal territories over the past four-hundred years but also effaces older maps of Native North American nations" (2004, 205). For a comprehensive analysis, see Andrews and Walton 2006.

3. For an analysis of King's tendency to mix fact and fantasy in his short fiction, see Gibert 2001.

4. King is well acquainted with the works of other Native writers who use the same motifs, for he remarked in his fourth Massey lecture: "Gerald Vizenor borrows traditional figures, such as the Trickster, re-imagines them within a contemporary context, and sets them loose in a sometimes modern, sometimes post-apocalyptic world" (2005c, III).

5. Speech is the predominant narrative mode even in King's first novel, *Medicine River*, where direct speech is indicated by a conventional use of quotation marks.

6. When Thomas King compared the film *Dances with Wolves* with one of Tomson Highway's plays, he emphasized his own and his coetaneous Native writers' determination to set their fiction in the present, adding: "When we do go to the past, it is not the 19th century of cowboys and Indians; it is to the past of oral stories and tribal traditions" (1991a).

7. When interviewed by Marie C. Davis upon the publication of *A Coyote Columbus Story*, King explicitly referred to his deliberate use of anachronism as a method "to tie the past with the present" (Davis 1996, 56).

8. King's short fiction is interspersed with amusing glimpses of outer space. See, for instance, "How Corporal Colin Sterling Saved Blossom, Alberta, and Most of the Rest of the World as Well" (1987), an ironically entitled short story about how all the Indians in North America become petrified and are subsequently taken away in spaceships by blue alien coyotes (1993b, 47–63).

WORKS CITED

Andrews, Jennifer, and Priscilla L. Walton. 2006. "Rethinking Canadian and American Nationality: Indigeneity and the 49th Parallel in Thomas King." *American Literary History* 18.3 (Fall): 600–617.

Andrews, Marke. 1992. "History by 'The Little Guy.'" Review of *A Coyote Columbus Story. Vancouver Sun*, 28 November, C15.

Atwood, Margaret. 1992. "A Double-Bladed Knife: Subversive Laughter in Two Stories by Thomas King." In *Native Writers and Canadian Writing*, edited by W. H. New, 243–50. 1990; Vancouver: University of British Columbia Press.

Davis, Marie C. 1996. "Parable, Parody, or 'Blip in the Canadian Literary Landscape': Tom King on *A Coyote Columbus Story.*" *Canadian Children's Literature* 22.4 (Winter): 47–64.

Gibert, Teresa. 2001. "Narrative Strategies in Thomas King's Short Stories." In *Telling Stories: Postcolonial Short Fiction in English*, edited by Jacqueline Bardolph, 67–76. Amsterdam: Rodopi.

———. 2006. "Written Orality in Thomas King's Short Fiction." *Journal of the Short Story in English* 47 (Autumn): 97–109.

King, Thomas. 1986. "Inventing the Indian: White Images, Native Oral Literature, and Contemporary Native Writers." Ph.D. diss., University of Utah, 1986.

———. 1990a. "Interview with Thomas King." Interview by Constance Rooke. *World Literature Written in English* 30.2 (Autumn): 62–76.

———. 1990b. *All My Relations: An Anthology of Contemporary Canadian Native Fiction*, edited by Thomas King. Toronto: McClelland.

———. 1990c. "Other Stories, Other Voices." *Toronto Star*, 31 March, M12.

———. 1991a. "Dances with the Truth." *Toronto Star*, 13 April, G1.

———. 1991b. Interview by Hartmut Lutz. 2 May 1990. In *Contemporary Challenges: Conversations with Canadian Native Authors*, by Hartmut Lutz, 107–16. Saskatoon: Fifth House.

———. 1991c. *Medicine River.* 1989; Toronto: Penguin.

———. 1992. *A Coyote Columbus Story.* Toronto: Groundwood.

———. 1993a. *Green Grass, Running Water.* Toronto: HarperCollins.

———. 1993b. *One Good Story, That One.* Toronto: HarperCollins.

———. 1997. "Godzilla vs. Post-Colonial." In *New Contexts of Canadian Criticism*, edited by Ajay Heble, Donna Palmateer Pennee, and J. R. (Tim) Struthers, 241–48. 1990; Peterborough, Ontario: Broadview.

———. 1998. "Coyote Lives: Thomas King." Interview by Jeffrey Canton. In *The Power to Bend Spoons: Interviews with Canadian Novelists,* edited by Beverley Daurio and Frank Davey, 90–97. 1994; Toronto: Mercury.

———. 1999a. "Peter Gzowski Interviews Thomas King on *Green Grass, Running Water.*" *Canadian Literature* 161–62 (Summer–Autumn): 65–76.

———. 1999b. "Teaching Dead Dog New Tricks." Interview by David Homel. *The Gazette,* 20 November, J4.

———. 1999c. *Truth and Bright Water.* Toronto: HarperFlamingoCanada.

———. 2005a. "Contributor's Note." In *Our Story: Aboriginal Voices on Canada's Past,* by Thomas King et al., 157–58. Doubleday/Anchor Canada.

———. 2005b. *A Short History of Indians in Canada.* Toronto: HarperCollins.

———. 2005c. *The Truth about Stories: A Native Narrative.* 2003; Minneapolis: University of Minnesota Press.

McCall, Sophie. 2004. "The Forty-Ninth Parallel and Other Borders: Recent Directions in Native North American Literary Criticism." *Canadian Review of American Studies* 34.2: 205–20.

Owens, Louis. 2001. *I Hear the Train: Reflections, Inventions, Refractions.* Norman: University of Oklahoma Press.

Silko, Leslie Marmon. 1977. *Ceremony.* New York: Penguin.

Indians in Sunday Clothes: The Imposturing Strategies of Grey Owl

A rchibald Stansfeld Belaney was born in Sussex, England, in September 1888 to a farmer family. He was raised by his grandmother and two maiden aunts. He is said to have expressed an interest in nature and American Indians at an early age. In 1906 he migrated to Canada to study agriculture. After a brief time in Toronto he moved to Temagami in northern Ontario and adopted an Indian identity (half Scottish, half Apache) under the name of Grey Owl. He worked as a fur trapper, wilderness guide, and forest ranger. During World War I he joined the 13th Montreal Battalion of the Black Watch. His unit was shipped to France, where he served as a sniper. He was wounded and sent to England for treatment. In 1917 he went back to Canada and was discharged with a disability pension. In 1925 he met Gertrude Bernard (whom he later called Anahareo), an Iroquois woman who encouraged him to stop trapping and start writing about wilderness life. His works attracted the attention of the Dominion Parks Services, for whom he began to work as a naturalist. Later he would also star in their movies. In 1935–37 he toured England in Ojibwa costume to promote his books and lecture about conservation. A year later he returned to his cabin at the Ajawaan Lake. He died on April 13, 1938. Doubts about his identity began appearing after his death. Eventually his imposture was exposed. Publication of his books ceased and donations to conservationist causes decreased.

■ 1

His imposture (pp. of *imponere* = to impose upon) went undetected for a long time, at least for those who were not close to him, because Archibald Stansfeld Belaney reinforced the essentialist categories of oppression upheld by the system of knowledge. In other words, the system that interprets the world hid the difference imposed upon him, his contradiction.

Contrary to Hegel, whose positive dialectics served reconciliation through the principle of the Spirit, Adorno's procedure of negative dialectics served contradiction: "The contradiction is the non-identical under the aspect of identity; the primacy of the principle of contradiction in dialectics measures what is heterogeneous in unitary thinking. By colliding against its own borders, it reaches beyond itself. Dialectics is the consistent consciousness of non-identity," he explains (1970, 16–18). Insofar as consciousness of nonidentity—achieved though confronting the system and the external to the system, the theoretical and the atheoretical, the concept and the thing—denies identity, it also prevents identifying judgments and, within the same movement, disavows the system:

> The slightest remainder of non-identity would suffice, according to its concept, to deny identity. The excrescences of the systems since the Cartesian pineal gland and the axioms and definitions of Spinoza, already filled to the brim with the entire rationalism which he deductively extracts, proclaim by their untruth that of the systems themselves, their madness. (32)

Yet Adorno's critique of idealism defends idealism to the extent that, despite the preponderance of the object, only "those who have had the undeserved

good fortune not to be completely adjusted in their inner intellectual composition to the prevailing norms" yield to the object (1970, 50). But what interests
me is that although Adorno speculates on the concept of the nonconceptual,
he understands this possibility as clearing away dialectics by constraining "the
entire world to the identical, to totality" (149). It is my argument, however,
that the difference does not necessarily have to perish in the concept. When
the concept defines itself as nonidentity, as in the case of the subaltern, the
signature of the contradiction persists in the substance of the identical.

On these grounds three extrapolations are made: First, the narrative of
colonization has been a narrative of imposture, built on concepts that repressed all qualitative referents. The subject—who was negated to simulate
an appearance of objectivity—imposed upon the other a look existing in his
mind and made the referent vanish into the concept. Perceptively, Vizenor
writes that "Indians are cultural narratives of an absence" (1998, 28), referring
to a long history of photographic ethnography and literary discourse that has
eviscerated Indians and thrown them away from the concept of indigeneity.
Second, imposture demands exposure, because if the spectator is deceived,
imposture ceases to exist as a promise of truth. Third, since identity aims at
mimesis and since "the concept cannot otherwise represent the thing which
it repressed, namely mimesis, than by appropriating something of this latter
into its own mode of conduct, without losing itself to it" (29), it is through
resistance to the nonconceptually mimetic, that is, in the compulsion for
remaining identical, that antagonism can be gleaned. In other words, im-
posturing does not completely supplant the self because rarely is anything so
perfectly hidden that it is never undetected. Ultimately, the self is always too
homogeneous within itself, within its knowledge, too "immutable" (140) to
resist exposure. However, when there is no thing to confront the concept
with, resistance must be looked for in the dominating principle of theory,
which becomes the thing itself.

■ 2

Theory. From Greek *theoria*, from *theoros* = spectator, from *thea* = a viewing
+ *oros* = seeing. Theory = perception.

"We imagine perception to be a photographic view of things," says Bergson (1991, 38), a photograph unencumbered by "the noise of Time," as Barthes puts it (1981, 15). To Barthes, in fact:

> Photography cannot signify (aim at a generality) except by assuming a mask. It is this word which Calvino correctly used to designate what makes a face into a product of a society and of its history. As in the portrait of William Casby, photographed by Avedon: the essence of slavery is here laid bare: the mask is the meaning, insofar as it is absolutely pure (as it was in the ancient theater). This is why the great photographers are great mythologists: Nadar (the French bourgeoisie), Sander (the Germans of pre-Nazi Germany), Avedon (New York's "upper crust"). (34)

He states further:

> The photograph of the Mask is in fact critical enough to disturb (in 1934, the Nazis censored Sander because "his faces of the period" did not correspond to the Nazi archetype of the race), but it is also too discreet (or too "distinguished") to constitute an authentic and effective social critique, at least according to the exigencies of militantism: what committed science would acknowledge the interest of Physiognomy? (36)

To Barthes who, like Hegel, considers the outer higher than the inner, and assumes that there is no justified concealment, the mask is the soul, and on it lies the possibility of truth. That the truth functions on the surface of the sign is said to have been true for Indians in the old times. Have we not been told that their resistance to being photographed was grounded on the belief that the photograph buried the soul they had been robbed of?

Together with Nadar, Sander and Avedon, Edward Curtis was also a great photographer. Between 1896 and 1930 he took over 40,000 negatives of people from 80 different nations that served as important historical documents. His Indian, however, was removed from the complex realities of twentieth-century life. He—most times it was a he—was "wild, free, noble, handsome, philosophical, eloquent, solitary" (King 2003, 79). He had no facial hair, kept his clothes on, and spoke "reasonable English" (82). Succinctly and eloquently Vizenor writes:

> Curtis paid his natives to pose; he selected ornaments, vestments, and he played the natural light, tone, picturesque reflections, and the solitary nature of natives in his pictures. The pictorial images of pensive warriors are simulations of the real; transmuted in visual analogies. The aesthetic poses of natives countered the cruelties of reservations and binaries of savagism and civilization. (2000, 5)

I guess Curtis would have loved to take a picture of Grey Owl, who would have loved to be captured by Curtis's lens, but he was not, though Grey Owl represented the type that was itself representative. In the photograph "*Wa-Sha-Quon-Asin*," inserted in his autobiography, *Pilgrims of the Wild*, he sits in full regalia, an axe in his left hand (was he left-handed?), looking his best:

> My idea of looking my best was to wear my hair long, have plenty of fringes on my buckskin, to allow one tassel of my Hudson Bay sash to hang behind like a tail, and to have the front of my shirt decorated with an oblique row of safety pins on each side, as a Cossack wears his ammunition, to be intriguingly glimpsed at times beneath a leather vest. (1973, 16)

For whom does he look his best? No photographer is acknowledged. Grey Owl, lean and brown, stares back at the spectator, aware of his image being taken, as if holding the privileged position of seeing what others cannot see. What strikes the eye is the immense whiteness of his clothes. They look disturbingly new, and big on him, for that matter. Note the detail of the cuff extending past his wrist, asking to be turned back to fit the length of his arm. In spite of this, or precisely because of this, Grey Owl looks much like an Indian. Yet, it is as if this excess of indigeneity tried to compensate for some kind of lack. Contrary to Barthes, who says that "the Photograph always carries its referent with itself" (1981, 5), I feel "Wa-Sha-Quon-Asin" does not refer. I feel it lacks a referent. My feeling is obviously conditioned by the knowledge that he was no Indian, that the photograph contains no living presence. A body without the quality of a soul. Did Belaney in his posing behind the mask of the Indian suffer from any discomfort of inauthenticity, as Barthes did when pictures of him were taken? "I constitute myself in the process of 'posing,' I instantly make another body for myself, I transform myself in advance into an image," says Barthes, too aware of the distance between his consciousness and his identity to lie to himself (10). I wonder if Belaney lied to himself, or if he believed that he was laying bare the essence of pure Nativeness through his images. Is his photograph in any way critical? I wonder why he chose to supplement his Indian photographs with writing. Why did he feel in need to narrativize his pictures?

To be sure, there was money, but there was something else. On the one hand, as Vizenor notes, "The creation of visual images . . . is represented by linguistic authority. Pointedly, photographic images are bound by the structure of language" (2000, 2). On the other hand, Native American autobiographies, like photography, are a postcontact form that has been predicated on absence and disappearance:

> Native American memoirs did not exist before the passage of the Indian Removal Act of 1830, which mandated the forced migration of the eastern tribes to locations west of the Mississippi River. The first Indian autobiography, the *Life of Ma-Ka-tai-me-she-kia-kiak or Black Hawk,* by the Sauk leader, appeared in 1833 after his defeat by federal troops in the campaign known as Black Hawk War. Native American autobiography has always been a solicited form, traditionally elicited and edited by a white person though narrated by its subject. . . . While nineteenth-century Native American autobiographies were the stories of defeated leaders, of heroes in the mold of Kit Carson or Sam Houston, twentieth-century works began to represent the process of Americanization. (Browder 2000, 126)

And on yet another hand, autobiography before Grey Owl had already served the purpose of ethnic reconstruction. In 1856 James P. Beckwourth, of black descent, rewrote himself into whiteness, passing as Crow in the story of his life and adventures. By 1928 Sylvester Long, a colored janitor born in North Carolina, had evolved into Chief Buffalo Long Lance through writing. Later, in 1976 Asa Carter would take on a Cherokee self in *The Education of Little Tree* as a way of leaving his racist reputation behind him. But most of all, to me, Belaney wrote to fill the hole in the photograph with the dynamics of a presence. In so doing he secretly exposed the identical that inhabited his representation, and flaunted his own photographic act of othering the self.

■ 3

In "The Pose of Imposture" Lee Edelman notes that "the image constitutive of a self-portrait demands that it be read in some relation to the original" (1986, 95). Although "the nature of the 'original' is often far from clear" (95), not so the representation to which the self-portrait points. In "The Mission of Hiawatha," within *Tales of an Empty Cabin*, Belaney clearly identifies James Fenimore Cooper and Henry Wadsworth Longfellow as the unequivocal models for his own portrayal. The former "lived a great deal closer to the days and affairs they described than we do" (1989, 80), and possessed deep knowledge of "the subtlety, the evasiveness, the stubbornness, the self-denying fortitude, and the inexplicable inconsistencies of Indian character" (80), despite his idealization of him "in rather exaggerated manner" (80). That Cooper's idealization covered contempt—in fact, the mechanisms that work in the celebration of the nonidentical are also employed by racism (Adorno 1970, 172–74)—goes unnoticed for Belaney, whose theoretical account of indigeneity shows the same disrespect, as shown below. For his part Longfellow "depicted an entirely opposite side of Indian life" (1989, 81). The story of Hiawatha is "allegorical and much is legend; yet the allegories can, in nearly every instance, be applied to conditions of modern life, and the legends, if barbaric, are often beautiful, and truly told. And for that matter, modern history books contain as fine a collection of fairy tales, as is to be found anywhere" (81). Far from discrediting history as downright falsehood, Belaney invests allegory with the power of truth:

With the exception of one or two mispronunciations, done intentionally in order to preserve the metre, all the Ojibwa words have been correctly rendered, and in some cases translated. So authentic is the treatment that the whole thing could have been written by an Indian had there been one skilled enough to do it. The peculiar wording used, the declamatory style, the imagery, the reiteration of a thought successfully in different ways, and the smooth-flowing, almost monotonous rhythm, make the work seem less like a poem than a chant, and reminds me of nothing so much as the intoning of some wise and aged Indian orator who, standing before some great assemblage of his people, recites, in well-selected phrase and measured utterance, the history of some great event of former days. (81)

He alleges that "The personification of animals and natural objects is typically Indian" (82), and concludes, "The delineations of Indian character are remarkably true to life . . . [and] can be found—though modified perhaps—in every Indian village, and their counterparts in nearly every community, everywhere" (83).

However authentic the model is, it is still an interpretation. As Edelman points out, the word *model* "implies a crucial *lack* of authenticity to the extent that it signifies a reproduction of some *other* object, a replica or a copy" (1986, 96). More crucial is a lack when that which it represents has been liquidated in the representation. Significantly, Belaney resists his literary antecedents in the attempt to become more original than the originals themselves:

I had noticed that, apart from the literary skill and carefully selected wording apparent in them, many of the narratives we read with such interest had very little meat on their bone, so to speak, when they were dissected. I had plenty of material, so I decided to write an article with lots of meat on it. So I commenced the welding process. This took about a week, and resulted in a production about six thousand words in length, very meaty, and in which I covered the greater part of Northern Canada, and touched with no light hand on every incident and animal common to that region. (1989, 137)

Yet the reality of his corporeal existence is not summoned up, so that by attempting to bypass Longfellow, Belaney only reproduces him—his words, phrases, motifs, images—all the more effectively. Ultimately, his book is a crusade of memory toward early time, a kind of pilgrim's regress to a time frozen and eternal, freed from "the seeming burden of centuries of wrong" (1989, 4). The memory is his and still not his, since Belaney only remembers what his readings allow him to remember. Because perception does not determine the appearance of memory, but rather memory spontaneously meets perception and conditions its appearance (Bergson 1991, 101), Belaney's perceptions are inevitably shut within a memory that his body has not stored up.

Incidentally Bergson, like Descartes, distinguishes two kinds of memory: memory as habit and memory as representation. The former acts out our past experience but does not call up its image, and does not involve a conscious mental picture. The latter, elevated to the status of "true memory" (1991, 151), conserves bygone images strung out along the course of time, "leaving to each fact its place and, consequently, marking its date, truly moving in the past and not, like the first, in an ever renewed present" (151). The images neglect no detail but lack duration. Inasmuch as they are "pure from all admixture of sensation" (141), they are independent from the body. So if bodily memory disfigures perception by expanding it with time and "digesting" it into movement (210), memory par excellence feeds on the substance of perception, contracting it "into a duration too narrow to permit the separation of its moments," and eventually disappearing "at the moment when motor activity tries to fix its outline" (87). Upon this memory rests the soul (220).

In his desire to be a "primitive," Barthes wishes to do away with true memory: "I dismiss all knowledge, all culture, I refuse to inherit anything from another eye than my own" (1981, 51). Yet how can you be without culture? His refusal hides an impossible performative. Like him, Belaney is so deeply sunk into the representation of the past that he cannot keep time. "So we live in the past and the rest of the world keeps goin [*sic*] by," he writes (1989, 92). His prenarrative time leaves out intuition of duration, which Bergson defines in terms of movement and heterogeneity. Motion there is in the narrative, which is basically a wandering through northern Ontario. And yet the landscape has the static quality of a painting. Because all the spaces he traverses look alike, and movement along the continuity of the same is no movement, appearance of movement coincides with immobility. So when halfway through the book, Belaney decides to give up traveling entirely, there is no significant change in the deathlike pace of the narrative: "To beings of our kind, cessation of travelling, the denial of that unappeasable urge to see what lays beyond the hills, meant stagnation, almost a cessation of living, and worse, long hours of idleness with their dark attendant introspection" (113). This "funereal immobility" (Barthes 1981, 5) transforms the narrative into a photographic image that cannot disappear if "to act is just to induce this memory to shrink, or rather to become thinned and sharpened" (Bergson 1991, 106).

The ecstatic effect of what cannot disappear becomes more precise by repetition at both structural and linguistic levels. The situation is one: the losing and recovery of the perceived object by the perceiving subject. The whole structure whirls around this *fort-da* game. On the other hand, the inflation of the book with synonyms discards the narrative aspects as inessential: "I was much preoccupied with this note book and the still-hunts in the trackless jungles of the book of synonyms, that at times I forgot to eat. I became vocabulary-conscious, began to use four and five dollar words, and often my conversation was unintelligible to my English-speaking friends," he confesses (1989, 215).

Where did he learn his unintelligible English? Belaney has previously written that

> most of my time from middle youth on, had been spent in solitude or largely amongst a people whose language was not English, and confused by regional dialects. Only a retentive memory and a passion for reading has kept alive this early training, and my precise and somewhat stilted English was, like a stiff and ceremonious suit of Sunday best, something to be taken out of the closet and worn on occasion, and its use ended, returned to the limbo of unneeded things. (15)

Precise, wealthy in detail, and stilted, unlike the vague and imprecise language spoken by "primitives" (Austin 1962, 51), his English was far more reasonable than the reasonable English Curtis made his Indians speak, as if Belaney was doing the writing to the exclusion of Grey Owl. So versus the mimetic language cognizant of its own time-space that Adorno's method attempts to rescue so as "to have the thing and the expression approach one another to the point of non-differentiability" (1970, 66), there are the empty declamations of Belaney, "the reiteration of a thought successfully in different ways" through synonyms that signify dissimulation. Civilization falls away like "a discarded garment" (1989, 40), storytellers are actors in mummery (12) and the past is an old cloth lying about their feet (138). In his anxiety over exposure, countries are all dressed up (145), watersheds are clothed "in a black forest of virgin pine" (158), and facts lie hidden "under a camouflage of ambiguities" (145). However, is not to conceal by pretense an inescapable need in a theatrical economy where everybody and everything looks at everybody and everything else? If "Photography touches art . . . by Theater" (Barthes 1981, 31), Belaney runs "a panorama theater animated" by trees that stare and clothes that look at the performance of animals who eye back at each other knowingly (1989, 31). Above them all stands the panoptical watcher of the prologue, who has the power of legitimizing another's existence through acknowledgment or withholding notice. In the prologue sits "a man, alert, silent, watchful" (1973, 3). In front of him

> and directed through the aperture into the building, is a motion picture camera, trained on the door. . . . Outside, in strategic positions commanding the door and the approach from the lake, are other men, holding cameras. Inside the building a man sits in a chair, waiting. Suddenly:
> "All right! Here he comes," cries the watcher.
> . . . over the threshold . . . [comes] a full-grown beaver . . . . Walking upright like a man. (3–4)

A larger beaver enters. "Meanwhile the man in the chair rises, shuts the door and resumes his seat" (5). Another beaver emerges. "The operator's face is a study; he is getting it all" (5). When the beavers finish their job "they run to the seated man and stand erect, looking up at him" (5). The beavers disappear under water and the film is over. "It has been very casual, in a way. No rehearsing has been done, no commands given; the actors have done just about as they liked" (6).

The watchful man is the man who watches the beavers, the cameras, the operators, and watches himself—an Englishman looking like an Indian—doing the watching, as if behind the camera, as if he, together with his surroundings, was no more than an image, agent and object of his own perception. Was it Belaney who captured Grey Owl in the full-regalia picture? When the camera is turned off, his ethereal voice solidifies into a first person, letting us see him as the origin of himself, his own father, and the origin of the story, which is basically the narration of his looking at himself looking "alert, silent, watchful," immobile, "much like Indians" (25).

The "gloomy half-breed" who is "so much like Indians" is for Belaney the genuine Indian. "He has assimilated much of the white man's knowledge whilst retaining nearly all the characteristics of his race" (55). He is melancholic and compassionate. Contrary to him, the "real Indians" (29), of full Indian blood, are indifferent to the sufferings of animals that provide the means to live (23). They are inattentive to others, and particularly "backward" (1989, 162). They are killers (1973, 21), brutal savages (29), cannibals capable of unthinkable cruelties. Also of full Indian blood, equally ignoble and perverted are the white Indians. Though well dressed, they are great thieves, says Belaney, proficient in the technique of deceit and vice (250–51). His open condemnation of full-blooded Indians aims at establishing his persona as the most authentic, but it does not serve as an index of truth if affect is to be subtracted from perception to get the image in its true purity (Bergson 1991, 58).

Nor can his conceptual arrangement eliminate contradictoriness. Grey Owl is a conservationist, and yet he is a mighty hunter: "Pride forbids me," says he, "to say how few wolves I killed that night, considering the amount of ammunition I used, but at forty dollars each as the bounty then was, I was able to buy me some long needed renewals in my outfit, and have some left over" (1989, 77). He is a seasoned adventurer, and yet his adventures are the result of his inexperience: "I might add here that adventures of nearly every kind are almost the outcome of either bad judgement or inexperience or both," he declares (99). The nature he inhabits is pre-civilized, and yet denatured:

"Man should enter the woods, not with any conquistador obsession or mighty hunter complex, neither in a spirit of braggadocio, but rather with the awe, and not a little of the veneration, of one who steps within the portals of some vast and ancient edifice of wondrous architecture," he admonishes (vii–viii). Although he declares that he has no intention "of enlisting the sympathy of an audience or a reader" with disclaimers of a self-deprecatory nature (259), he cannot stop apologizing for his greenness as a writer: "And because it is a tale of ways and means and a manner of living which you may be unfamiliar with, its strangeness may compensate in some degree for my lack of skill in the telling of it," he writes in the prologue to his autobiography (1973, 7). But even though he decides to write "not a personal biography, as requested, but a series of essays of the North itself," it seems to him that "a few good healthy unequivocating 'I's' standing up honestly on their own hind legs, would do no harm whatever" (185). A few too many, it seems to me, for he ends up writing a navel-staring account of a man's search for glory and eternal life. Not in vain does Adorno write that the capacity to distance oneself and rise above things by being a spectator is the immortal part of what is human (1970, 354–58). At the end of the prologue he insists: "I do not draw comparisons between man and beast. . . . Nor do I ascribe human attributes to animals" (xv), yet the paws of his beavers are like hands (45), their language is human (93), and their voices those of a child (192). In point of fact, the ways of these "little people" (42) are so very human that they eventually outdo humans in their humanity.

■ 4

In *Pilgrims of the Wild* Belaney repeats the absence in the photograph but translates his soul into language. "The peculiar wording used, the declamatory style, the imagery, the reiteration of a thought successfully in different ways . . . the smooth-flowing, almost monotonous rhythm" (1989, 81), the prefabricated categories, and dogmatization are not Sunday best worn for the occasion, but ordinary clothes that make the nonidentical the same, and in the making reproduce the contradiction that they stamp out: an Indian posing like an Englishman.

■ 5

Maybe Belaney did not suffer the discomfort of inauthenticity because he believed his own fabrication. But, on the other hand, I think he could not have lied to himself. Can one lie to oneself? "One must not lie to oneself," says Derrida, "the liar knows the truth of what he thinks, he knows what he *means to say*, he knows the difference between what he thinks and what he says: he knows that he is lying" (2002, 41). Moreover, "A lie always harms another; if not some other human being, then it nevertheless does harm to humanity in general, inasmuch as it vitiates the very source of right," Kant dictates (1981, 64–65). Karl Abraham tells the story of another impostor called N. However much N., who othered himself many times, wanted to believe that he was saying the truth, his belief was suspended each time he was charged with fraud and sent to prison. N. was an artist, Abraham concludes, driven by ambivalent impulses: avoidance of exposure and the need of being exposed. His pleasure, he says, derived not only from deceiving others but from gaining their admiration of himself as an artist. Did Belaney, who created himself as a work of art and deceived everybody, also mean to say in his writing what he sought to deny in his pictures so as not to vitiate the very source of right? He lied too much. In strictest terms, he told too many stories.

Storia = Narrative of fictitious events meant to entertain. As euphemism for a lie it dates from 1697.

"To lie," says Rousseau, "is to conceal a truth we ought to make manifest" (2000, 29). One of the questions that arises from his examination is when we owe a truth to another. He finds the answer in intention and sacrifice. The truthful man seeks to deceive no one. So "the fiction writer who merely sets forth a fable as a fable in no way lies" (32): "Fictions which have a moral purpose are called allegories or fables, and as their purpose is or ought to be to wrap useful truths in easily perceived and pleasing forms, in such cases we hardly care about hiding the *de facto* lie, which is only the cloak of truth" (32). The storyteller, then, who by definition has no intention to pass a deceitful content as truth, is a truthful man. As a truthful man he sacrifices his inclinations to the ethics of veracity, which "is always a sacral ethics of sacrifice" (Derrida 2002, 33). Belaney, however, in his commitment to the truth of indigeneity—to what he in good faith had learned its essence was—did not sacrifice himself. Hence the imposture. Not the imposture of passing off as Indian but the imposture of not having dispossessed himself of the truth-content of himself.

WORKS CITED

Adorno, Theodor. 1970. *Negative Dialectics.* Translated by Denis Redmond. Frankfurt am Main: Suhrkamp Verlag.

Abraham, Karl. 1935. "The History of an Impostor in the Light of Psychoanalytic Knowledge." *The Psychoanalytic Quarterly* 4: 570–87.

Austin, J. L. 1962. *How to Do Things with Words.* Cambridge: Cambridge University Press.

Barthes, Roland. 1981. *Camera Lucida. Reflections on Photography.* Translated by Richard Howard. New York: Hill and Wang.

Bergson, Henri. 1991. *Matter and Memory.* Translated by N. M. Paul and W. S. Palmer. New York: Zone Books.

Browder, Laura. 2000. *Slippery Characters: Ethnic Impersonators and American Identities.* Chapel Hill: University of North Carolina Press.

Derrida, Jacques. 2002. "History of the Lie: Prolegomena." In *Without Alibi,* translated by Peggy Kamuf, 28–70. Stanford, Calif.: Stanford University Press.

Edelman, Lee. 1986. "The Pose of Imposture: Ashberry's 'Self-Portrait in a Convex Mirror.'" *Twentieth-Century Journal* 32.1: 95–114.

Grey Owl. 1973. *Pilgrims of the Wild.* 1935; Toronto: Macmillan.

———. 1989. *Tales of an Empty Cabin: Stories of the Early Days in Canada's North.* 1936; Toronto: Macmillan.

Kant, Immanuel. 1981. *Grounding for the Metaphysics of Morals* with *On a Supposed Right to Lie Because of Philanthropic Concerns.* Translated by James W. Ellington. Indianapolis: Hackett.

King, Thomas. 2003. *The Truth about Stories: A Native Narrative.* Toronto: Anansi.

Rousseau, Jean-Jacques. 2000. "Fourth Walk." In *The Reveries of a Solitary Walker, Botanical Writings,* and *Letter to Flanquières,* edited by Cristopher Kelly, translated by Charles E. Butterworth, 28–40. Hanover, N.H.: University Press of New England.

Vizenor, Gerald. 1998. *Fugitive Poses: Native American Indian Scenes of Absence and*

Presence. Lincoln: University of Nebraska Press.

———. 2000. "Edward Curtis: Pictorialist and Ethnographic Adventurist." *October.* http://memory.loc.gov/ammen/award98/ienhtml/essay3.html.

The Eagleheart Narratives: Contexts, Process, Representation, and Ceremony in Making Texts

GORDON D. HENRY JR.

ver the course of twenty-four years Montana scholar Nicolas Vrooman and I have interviewed Turtle Mountain elder Francis Cree—also known as Eagleheart. From these oral, taped interviews we have put together draft texts of written transcriptions that we will edit for a book. This book has been in the works for well over eight years now. It has proven a struggle in process, to provide context, in terms of representation and in negotiating how, or even whether, to represent Eagleheart, his words, the ceremonies he discusses and the communities and people he speaks of and through.

In the introduction to a special issue of the *American Indian Quarterly*, Devon Mihesuah quotes Elizabeth Cook Lynn's concerns about the Nebraska series on "American Indian Lives."

I think the ethnographic biography is not an Indian story at all . . . the writer almost always takes sides with the informant "with the result being" a manuscript to a publisher which will satisfy any voyeur's curiosity; manuscripts which are by and large fantasies of Indians as non-conformists to American cultural restrictions. (1996, 9)

From some viewpoints, Cook Lynn's perspective, while contentious and interestingly provocative, also seems speculative—though not of someone on the outside looking in—and presumptuous on a number of fronts. Who can say if writing on American Indian lives ever falls under the restrictive, mechanical categories of ethnographic or biographic? It may be possible, for example, that *ethno* and *bio* are terms an Indian would never consider when writing or speaking in reference to self, community, or story.

In *Indigenous Aesthetics* Steven Leuthold argues for attempting to view Native culture production as intercultural, yet uniquely related to "the stated goals of contemporary indigenous peoples: self-determination, cultural continuity, cultural distinctiveness from the larger dominant culture, and so on" (1998, 3). Leuthold goes on to advocate aesthetic expression as important to the creation—and I would add—the continued engagement with "national, tribal and group identity," expression that develops from "dance, music, song, the visual arts, literature, drama and storytelling" (5). It's also very likely that the ethno/bio/cultural/Indian story will neither transgress the bounded limits nor entail the definitive Indian story contested in Cook Lynn's terms of critique. More simply the graphic representation of a life of an Indian person may not match anyone's rubric for an Indian story. From Leuthold's perspective a systems approach to aesthetics offers more interesting possibilities for social practices and cultural productions.

> The term "aesthetic" refers to real aspects of lived experience that have a social dimension. Linking ethics, religion, or politics and aesthetics reveals how value systems are embedded in our physical and emotional relationships to the world in which we live. Aesthetic experience is bodily, sensory; it is not just abstract and theoretical.
>
> . . . In the context of indigenous aesthetics a conceptual explanation of a belief or value system may not be the only source of discovering aesthetic ideas; rather beliefs and values are lived, embedded in social relationships. (1998, 6)

I would add to Leuthold's view that an indigenous aesthetic might also offer unique ways for viewing, sensing, transmitting, receiving, and addressing the complexities of lived social relationships.

As for the writer "taking sides with the informant," I would imagine that in many cases that would be the best one could do if the writer and the informant were not one and the same, and an interesting accomplishment if the writer and informant were the same person. What would it entail for a writer to take the side of an informant? How does one become an informant? How can one be sure one is informing or being informed? With the terms *writer*, *informant*, we must imagine more, it seems, the heavy historical baggage of anthropology and ghosts of literary Native lives, rather than more interesting contestations, such as the agonistics of learning out of context at another site, or with an imagined other before us. Further, a manuscript that could satisfy any voyeur's curiosity might be worth looking into even if the writer and publisher had produced the work with some other nonvoyeuristic fantasy in mind. Such a fantasy, it seems, would have to be another's exo-formed fantasy, perhaps a non-Indian's fantasy of an Indian life. At the same time, under Cook Lynn's critiques we would have to assume Indians do not read Indian lives, unless those Indians are also voyeurs, waiting for the next work in a series of glimpses into lives, not their own. In some broader sense, to address Cook Lynn's concerns we would have to understand how other people write and read lives into categories of life/story/Indian, among other terms of difference. And perhaps no writer or informant can do that except for maybe Jorge Luis Borges, Gerald Vizenor, Walt Whitman, Gertrude Stein, Wallace Stevens, Gilles Deleuze, Aristotle . . . Perhaps instead our life stories as Indians, writers, informants, or voyeurs must be read otherwise, under the unrestricted gaze of an appropriate Indian critic, a critical guide, at best, or a consensually produced cultural concordance at worst. Best and worst, and everything in between, leaves little to the trust or imagination of the reader, writer, informant, voyeur, critic.

With all this before us, I will not back off from Cook Lynn's concern about a writer being on the side of "the informant." (Though Francis Cree is much more to me than anything an informant might encompass, he has been a spiritual mentor to me, a friend and an advisor, as well as a source of information—though for many people the term *information* might lean too heavily into associations with different technologies of transmission.)

Thus, I wrote in a note submitted with my book proposal to the University of Nebraska Press:

In 1998 I gave Francis tobacco to request his permission to write a book about him. He accepted the tobacco and thus sanctioned the book project. With that sanction, I would like to honor Francis Cree. I have known Francis for over twenty years. During that time Francis shared ceremonies, spiritual teachings, his home, his time, and his heart with me and hundreds of other people. He did this with great patience and a powerful unspoken love. As a human being, Francis helped me to have courage and find strength in myself. As an Anishinabe he opened many of us to cultural and spiritual perspectives which will inform the survival of our families and communities.

Throughout the years that I've known him, Francis has passed ceremonies on to me: he blessed my pipe, he gave me instructions for the sweat lodge ceremony; he conferred songs, passed on the naming ceremony; he named my children, and my wife; and in 1993, he honored four other men and myself when he passed the thirsty dance ceremony to us. I am honored by this, of course. I am more honored, to be one who Francis calls "my son." I am still more honored to be part of his life, to have known a man who has been a model for compassion, respect, peace, unity and love—those attributes which he says should be at the center of our education. For these reasons, and many more, I would like to honor the life of Francis Cree and his family by helping to complete this book project. Professor LeBeau has also participated in the thirsty dance under Francis' guidance and like Francis, LeBeau has family at Turtle Mountain. He and his family members were also given names by Francis Cree in 1994. So this project holds important personal and cultural significance for him as well. Let me also add here, that while I may write accounts of some of the stories and practices Francis committed to interview, I also learned many of these stories and I have participated in and learned many of the practices Francis details in his interviews.

Beyond my personal interest and cultural affiliations, Eagleheart's experiences seem interesting enough on the surface to be a worthy subject for a book. His lived social relationships and his ways of relating to living may even suggest a set of social practices as aesthetic behavior.[1]

For most readers, voyeurs and otherwise, Eagleheart's story will offer rare insights into the history, the lives, the beliefs, and the ceremonial spirit of the Plains Anishinabeg. Francis's life has spanned, and been influenced by, every important U.S. governmental policy related to American Indian people of the twentieth century. Francis was born in 1918, so his birth came before the American Indian Citizenship Act. He also lived among, knew, and spoke with people who were present at the establishment of the Turtle Mountain Reservation in *1865*. As a young child, he lived through the allotment experience and its devastating effects on the land-base of his people. In later years Eagleheart witnessed the deterioration of ceremonial life, deforestation of tribal lands, and the damages of poverty and alcoholism among his people.

By 1930 he was sanctioned to lead the Thirsty Dance Ceremony as passed down from Many Eagles Set, through a family lineage from his Uncle Standing Chief to him. Discouraged by what he termed lack of respect for the ceremonies, Francis studied to be a preacher at a the Moka-um Bible School in Bagley, Minnesota, in 1958. From 1960 to 1962 Francis served as tribal chairman for the Turtle Mountain Chippewa. In spring 1962 he was selected to go with a group of tribal leaders to meet with John Kennedy, on issues of American Indian rights.

In the middle to late 1980s, Eagleheart worked to reintroduce the pipe, the sweat lodge, and the thirsty dance to generations of Anishinabeg who had little or no connection to those elements of their Ojibwa heritage. Eagleheart also became a leader in tribal politics and on treaty issues and tribal sovereignty. In some cases his knowledge and experience drew him to national, pan-Indian concerns. Eagleheart was one of a number of traditional elders invited to participate in the North American Indian Elders and Youth Circle, a group that included Leon Shenandoah, Thomas Banyaca, Phillip Deer, Joe Medicine Crow, Oren Lyons, and Jake Swamp, among others. Francis and the other leaders in that circle shared spiritual teachings, stories across generations, intertribally and interculturally. His work on repatriation of American Indian remains took him to various venues to speak and, on occasion, to assist in reburials.

From another perspective, Francis is one of the last living human transmitters for such a breadth of specific cultural practices. From the age of seven years old, he has been engaged in important spiritual and cultural ceremonies, to the exclusion of formal education in tribal boarding schools and day schools. He attended school only until the third grade. Instead Eagleheart has received instruction in other contexts and teaching situations. So he is familiar with a myriad of practices, including the naming ceremony, the pipe ceremony (*pwawgun*), the sweat lodge ceremony (*manido wadiswan*), the trader dance, the marriage ceremony, the fasting ceremony, and the thirsty dance (*nibagwe shimowin*), (a ceremony that is similar to the sun dance of other Plains cultures, but which retains structural, historical, and spiritual elements unique to the Plains Anishinabeg). Many of these ceremonies were passed on to Francis by his elders, through lineage, or in accordance with Plains Anishinabeg and Cree ways, through spiritual vision and through certain affiliations. While Francis has the knowledge to conduct and share these ceremonies, he also knows the tribal stories, the songs, the historical background, and the significance of structural elements of the ceremonies. Since some of these ceremonies were no longer practiced, for some time, Eagleheart's accounts of such practices reflect a connection to one of the last sources of the human and cultural vision associated with these ceremonies. On one important front, then, the Eagleheart narratives will serve as a cultural resource, preserving information about cultural and spiritual perspectives that might otherwise be forgotten, fragmented, or subsumed to insignificance in smaller concerns of assimilative cultural considerations. As importantly, Francis's survival is a testament to the resilience of the Plains Anishinabeg and their spiritual teachings. His work is a testament to the power of an *oshkawbewis*, a helper in service to the people.

At this time we have formulated four sections for presenting edited transcriptions of Francis's interviews. The first section engenders Francis personal stories, or his narrative accounts of his individual experiences. The second section will include personal family narrative and intergenerational accounts of ceremonial practices and origins. The third section will revolve around tribal and pantribal historical narratives. And the fourth section will provide accounts of oral stories Francis has learned over the course of his life.

While Cook Lynn might categorize some of the narratives and sections we've set up as ethnographic or biographic, each section works beyond the boundaries of categories either we or Cook Lynn has set forth. We are also fairly certain that the *Eagleheart Narratives* are not simply windows for voyeurs. Edward Said claims

> the contemporary critical consciousness stands between the temptations represented by two formidable and related powers engaging critical attention. One is the culture to which critics are bound filiatively (by birth, nationality, profession); the other is the method or system acquired affiliatively (by social and political conviction, economic and historical circumstances, voluntary effort and willed deliberation). (1983, 25)

While we don't, or can't, adhere to all of Said's prescriptions for applying affiliation to our work with Eagleheart, we do want to stress the ways in which affiliation offers opportunities to reposition and reauthorize the transmission and reception of texts produced out of, and transmitted through, American Indian experiences. For example, Julie Cruikshank contends that "an enduring value of informal storytelling is to subvert official orthodoxies and to challenge conventional ways of thinking" (1998, xiii). Further, beyond offering "views in" from the outside, we hope to enforce certain cultural aesthetics, associated with "informal storytelling."

To be sure, Francis establishes his own filiations and affiliations through narrative. In one section on family, he connects his lineage with known history and territory and untold names and circumstances.

> [We're] Chippewa. By gosh, they call us Cree, but we're not Crees. My dad's name was Little Boy and my dad's dad, his name was Young Man.
> My great-grandfather was a Cree chief, 1831. There's only three of them that left there, 1831. Broken Arm, Either Eye, and there was an Assiniboine-Sioux's name was The Light. The Light. Got two names. That Assiniboine, he had two names, was Either Eye and The Light.

There was another unknown name, in Soodoo [Saulteaux, French name for the Anishinabe]. He was with Sacajawea and Charbonneau. Yeah, they went down on the steamboat, that's when this picture, he drawed it, 1831. I discovered him in Washington at the archives. I done a lot of research of the history. That's where I found him. Well, Broken Arm, Either Eye was a Cree chief. Yeah, the same man with two different names. Had two different names. My great grandpa's name was Either Eye and Broken Arm, and this one Chippewa, they did not know his name, unknown name, Saulteaux. He was a Chippewa, and Sacajawea's husband, Charbonneau, was a Frenchman, he was the interpreter, they're the ones that left from Fort Union on a steamboat to go to Washington and establish their reservations, territories. But this has never been brought up, any way at all. But I've done research work in Washington and I found all these things. Actually the place where they taken the, their territories, this and that, that's in 1831, that's quite a few years back and I got documents and pictures. The pictures were, at that time, was an artist by the name of George Catlin. He was the artist, drew all these people.[2]

In another chapter Eagleheart contextualizes his filiation[3] not through lineage and history, but through remembrance of place—an indigeneity if you will—the actions of parents and in song, movement and a strong sense of difference, a self-conscious affiliation with his own strangeness, initially designated by another, through song. (Perhaps that is another unrestricted possibility for an Indian story.) In some other way, Francis has also recognized through his narrative that his life, his cultural life remains composed of the strangeness of a personal life through a life of cultural affiliation.

I remember from since I was three months old. I remember when I was three months old, where we lived, and the house, the way the house was made out of. Our house was made out of lumber, was no log house, I don't know how we got a hold of this lumber, but my dad had made a lumber house. And I think that house must have been about fourteen by sixteen. Just a one-room house.

It's west here. It's west, where my sister lives there, then south there. Right below the hill there, just a little bit on a side hill there, high spot there, is where the house was built. And it was in the fall like this here, was in the fall, my dad, then, went to town and my grandpa was keeping me. And my grandpa was not a heavy-set man, he was kind of a short, light guy, he wore suspender overalls. I remember his suspender overalls he wore. And he was, had those, kind of a, what they call denim shirts. That kind, he had that kind of shirt on.

And the house was facing, the door facing east, facing east and there was two windows on the south side, one on the west. And the spring was the north-east side of the house. Cook stove was a black old Monarch stove. That's all, we didn't have no heater. And the bed was on the northwest side of the house, inside.

And I remember my dad and them went to town and my grandpa was keeping me. I must have been giving him a rough time 'cause he was carrying me back and forth on the floor. And he was singing this song here. He was singing this Indian song. I remember that song. I remember that song he was singing. And the way that song goes the words in it, he says, "This strange little boy here," he said, "this strange little boy here I'm carrying." That's the way the words went in that song in the Indian language, it was in the Cree, he sang them words in the Cree language. Walking back and forth, back and forth on the floor.

In the process of making this book, of continuing to try to make this book, to make interviews into text, we believe we, the writers, as writers, editors, transcribers, students, friends, are also establishing and maintaining an affiliation that extends beyond our professional commitments and academic appointments.

In this sense, in the case of our work with Francis Cree, Elizabeth Cook Lynn may be more right about writers "taking sides" than she might have intended. As you may have guessed by earlier statements, we have made a conscious effort to affiliate ourselves with Francis Cree, even prior to considering making a book. To this point I would like to build further from a few ideas offered by Edward Said:

Affiliation is what enables text to maintain itself as text, and this is covered by a range of circumstances: status of the author, historical moment, conditions of publication, diffusion and reception, values drawn
upon, values and ideas assumed, a framework of consensually held tacit
assumptions, presumed background and so on and so on . . . to study
affiliation is to study and to recreate the bonds between texts and the
world, bonds that specialization and institutions of literature have all but
effaced. Every text is an act of will to some extent, but what has not been
very much studied is the degree to which texts are made permissible.
To recreate the affiliative network is therefore to make visible, to give
materiality back to, the strands holding the text to society, author and
culture. (1983, 174–75)

While Said may be positioning literary critics and cultural theorists to face,
with awareness, their "intellectual" affiliations[4] with "the way authority is
carried from the state down into society" (172), we might also acknowledge
his views as an opportunity for us to use whatever technical skill, cultural
practices, intercultural credentials, and social relationships we have in arms
to uphold the authority of individuals, knowledge systems, and cultural practices that legitimize our preferences for involvement with communities and
people of interest, outside and beyond restrictive affiliations with institutions,
discourse models and disciplines of dominant culture in their affirmations of
certain authorized values.

So under another discourse model we turn to a story, a narrative that illustrates a trail of affiliation that engenders shifting contexts of experience and
language. In this case the narrative, story, establishes intercultural affiliations
in the ongoing life of the intergenerational, multiple context transmission of
narrative. That is, the story, initially transmitted through filiations, continues
through affiliation.

■ Contexts and Affiliations: Eagleheart's Father's Story

My dad said, Look, he said, I was a little boy here, I must have been about ten years old, he says, when these Nez Perce people they were fighting south of Chinook right here, big war there. That was Chief Joseph, see? And after that fight we was living down here in Milk River, right down the Milk River. There was a lot of trees there and everything, rough-looking place, the Milk River all the way down. We was living right there, my dad said, that two big tracks meet, he said. But the cavalry didn't bother us, he said, they didn't bother us, didn't bother us. They'd come through there, from Fort Assiniboine. These cavalries, they didn't bother us, he said. And we was living nears.

And then one night, all of a sudden there was a group of people they come, there must have been about thirty of them, maybe more. At night, a group of people they were on foot, leading horses, they come down there. They seen these tipis and then my dad went out there, he said, he was talking to 'em sign language. And this guy was the leader, kind of young guy, young man, kind of tall. He made a motion; they never ate for three days or more, he said, because they were busy having war down south. They were having war; they didn't have time to hunt. And that's why, see, if you can get something to eat.

And my dad told him, he said, help yourself, eat all what you want to eat, he says. So they stayed there three nights and in the daytime they'd hide in the bush, they'd hide in the bush. Kids said they were bags, big round bags on them horses, saddlebags like each side the horses, bunch of kids in there, three, four kids in there, hides. There's one old lady there, she was about eighty some years old. She got pretty sick right there; she had the fat meat too soon, too much at one time. Well, anyways, they stayed there three nights, he said. And my dad told him you can have all the meat you want. They helped themselves.

Then he said, one day they told 'em, which way is the Canadian border? And he told 'em, straight north, this is north, that way. And he told 'em, you camp maybe twice then you'll be in this Canadian border. That direction. So that night they planned on leaving, and they gave my dad two army rifles, two army rifles and two belts with shells, plum full, he said. Gave him those, gave to my dad. So my dad went with them part way, that night, showing them directions. So they struck off that way. That was Chief Joseph people, yeah.

That was in Milk River there south of Chinook, Montana. That's what my dad's telling us there cause we camped there. He was born around in the '67, somewhere's around there. That's why, I said, he was about ten years old. And Chief Joseph, his battle there was in '77, I think? Somewhere's in there?

To derive a sense of context for this text in progress, let us turn to a model of the trail of transmission of Eagleheart's father's story.

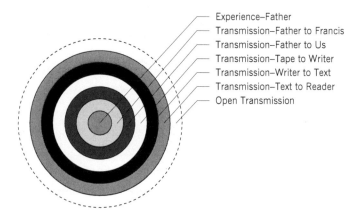

Experience–Father
Transmission–Father to Francis
Transmission–Father to Us
Transmission–Tape to Writer
Transmission–Writer to Text
Transmission–Text to Reader
Open Transmission

James (Sakej) Youngblood Henderson's work may help to inform this model. In an article titled "The Context of the State of Nature," Youngblood Henderson refers to Brazilian legal scholar Roberto Unger when he states, "If a context allows people to move within it to discover everything about the world they can discover, then it is a 'natural' context. If the context does not allow such natural movement, then it is an artificial context, derived from selected assumptions" (2000, 12). Youngblood Henderson goes on to claim "that all major aspects of human empowerment or self-assertion depend on our success at diminishing the distance between context preserving routines (law) and context-transforming conflict" (14). This may happen through contexts, or sites of struggle.

In some respects then, the transmission of "Eagleheart's Father's Story" works through diminishing contexts of experience. Under Unger's view, the deepest context occurred when Francis's father actually met with Chief Joseph's people. The account of that experience, through narrative, eventually to print, diminishes the experience through artificial context and through certain assumptions required in the way experience is represented in the printed context. To put it another way, though a story remains, the context of the story, the modes of transmission of the story and the distance between the experience and the story, preserve aspects of the story/experience that are markedly different from the experience of the story. Still, the story takes on a life beyond the context of experience to produce expression and reception in different unrelated contexts. All of this extra transmission through different contexts re-creates the story and transforms affiliations. To put it another way, the story provides a way for extending affiliation through an intersubjective range of contexts. Further, the story's transmission may produce "context-transforming conflicts" at various stages in production and reception of the "text."

While much of this may seem problematic on a number of levels, if, as Julie Cruikshank contends, stories have social lives, then their lives depend on conductors, transmitters, receivers and contexts. The continuing life of a story may depend on humans, perhaps even events, invested with enough energy in the life of stories to conduct stories to their lives as story carriers, or transmitters. These transmissions will reveal not only affiliations, but tendencies. In reference to Deleuze's critique of transcendental illusion, Constantin V. Boundas writes:

> The possibility of transcendental illusion is now accounted for, not in terms of mental faculties mistaken about jurisdictions and territories, but in terms of tendencies rooted in things themselves, and being actualized in ways that bring them into conflict with each other. (1996, 85)

In view of Francis's father's story we see how a story/life may transcend certain fixed assumptions and tend from experiences of varied transmissions to create new contexts for itself, through affiliation and multiple sites of cultural transmission. Stories and songs know no distance; they tend to transcend distance and context. Story and songs are not subject to the jurisdiction or the fixed, forced inscriptions of institution or law. Stories and songs have the capacity to move, live, and pass interculturally through varied communicative methods and modes to find affiliates for the practices and cultural characteristics the stories subtend, to expand the possibility for affiliation beyond any known cultural context. Like a seemingly dislocated band moving beyond borders, driven from home and family, stories and songs continue with other bands and families, to live on, in ever-extending sites of struggle where the spirit of affiliation develops anew, to energize and empower people, in an on-going development of faculties, for understanding themselves, ourselves and others.

NOTES

1. Leuthold claims that "aesthetic behavior is a set of social practices" (1998, 6).
2. Editors note he was painted by George Catlin
3. "2 a: descent or derivation from culture or language, b: the act or process for determining such relationship" (*Websters Collegiate Dictionary*, 1993).
4. *Longman Dictionary of Contemporary English*: "affiliate . . . to join, or connect" (15).

WORKS CITED

Boundas, Constantin. V. 1996. "Deleuze–Bergson: An Ontology of the Virtual." In *Deleuze: A Critical Reader,* edited by Paul Patton, 81–106. Blackwell: Oxford.

Cruikshank, Julie. 1998. *The Social Life of Stories: Narrative and Knowledge in the Yukon Territories.* Lincoln: University of Nebraska Press.

Leuthold, Steven. 1998. *Indigenous Aesthetics: Native Art, Media, and Identity.* Austin: University of Texas Press.

Mihesuah, Devon A. 1996. "Voices, Interpretations and 'The New Indian History': Comment on the 'American Indian Quarterly's' Special Issue Writing about (Writing about) American Indians." *American Indian Quarterly* 20 (Winter): 91–108.

Said, Edward. 1983. *The World, the Text and the Critic*. Cambridge: Harvard University Press.

Youngblood Henderson, James (Sákéj). 2000. "The Context of the State of Nature." In *Reclaiming Indigenous Voice and Vision*, edited by Marie Batiste, 11–38. Vancouver: University of British Columbia Press.

Origin-of-Poem Story: Origin and Ownership of an Indian Poem, "Earth Death"

PATRICK R. LEBEAU

This American Indian poet's creative instincts draw from a storehouse of memories and experiences, elusive or graspable at fleeting moments, and sometimes captured and rendered in an organizational construct identified as poem, story, essay, or song. Mostly from memory themes emerge and choices are made to communicate an idea, an emotion or scene but to explain this process as inspiration perpetrated by an immutable, intangible muse is to deflect from the stories that are behind the origin of many "Indian" poems.

The story behind the origin of my poem "Earth Death" for example, offers not only a greater contextual world of meaning but also a human and ancestral connection to place and politics, memory and imagination, which puts into question the concept of intellectual property and creative ownership. Sole proprietorship runs counter to ideas of my Native community and family, especially when the origin-of-poem story is told. A kind of shared "ownership," or more likely, a shared responsibility, links the memory to the experience and the experience to the poem. My writing of the "Earth Death" is a way of remembering a story in my own way and sharing that memory with others in a short concise manner that highlights what I believe was most important at the time of writing.

However, to dismiss the power of a Western idea of a muse is to also ignore the motivation for this particular exploration of the origin-of-poem story, which sprang from questions posed to me by Susana Onega (Catedrática de Universidad and chair, Departamento de Filología Inglesa y Alemana, Universidad De Zaragoza) on March 9, 2004, after a reading of the poem, "Earth Death." She wanted me to explain the origin of the poem, but, more importantly, she wanted to know my level of ownership. She wanted to know if I owed any obligation to some other source or inspiration. She wanted to know if I claimed what I wrote was my own creative story or if the story was from somebody else, like an ancestor, which is a valid question of ownership. I was surprised that I did not hesitate to answer in a manner that explained, seemingly, more to me than to the audience, for a story emerged, which explained the origin but also touched on memories I thought irrelevant to the creative act of the composition of the poem. To that point of about twenty years of reading my own creative work, I never added any more information other than the words organized to create the poem itself. I thought context and explanation were superfluous to the overall power and purpose of the poem's identity. Susana Onega's questions changed that perspective as she challenged my ownership of such ideas that clearly were from a multitude of sources, which inspired the spontaneous but albeit fragmented story that became my answer to queries and the larger, more contextualized story that follows.

However, the poem, as part of a published collection, must stand on its own merit; therefore, the origin-of-poem story herein serves as a form of literary critique and as an answer to questions of origin, originality, and ownership. The story explicates the connection between the Native American archetypal sources (e.g., the North American landscape, rhythm and repetition, and oral tradition/storytelling) and Western forms of literature (e.g., essay, short story, and poem). By bridging the oral tradition with the written word, Native authors manipulate the language and literary forms of the colonizer, the conqueror, to tell a Native American story from a Native American perspective to listeners and readers well beyond the Native American community itself. In this way, Native American authors take responsibility and possession of their own stories and histories rather than continue to let others control the way the story of Native

Americans is told. The result is a Native Americanization of Western forms of literature, a facing eastward so to speak, a shifting of direction and perspective.

My overall essay will expand on the ideas expressed in the paragraphs above, will include a short creative nonfiction piece, which tells of the origin of the "Earth Death" poem, and will conclude with the "Earth Death" poem itself. The origin-of-poem story is a combination of history, memory, and landscape centered on a childhood experience. In brief, the story is about a human skeleton, washed up on the shore of the Missouri River, which is found by my grandfather's best friend, and the subsequent discussion and thoughts of these two old people about the origin and meaning of this unusual discovery. Many years later, I write the poem, "Earth Death," based on this memory and experience. The essay shows how this story can serve as a way of interpreting the poem by providing a greater archetypal and cultural background.

However, as an undergraduate and graduate student, I have conducted many years of research into repatriation and issues surrounding the scaffold burial practices of the Lakota and Dakota, my paternal ancestors, and I have been involved in many civic actions and protests to address these issues of Native repatriation in public forums and to reclaim bodies and body parts, especially from universities. In some ways, the "Earth Death" poem is political protest; more importantly, the personal and ancestral memory combines with the memory of archival records, laws, and statutes, which results in a poem in the Western form that must within the context of the story be more than a poem.

Even to this day, I can still imagine the two old men coughing back and forth and discussing the political, moral, and ethical issues of Lakota burial practices.

■ Origin-of-Poem-Story

He remembered the saying "old jalopy," referring to that old white Ford pickup truck with the loose springs and ramshackle condition making the bouncing and gyrating of its cab an interesting and sometimes dangerous ride for a seven-year-old boy riding with his Lakota grandfather who brought along his namesake to visit an old friend and asked him to drive.

"Yep, you can go as slow as your fear of rocks and rivers and mothers and mares and gears and gravel makes you. Nothing better than learning to drive on the fly as the flies bother you," he said, taking a sip from an elongated buffalo horn, with a cork lid like a powder horn, filled with a smelly liquid and then gumming a piece of jerky held tightly in a wringed-out hand. The road, wet and slippery from a vicious thunderstorm the night before, spangled with rain-filled potholes and glistened with flat and misshaped stones revealed from the runoff.

As he changed places by sliding over his grandfather's lap, he remembered the time he had to test-drive the racing car built for kids by his mechanically minded father, who fashioned a yellow car in the style of 1950s Edmonds midget race cars out of scrap medal and a lawnmower engine. A lever with a red knob attached to the right inner side of the cockpit stood erect next to a group of frenzied white letters making lazy declarations of stop, idle, and fast. In between idle and fast, his father said, "You can speed up or slow down," apparently not remembering he was left-handed. The test drive around the gumbo track lasted one lap with the torpedoed crash into his grandmother's front porch.

After that, the look down the craggy breaks colored with bands of browns, reds, grays, and yellows and the curvy roads cutting through the domes, buttes, pyramids, and cones, collectively named badlands, projecting down to the Missouri River, seemed easy going. No looks or stares—no words or shouts. Only the sandstone, shale, and clay valley before him and the gentle-mannered and cragged-faced old man beside him stood to remind him of his abilities and triumphs, for he was an expert of navigation and the old man's favorite. When he was in this place in the accompaniment of his grandfather, he possessed bearing; he felt like a boot stuck in gumbo, the wet soil of his grandfather's cattle ranch, the stuff of play and tumble.

He navigated the rickety and battered truck around the gravel mounds, tea cup-shaped hills, flattened anvil-like causeways, and the many descending curves that suddenly climb and then down, down and down again; and the mind of the seven-year-old thinking of 7-Up bottles and beef jerky kept fresh and cold inside the unlocked pop machine at the last stop, listening to grandpa tell stories.

As the gas spilled into the tank and as he chewed and sipped, his grandfather asked, "Patrick, hold out your hands."

First he squatted to situate and balance the jerky on the lip rim of the 7-Up bottle placed on the ground and then he sprang forward toward his grandfather, the momentum propelling his arms upward; his palms turned up. At once, his grandfather grabbed them, one-handed, in a tangle and then weave of fingers that froze him in a cramped bended position reminding him of throwing up, the flue, the measles, the chicken pox, fevers and shakes—many the names of illness of remembrance and not a diagnosis of present times. Not pain as much as immobility—not sickness but stillness.

"Hey Little Racer! You see the tricky old warrior fools the youthful snake. Hah! The snake squirms and twists but cannot escape. No matter! No matter, Little Racer, the trick is flawed, for when I release, the snake can escape or strike back. The old warrior must have friends for this little trick to work beyond the snare. You know, my friend, with that rattling sound for speech, is the person I take you to meet. He taught me this trick a long time ago."

That friend he knew was a singer, and the memory of his drumming filled the boy's mind as he jumped from the idling truck to lift the barbed-wire hoop over the post to release the gate for their chitty-chitty-bang-bang entrance: the backfire sparked another memory of a school play where he entered a wooden stage driving a cardboard car.

He skipped rocks as he drifted farther away from the truck, parked some distance from the house of the friend his grandfather called Snare Drum. At that place, the curve of the road touched the east bank of the Missouri and following its path, the eye stretched about a hundred yards upward to the small wind-battered house, with a long wooden porch, sprinkled with rain-soaked furniture. A manlike figure stood atop the steps peering down, a hand salute-like over his eyebrows. The old man rolled a cigarette carefully over his lap so as not to waste dregs to the wind or careless fingers; glancing upward toward the house, mumbling a private prayer, he looked after the boy, now getting his feet wet in the lapping waves driven by a westward wind.

The old man yelled, "Little Racer, over near that western bank was the old town of Cheyenne; our old home is there, under the water: The U.S. Army Corps of Engineers built many dams along this river; the dams flooded out the river bottom Indians and made them plains people. If you look closely you can still see the roofs. Your grandmother Swiftbird grew many fine vegetables and flowers in her prized garden; now she grows chickens and tumble weeds."

"Hey Boot Horn, whatcha got with you, a straggle calf or drift dog?" rattled the man on the porch step, as he waved the two on. The truck, now pointing toward the shore where they had just been, required attention, so the boy, stopped in his tracks with an unvoiced wave of a wrinkled hand, wedged flat river rocks under the tires as his grandfather instructed him in selection and position.

"No, no, he is a Little Racer, a refugee of a circuit track he drove in a straight line; I had him drive me here, one way, because I now know his driving abilities. He can swing a club as well with no great strength but the new and different places he puts the ball tells me he is strong. You have met him before when he went by a different name," the old man, Boot Horn, explained.

Little Racer by this time stood still, a step from the risers, hoping what he saw was not a specter, a riser from the dark shadows of Snare Drum's covered porch. He tried to step back but he froze, not wanting but waiting, foot in air—big yellow brown boot with steel reinforcements started to shake—avoiding the step: for on the porch towards the left a yellowed and brown skeleton sat peacefully in Snare Drum's rocking chair, bobbing due to the strong westward storm winds still a-blowing, kicking up dust and chaff at flippant occasions, spewing dust-devils, tiny tornadoes, and disgorging the celebratory tumbleweeds from hidden prairie sources.

"Yeah, yeah, I found the bones on the east side of river after the big storms last night. I don't know why but I tied them together, as best I could, with the left-over red ribbon from this spring, into what I thought was a human shape. I drug him up and sat him over there, in my chair, in my rocking chair. I placed tobacco on his skull, hands, and feet." Snare Drum's shaking lament left Boot Horn stunned and in silence for long time, depending on how the loose and wrinkled face drooped or tightened, drooped or tightened, according to what must have been some kind of unsaid thought.

Snare Drum, clearly not liking to admit he had touched the dead, continued: "He is old 'cause I found traces of buffalo hide, brass beads, and hummingbirds adorned and tied in a fashion that they themselves looked like a warrior's adornment or even war weapons by the way the beaks resemble bar darts or killing projectiles: as you can see, they are tied to his arms with blue ribbon. What else could I do?"

They talked in the low guttural murmurs of his grandfather and the rasping and vibrating sounds of Snare Drum of the many Lakota/Dakota burial sites along the Missouri, often situated on high promontories—lofty lookouts, high-up watchtower positions—affording, commanding, the dead spectators a grandiose view of the world below and the night and day sky above, reaching up, as the Christians say, to the heavens.

Their voices merging together in Little Racer's head: "The dead were clothed in their finest regalia and enclosed within a luxurious blanket. Back not too many years ago, people were lifted into the sky on burial scaffolds or in other areas placed in a many-branched and tall tree to remain over the winter, waiting for the proper time for burial in the ground in shallow graves, graves marked by long, singular posts, at the head and at the feat, sometimes painted, sometimes not. I have seen long streamers of white silk and red ribbon attached to such poles in the manner of sacred flags. The brilliantly colored cloth flags mark the burial ground in a most conspicuous manner. The Elders, Eagle Eye and Mad Bear, said the people, if provided the time, would build sturdy and enduring burial scaffolds to prolong the moment before the departed would return to the earth. So a long, long time ago, the people buried in the sky were left there until the earth reclaimed them through natural decay of the scaffold and of the body, after many years of sun, wind, snow and rain, crumbling and falling to pieces and bones scattered upon the ground. Only then, their bones and remains would be gathered together and buried or more likely heaped and the grave mound marked with posts and flags."

As the men talked, the boy, steel shoe descending, stepped quickly to the door jam, placing the old men between him and the yellow-boned Lakota stranger on the far end of the porch, and then disappearing into the darkness of the house to take off his shoes and to find the comfortable bear skin in which to lounge and perhaps to sleep. The throaty and rasping noises, once he stretched out, slowly changed to melodious and soft chirps and twitters of songbirds, like the finch in an early morning on a warm spring day, the colorful plumage invading his imagination.

Through the open window, the sky, without a single cloud, blazed away in the noonday sun, slowly evaporating the lingering morning mists still clinging to low spots in and around the hills, as if the mists refused the let go of their loving embrace of the mounds and grasses below them.

Reclined and stupefied, Little Racer continued to listen to the shorted gasps and breath of the speech of his elderly patrons: "Many of the early Christian missionaries erected their churches close to such grave sites and over time burial in scaffolds was outlawed. Yet, as I have been told, many Lakota heaved Christian-like coffins onto the traditional scaffold for a respectful period of time before burying the body and coffin in a Christian grave. Sometimes, they'd just leave the coffin up there, in the sky, until the ministers or priests would take them down and bury them themselves."

Bitterness entered the voice breaths of the old men; spittle rained in the sunbeamed light slicing through the threshold, as Little Racer watched the droplets merge with the dust and shadows. "Members of the local Masonic lodge have been known to claim Lakota scaffold burial grounds as their own as if to erase the sacred presence of our ancestors in favor of the Masons and their families. They said our burial rituals were blasphemous to what they said was the 'knowledge of the true God,' even when the people yearned to be buried in the sky, the winter rest and respect due the people of the plains and of the land of the big sky."

"Yes, yes, yes (not really knowing who is talking) . . . the bone stealers would come as well. Take the bones, cramming them into wooden crates. Some of these white people are always digging around, taking the bones they find to some far-off place, especially the bones of strange-looking creatures, dinosaurs like the huge fake ones standing out in front of those green-signed gas stations, a place for tourists and the curious. In the 1920s, local high school pranksters, or were they college students [hell, they could have been anthropologists], but they all were really unknowing grave robbers, came out here to dig up the bones of Indian 'chiefs,' wherever they can, always drunk and on some initiation mission to prove their prowess and manliness. As long as I can remember, beer drinking and the stealing of our ancestor's skulls go hand in hand. Odd, they think they can take the dead away from their burial land by taking the bones; they never consider: What was around the bones. Where are the flesh, hair, eyelashes, hearts, and intestines? Moving the bones does not change the land. Is it possible to get the dead out of the dirt? The skin and the hair are in the dirt."

Snare Drum rattled with tear-shacked coughs: "You know, I feel bad about those people buried in coffins; how does their skin get into the dirt? What about us? Are we to be buried in the ground without even a brief moment in the sky?"

On the battered old and wooden bed of the pickup truck, his silhouette showed the oddly bent back of a spear thrower but upon further inspection, just a boy getting ready to throw a line out into the blue sky toward the river far below, never intending to reach the wind-blown water, not a spear but a long fishing pole, the hook replaced by a rubber, tear-shaped, practice weight designed for casting.

Behind him, the old men carried a Pendleton-like blanket, rolled lengthwise, and tied with red and blue ribbon, up toward a humped promontory, flatted at its peak; the trail a bit wet in places but drying in a wind growing more fierce as white thunderheads approached from the far western horizon. "Hey Little Racer," looking over his shoulder, "not to worry, a long way off and probably veering south." The tall clouds below, with a seemingly endless expanse of land between them and the storm, sparked and flickered with hidden flashes and buried discharges of atmospheric energy, in and between the white and gray clouds, a long and silent distance away. Too far to worry the small boy casting into the wind, a wind kicking and swirling the surface dirt and arching and fighting the line in unpredictable, uncontrollable gusts, forcing the weight away from the boy's target and causing a tedious and resistant reel.

The blood flowed down the left arm, just below the circular vaccination scar, weathered in the old man's skin. Snare Drum worked silently and efficiently with a bone-handled knife, as he removed small square pieces of skin from Boot Horn's arm, they both called offerings, and placing them in a square of dark blue cloth; his own arms streaked with drying blood, and the lines of tiny wounds patched over with twists of tobacco, clotting and scabbing with the blood, the loose dregs falling to the earth, which now had a grave dug shallowly into the promontory ground, inside the rolled and tied blanket.

A tom tom of drumming started with a tom, tom, tom ta´tom rattling and a slow song broke forth, mellowing into a *cheya'ya,* a crying lament, repeating four times:

> Wan na yan mah nii yeh
> Wan na yan mah nii yeh
> Tatanka wan mah nii yeh
> Tatanka wan mah nii yeh
> Ah tey hey ye lo
> Ah tey hey ye lo
>
> Wan na yan mah nii yeh
> Wan na yan mah nii yeh
> Tatanka wan mah nii yeh
> Tatanka wan mah nii yeh
> Ah tey hey yeh lo
> Ah tey hey y lo
>
> Wan na yan mah nii yeh
> Wan na yan mah nii yeh
> Tatanka wan mah nii yeh
> Tatanka wan mah nii yeh
> Ah tey hey ye lo
> Ah tey hey ye lo
>
> Wan na yan mah nii yeh
> Wan na yan mah nii yeh
> Tatanka wan mah nii yeh
> Tatanka wan mah nii yeh
> Ah tey hey yeh lo
> Ah tey hey y lo

The preceding not only explains the origin and ownership of the poem "Earth Death," but also tells how oral traditions that include the stories, memories and history of a particular family, community and people, and the ordinary, though complicated and multilayered, can be organized in fixed rhetorical patterns. As an adult and after many years of exploration in the art of poetics, including the graceful and elegiac, the sonnet and the haiku, the idea of the poem as a way to render the voice of those stories into a recognizable verse and pattern came to mind and became a method to explore my own personal history as that history reflects the culture of my community, including the political and social conflicts inherent in a colonized people. The scraps and fragments of memories sparked by family stories, the remembrance of the words of ancestors now long dead, the oral traditions of people revealing the ritual practices and beliefs, the written histories of known conflicts between Westerners and the Lakota, especially with repatriation and burial practices, graveyards and bone collections, allow for a manipulation of the Western form of literature called poem from a uniquely Lakota perspective, albeit much of the story remains hidden in metaphor, imagery, and figurative language. To read the multilayered depth and quality of the poem "Earth Death," "The Origin-of-Poem Story" helps but, more importantly, the story makes known the memories and stories held by the author, and his cultural background should be considered in any interpretation and analysis. The words themselves may have many owners, and the story itself is what has created this poem:

EARTH DEATH
somebody spoke
he heard his name
somebody spoke
he heard his name

existing, he spoke
existing, he spoke
dancing, dancing he

heard his words

"not the earth"
"not the earth"
he dreamed of the sky

"not the earth"
"not the earth"
he dreamed of dying in the sky

somebody spoke
he pulled at his ears
somebody spoke
he tried pulling off his ears

not beneath this earth
not beneath this earth
or beneath the surface of the sky

"please bury me in the sky"
"please bury me in the sky"

the ground is cold, colder than the sky
somebody spoke, he heard his name,
he heard his name

"not the cold, only the sky"
"not the cold, only the sky"

somebody spoke
he refused to hear
somebody spoke,
he refused to hear

"not the cold, give me the sky"
"not the cold, give me the sky"

somebody spoke
existing he spoke
"please, please bury me in the sky"

dancing on the surface, he jumped into the sky
dancing on the surface, he jumped into the sky

jumping, jumping, he slowly died

WORK CITED

LeBeau, Patrick R. *Stands Alone, Faces, and Other Poems.* East Lansing: Michigan State
    University Press, 1999.

Contributors

Rob Appleford is associate professor in the English and Film Studies Department at the University of Alberta, Canada. He teaches and researches in the areas of Canadian Aboriginal/First Nations literatures and Native American literatures, with an emphasis on contemporary and emergent writing and critical theory. His published articles have appeared in the *American Indian Culture and Research Journal*, *Canadian Theatre Review*, *Modern Drama*, *Theatre Research in Canada/Récherches Théâtrales au Canada*, *Canadian Literature*, and in the book collections *Native America: Portrait of the Peoples*, *Siting the Other: Marginal Identities in Australian and Canadian Drama*, *Crucible of Cultures: Anglophone Drama at the Dawn of a New Millennium*, and *Canadian Author Series: Drew Hayden Taylor*. He has edited a collection of essays *Aboriginal Drama and Theatre* (2005). Currently, he is at work on a book-length study of Aboriginal literatures and critical theory entitled *The Ghost/Dance of North American Aboriginal Literature*.

Susan Berry Brill de Ramírez is Caterpillar Inc. Professor of English at Bradley University, where she teaches Native American literatures, environmental literatures, ecocomposition, folklore, and literary criticism and theory. Author of *Wittgenstein and Critical Theory* (1995), *Contemporary American Indian Literatures and the Oral Tradition* (1999), and *Native American Life-History Narratives: Colonial and Postcolonial Navajo Ethnography* (2007), and co-editor with Evelina Zuni Lucero for the recent volume *Simon J. Ortiz: A Poetic Legacy of Indigenous Continuance* (2009), Brill de Ramírez is currently completing a monograph on Native American women's ethnography and exploring the concepts of the conversive and "geographies of belonging" in Indigenous and diasporic literatures.

Harry Brown is associate professor of English at DePauw University, where he teaches courses in American literature, Native literatures, and digital culture. His publications include *The Native American in Short Fiction in The Saturday Evening Post* (2001), *Injun Joe's Ghost: The Indian Mixed-Blood in American Writing* (2004), and *Videogames and Education* (2008). He has also authored articles on James Fenimore Cooper, William Apess, Mary Jemison, John Rollin Ridge, and the dime western. His current research focuses on early American missionary narratives.

Teresa Gibert is professor of English at the Spanish National University of Distance Education (UNED) in Madrid, Spain, where she is Head of the Department of Foreign Languages and teaches courses on American and Canadian literature. Her publications include several essays about Thomas King ("Narrative Strategies in Thomas King's Short Stories," 2001; "Written Orality in Thomas King's Short Fiction," 2006; "Subverting the Master Narrative of Heroic Conquest: Thomas King's *A Coyote Columbus Story* (1992)," 2008; and "The Politics and Poetics of Thomas King's Textual Hauntings," forthcoming). Professor Gibert also wrote the chapter "'Ghost Stories': Fictions of History and Myth" for the volume *The Cambridge History of Canadian Literature* (2009).

P. Jane Hafen (Taos Pueblo) is a Professor of English at the University of Nevada, Las Vegas. She serves on the editorial boards of the Western Writers

Series, Boise State University, and American Indian Studies of Michigan State University Press, as an advisory editor of *Great Plains Quarterly*, on the board of the Charles Redd Center for Western Studies, and is an associate fellow at the Center for Great Plains Studies. She is a Frances C. Allen Fellow, D'Arcy McNickle Center for the History of the American Indian, The Newberry Library. Dr. Hafen is author of *Reading Louise Erdrich's Love Medicine*, editor of *Dreams and Thunder: Stories, Poems, and The Sun Dance Opera by Zitkala-Sa*, and coeditor of *The Great Plains Reader*.

Jane Haladay is currently assistant professor of American Indian Studies at the University of North Carolina at Pembroke, in the heart of the Lumbee Nation. Dr. Haladay holds a Ph.D. in Native American Studies with an emphasis in feminist theory and research from the University of California–Davis, and an M.A. in American Indian Studies from the University of Arizona. A native of California, Dr. Haladay taught high school English in the San Francisco Bay Area for eight years before beginning her career in postsecondary education. Dr. Haladay's scholarship and teaching focus on literary practices of decolonization, indigenous self-determination, the role of narrative in addressing violence against women, and the subversion of ethnic and gender stereotypes in the writings of contemporary Native North American authors.

Both poet and novelist, **Gordon D. Henry Jr.** is an enrolled member of the White Earth Chippewa Tribe of Minnesota. A professor of English and American Studies at Michigan State University, he now lives near Stanwood, Michigan. In 2006 he was appointed senior editor of the American Indian Studies Series at Michigan State University Press. His first novel, *The Light People*, won an American Book Award in 1995 and has recently been reissued by the Michigan State University Press. Henry's poetry and fiction is anthologized in various collections including *Songs From This Earth on Turtle's Back; Earth Song, Sky Spirit; Stories Migrating Home; Returning the Gift; Children of the Dragonfly;* and *Nothing But the Truth*. In 2004, Henry and George Cornell co-authored a middle-school text on the Ojibway. His mixed-genre work, *The Failure of Certain Charms and Other Disparate Signs of Life*, was published in 2007. His poetry, fiction, and interviews have been translated and published in Spain, Italy, and Greece. He is currently at work on a second novel and on biographical work on Turtle Mountain spiritual leader Francis Cree. For over twenty-five years Professor Henry has participated in the Nibaagwe Shimowin Ceremony, as passed on by Francis Cree. In 1994 Cree passed that ceremony to Gordon. Gordon has three crazy and beautiful daughters, Kehli, Mira, and Emily. He lives in Michigan with his wife Mary Anne and three lazy dogs, Hershey, Mocha, and Griffin.

Patrick R. LeBeau has been teaching and lecturing in the area of Native American Studies since high school, when he developed a travelling exhibit for the Kingman Museum, an affiliate of the Battle Creek, Michigan, school system. In college, he specialized in American and Native American studies. He earned B.A. and M.A. degrees from Michigan State University and a doctorate from the University of Michigan. At Michigan State University, he has served as director of the American Indian Studies Program and is currently professor of Writing, Rhetoric and American Cultures, where he teaches writing composition and Native American studies. He has taught the courses Native American Literature, Images of Native Americans in Hollywood Films, Race, Ethnicity, and Gender in Hollywood Films, Native American History, Native American Contemporary Issues, and Native American Philosophy. He has published several articles and made many presentations on general topics of Native American history and culture, including the chapter "The Fighting Braves of Michigamua: Adopting the Visage of American Indian Warriors in the Halls of Academia," in *Team Spirits: The Native American Mascot Controversy* (2001). Michigan State University Press published his first book of poetry, *Stands Alone, Faces, and Other Poems*, in 1999. One of the poems published in the book, "Fear of Bears," won first place in the category Poems in English and won the grand prize in the classification Poetry at the 1994 Annual Indian Market Poetry Awards (judges Gloria Bird and Barney Bush). His book *Rethinking Michigan Indian History* (2005) explores and challenges the way Michigan Indian history is taught in Michigan's educational institutions. His third book, *Term Paper Resource Guide to American Indian History* (2009), covers the most significant topics in American Indian history from first contact to recent years. The ultimate goal of the book is to have those topics serve as signposts to point and lead students to a greater and richer knowledge of the story of American Indians rather than to tell the complete story. He is an enrolled member of the Cheyenne River Sioux Indian Reservation of South Dakota, where his father is from. His mother is from Turtle Mountain Indian Reservation, North Dakota.

Silvia Martínez-Falquina is assistant professor of English in the Department of English and German Philology of the University of Zaragoza. After completing her bachelor's degree in English philology at the University of Oviedo, for which she was awarded the Extraordinary Degree Award in January 2002, she obtained a competitive national scholarship to pursue her doctoral studies at the University of Oviedo, and she was a long-term research scholar at Michigan State University (predoctoral) and Glasgow University (postdoctoral). Her Ph.D. dissertation was awarded the Extraordinary Doctorate Award by the University of Oviedo in January 2005, and was published by Oviedo University Press in 2002 as *Ceremonias postindias: Transgresión y re/visión de fronteras en la narrativa de Louise Erdrich* (Postindian Ceremonies: Border Transgression and Re/vision in Louise Erdrich's Narratives). She has held various teaching positions at the University of Oviedo, Saginaw Chippewa Tribal College, Glasgow University and the University of Zaragoza, where she currently teaches contemporary U.S. literature. Her research focuses on contemporary Native American literatures and a comparative approach to the literatures of the United States, with a special emphasis on theories of ethnicity, gender, ethics, and, most recently, the short story cycle. Her book *Indias y fronteras: El discurso en torno a la mujer étnica* (Indian women and the border: The ethnic woman's discourse; 2004) was the recipient of the I AUDEM Award for Young Women Researchers. Together with Bárbara Arizti, she has co-edited the volume of essays *On the Turn: The Ethics of Fiction in Contemporary Narrative in English* (2007). She is part of a competitive research team currently working on the articulation of trauma and ethics in contemporary narrative in English at the University of Zaragoza.

Born and raised in Minneapolis, Minnesota, **Molly McGlennen** (mixed-blood Anishinaabe) is an assistant professor of English and Native American studies at Vassar College. She received her Ph.D. in Native American studies from

University of California–Davis in 2005, with her dissertation work on contemporary indigenous women's poetry. She also earned her M.F.A. in creative writing from Mills College in 1998. Her writing has appeared in *Studies in American Indian Literatures, American Indian Culture and Research Journal,* and *Midwestern Miscellany.* Most recently her poetry has been published in *Genocide of the Mind: New Native American Writing, Shenandoah,* and *Frontiers.* Her collection of poetry, *Like Fried Fish and Flour Biscuits,* is forthcoming.

Elvira Pulitano is an assistant professor in the Ethnic Studies department at California Polytechnic State University. Her research and teaching interests include Indigenous Studies, African diaspora literatures, Caribbean literature, theories of race and ethnicity, migration, and human rights discourse. A Fulbright scholar from Italy, she holds a Ph.D. in English from the University of New Mexico. She is the author of *Toward a Native American Critical Theory* (2003) and has published essays on the work of Gerald Vizenor, Louis Owens, V. S. Naipaul, Caryl Phillips, and Edwidge Danticat. She is also the editor of *Transatlantic Voices: Interpretations of Native North American Literatures* (2007). Current works in progress include a monograph exploring literary representations of diaspora in Caribbean-born writers living in the United States and an edited volume on the United Nations Declaration on the Rights of Indigenous Peoples. Before her current appointment at Cal Poly, she taught postcolonial literatures and theory at the Universities of Geneva and Lausanne, in Switzerland.

Niigonwedom James Sinclair is a graduate of the Native American Literatures program at the University of Oklahoma and is currently a Ph.D. candidate in the Department of English at the University of British Columbia. His dissertation is an Anishinaabeg Literary History. Niigon is originally from Ste. Peter's Indian Reserve in Manitoba, Canada, but now makes his home in Winnipeg. His creative work has appeared in *Prairie Fire, juice, WLT2,* and *Tales from Moccasin Avenue: An Anthology of Native Stories.* His critical work will appear in the collections *Across Cultures/Across Borders: Canadian Aboriginal and Native American Literatures* (2009) and *Troubling Tricksters:*

Revisiting Critical Conversations (2009). Niigon also writes a monthly column entitled "Birchbark Bitings" in *Urban NDN*, Manitoba's alternative Aboriginal newspaper.

Nieves Pascual Soler graduated from the University of Granada in English Philology in 1989. She obtained her Ph.D. at the Complutense University in Madrid. She is associate professor of North American Literature at the University of Jaén, Spain. For some years she has been working on the effects of illness and imposture on the process of creation and has published her research in *Style, Mosaic, Revista Canaria de Estudios Ingleses*, and the *Journal of Intercultural Studies*. She is currently working on a monograph on postcolonial literatures.

Michael Wilson is associate professor at the University of Wisconsin–Milwaukee, where he teaches courses on indigenous literatures. He grew up in Oklahoma and is a member of the Choctaw Nation of Oklahoma. He received is B.A. in English from Oklahoma State University, and an M.A. and Ph.D. in English language and literature from Cornell University. His research interests include indigenous fiction, representations of indigenous people in literary and popular culture, postcolonial theory, and the history of struggles for freedom and independence by indigenous nations. His publications include "'A Communion of Unmerged Souls': Dialogism in Toni Morrison's *Sula*" in *Midwestern Miscellany*, "Speaking of Home: The Idea of the Center in Some Contemporary American Indian Writing" in the *Wicazo Sa Review*; "Writing a Friendship Dance: Orality in Mourning Dove's *Cogewea*" in *American Indian Culture and Research Journal*. Professor Wilson's teaching areas include indigenous fiction and poetry, images of indigenous peoples, postcolonialism and indigenous literatures, oral traditions and contemporary indigenous fiction, and the history, sovereignty and literature of Wisconsin tribes.